THE ULTIMATE CHICAGO PIZZA GUIDE

Go try some new pie!

THE ULTIMATE CHICAGO PIZZA GUIDE

A HISTORY OF *Squares & Slices* IN THE WINDY CITY

STEVE DOLINSKY

Northwestern University Press
Evanston, Illinois

Northwestern University Press
www.nupress.northwestern.edu

Contemporary photographs by Steve Dolinsky, unless otherwise noted.

Printed in Canada

10 9 8 7 6 5 4 3 2

Library of Congress Cataloging-in-Publication Data

Names: Dolinsky, Steve, author.
Title: The ultimate Chicago pizza guide : a history of squares & slices in the Windy City / Steve Dolinsky.
Other titles: History of squares & slices in the Windy City
Description: Evanston, Illinois : Northwestern University Press, 2021. | Includes index.
Identifiers: LCCN 2021010080 | ISBN 9780810144286 (paperback) | ISBN 9780810144293 (ebook)
Subjects: LCSH: Pizza—Illinois—Chicago—History | Pizzerias—Illinois—Chicago. | Chicago (Ill.)—Social life and customs.
Classification: LCC TX909.2.I32 D65 2021 | DDC 641.82/480977311—dc23
LC record available at https://lccn.loc.gov/2021010080

For Amy, Madeline & Max—always willing to schlep somewhere with me for a pizza, curry, ceviche, or Korean barbecue.

You inspire me every day. Thank you for your love and support.

And now . . . I'm done.

CONTENTS

THE ULTIMATE CHICAGO PIZZA GUIDE

INTRODUCTION

It's truly amazing what a pandemic can do for pizza. Already one of our nation's favorite foods, pizza has only skyrocketed in popularity over the past year and a half. While many restaurants struggled to stay afloat with mandatory closings limiting their business to pickup and delivery, the pizza makers could barely keep up. For every chef who told me they were down 70 percent from the year before, three pizzeria owners would tell me they were up 25 to 40 percent, or in the case of Giordano's, an eye-popping 200 percent increase year over year. That's a ton of mozzarella.

Pizza's business model was ideally suited to this shift in the way we procure food. Most stores already had pickup or delivery hard-wired into their DNA. Pizza is approachable, uncomplicated, and, for the most part, delicious. It crosses all sorts of boundaries and checks all the boxes—vegetarian, pork fiend, meat lover, picky kid, vegan, even gluten-free with more frequency lately (more on that at the end of the book). With unemployment soaring in 2020 and the loss of many local neighborhood restaurants, pizza also makes sense economically. The fact that you can feed a family of four for about thirty dollars is the proverbial Parmigiano-Reggiano icing on the cheese-and-sausage-laden cake.

So why write *another* book about Chicago's pizza scene? Because since I finished my first book—*Pizza City, USA: 101 Reasons Why Chicago Is America's Greatest Pizza Town* (published in the fall of 2018)—a lot has happened here. In that first book, I attempted to lay out my reasoning why the Second City was #1 when it came to the various styles of pizza offered. Not all in one place, like Tony's in San Francisco, where seven ovens produce upward of a dozen different regional styles. But rather, as a region. Because we have pizza *everywhere*, and it's rarely the above-ground pools New Yorkers love to mock. There's pizza in every one of the seventy-seven neighborhoods, and it's not all deep-dish. It's in touristy River North near Michigan Avenue, close to nightclubs, next to stadiums and bodegas, adjacent to shopping malls, side by side with currency exchanges, and hidden away inside Mexican restaurants.

New Yorkers have some outstanding pizza, no doubt about it. But most of it is limited to a narrow range of styles: giant slices—either wedges cut from eighteen-inch pies or squares cut from rectangular pans—plus a fair number of Neapolitans and some swanky artisan pies with farmers' market–driven ingredients. There are just a handful of Roman and Detroit-style pizzas and even fewer Chicago-style ones. In fact, I could count on one hand the number of recommendable deep-dish, stuffed, and Midwestern tavern-style pizzas in the New York City metro area. Don't believe me? Ask the local experts Adam Kuban (@akuban), Arthur Bovino (@nycbestpizza), or Scott Wiener (@scottspizzatours).

We are a city that embraces change and accepts the newness and the possibilities of something we've never seen before. Remember, we literally started from scratch in 1871 after the Great Fire. But we've always been like that, whether it was Daniel Burnham's skyscrapers in the late 1800s or Mies van der Rohe's modernist gems on Lake Shore Drive in the 1950s; Broadway producers bringing their shows here first for dry runs before launching them near Times Square; or chefs like Grant Achatz, Rick Bayless, and Paul Kahan (and Charlie Trotter before them, in the late '80s) knowing they'd have the creative freedom to express themselves to an audience more than willing to give it a go. Just as we don't rest on our laurels, we don't eat deep-dish every day. When Rome's Gabrielle Bonci—a favorite of the late Anthony Bourdain—decided to open his first *al taglio* pizzeria outside of Italy, guess where he decided to plant his flag? The West Loop. When I asked his American business partner why they chose Chicago, the answer was simple: "Because Chicagoans love to eat."

I identified ten different styles of pizza in that first book, highlighting 101 different places after six months of tasting through a gut-busting 185 locations (yes, there is a lot of bad pizza out there, and thank God for CorePower Yoga). But since I turned that book over to the publisher in late 2017, a wave of pizzerias has crashed upon our Italian beef-and-giardiniera-strewn streets like nothing I've seen in my thirty years of living here. The first book also led to the launch of my weekly tour business—Pizza City USA Tours—and my bimonthly podcast, Pizza City, which goes behind the scenes of some of the country's greatest pizzerias (www.pizzacityusa.com). For this part *due*, I managed to include 103 pizzas—almost half of which are new entries.

THE FIRST TWO CHICAGO PIZZA WAVES

Most locals really only think about the first two waves of pizza in Chicago. The first—Prohibition through post–World War II—featured the square-cut, thin-and-crispy pizzas most Chicagoans will tell you they grew up on. Doesn't matter if they're from Waukegan or Flossmoor. Unless you grew up in River North in the 1940s, chances are pretty good that if you're a kid from Chicagoland, you will have sharp, embedded memories, burned in like Neo's Matrix-generated childhood, of large, round pizzas cut into tiny squares. This is what I refer to in Pizza City as PIGUE (Pizza I Grew Up Eating) Syndrome. Others have referred to it as the Pizza Cognition Theory. Even a respected New York City chef such as Greg Baxtrom (Olmsted, Maison Yaki) will rhapsodize about the Aurelio's of his childhood, growing up in the southwestern suburbs. Sure, he'll talk up a classic slice from the likes of L'Industrie or Paulie Gee's in Brooklyn, but gun to the head, I'll bet you anything he'd say a sausage pie from Aurelio's triggers a Pavlovian response like ratatouille does for Anton Ego. I'll discuss the historical significance of these "Chicago-style thin" pizzas in chapter 4.

The second wave was undoubtedly the 1970s. By then, the city had only a handful of deep-dish places, 95 percent of them concentrated in River North, which meant they were the domain of tourists or locals seeking a special night out. This was the equivalent of eating at Famous Amadeus or Radio City Pizza in Times Square beneath a giant LCD display and saying it represented New York

City pizza. Larry Aronson was one of those local kids who loved going to River North's Uno—the birthplace of deep-dish in 1943—and wound up making his own version into a business called My Pi. But 1971 proved to be a watershed, and it's only fitting that the release of this book is timed to coincide with the fiftieth anniversary of that landmark year.

In early 1971, Burt Katz had just opened a place called Pequod's in Morton Grove, where he was making a modified deep-dish he called a "pan" pizza. That is, using the same deep pan, instead of pinching and lifting the dough up along the inner walls, he would simply let the dough proof in the pan and then place his mozzarella over it, so that parts of the cheese would also kiss the inner wall. When the pizza baked, the outer edge of the cheese would caramelize and char, offering a textural contrast, much like the Detroit-style pizzas that had been around since 1946. A few months later, on St. Patrick's Day, Lou Malnati opened his eponymous restaurant in a Swiss chalet–like building in Lincolnwood. Five months later, Larry Aronson opened My Pi on Loyola's campus, while at the same time, Rocco Palese was opening Nancy's on the Northwest Side, making a "stuffed" pizza no one had ever heard of before. It was unquestionably the dawn of the golden age of pizza in Chicago. Apollo 14 lands on the moon, America is introduced to Archie Bunker on CBS, and the Windy City is having a pizza gold rush as if it's Coloma, California, in 1849.

The second pizza wave also caused many pizzerias to expand their menus. Even if they were tavern-style specialists, they would suddenly offer deep-dish or stuffed or double-dough or Sicilian or possibly all of the above. It's like that quaint Thai place down the street trying to cook Chinese, Japanese, run a sushi bar, and also do justice to their khao soi and pad thai. Stretched too thin, chefs make a lot of marginal food rather than excelling at just a couple of things. Such was the case with Chicago pizzerias in the eighties and nineties, as they attempted to be one-stop shopping for every possible pizza craving while we watched Bulls playoff games seemingly every year. I still see this trend today at places like Pizza Bella in Palatine, where they offer no less than *six* styles of pizza: thin crust, double-dough, cheese-stuffed sliced crust, deep-dish, stuffed, and Detroit-style. How is anyone supposed to know which style is their specialty? If you have a less than stellar experience with one of those styles, would you go back a second time to give another one a try?

The excess of the eighties and lethargy of the nineties and aughts gave way to a comingling of deep-dish and stuffed (yes, there's a big difference, but out-of-towners and many locals still don't realize it). Some local mini-chains began expanding rather than focusing on one store. Quality and creativity dipped, giving the tourists and late-night comedians plenty of material with which to criticize the city's pizza. It didn't help that most visitors limited their excursions to Michigan Avenue, feeding a self-fulfilling prophecy of the same three or four pizza experiences, while locals were stuck primarily on the tavern-style pizzas from one of just four places:

- Near where they grew up
- On their way home from work
- Close to their kids' school
- Closest to home

THE THIRD WAVE

It's the third pizza wave I've been giving more thought to lately. Having the benefit of a little giardiniera-fueled hindsight, I see now that the city's most recent wave began around 2014. In the mid-teens, Labriola and its sister restaurant La Barra, founded by a commercial baker, began

I have had to figure out how to murder people, on a few occasions—strictly in the pages of novels. I was writing a political comedy called *Windy City* (not a satire, because Chicago politics is beyond satire), and was determined to open the story with the death of a Chicago political figure in the most flagrantly Chicago manner possible. Our local history does not, sadly, lack for examples. But the opinion from historians, literary figures, and opinionated readers seemed unanimous: it had to be a Chicago pizza, and it should be heavy and thick as a manhole cover. I heartily enjoyed the research.

Chicago today is blessed by scores of Beard-award laureled chefs and Michelin star kitchen stars, and thousands more in neighborhood spots around the city in which their talents reflect the human wealth of the world that calls Chicago home. And in a way, that's just confirmed the signature role of pizza in the food skyline. Chicago took something familiar, and shook it up with its own flair, innovation, style, and character.

One hot summer day a few years ago, my family had to report to a mortuary for my mother to be interred. We would wait a few months for a proper memorial. But our immediate family and a few friends gathered to bid good-bye to my mother, who so loved all things Chicago. At the ceremony's end, we were wistful, sad—and hungry. It took just a minute for someone to ask, "Pizza?" It was the obvious way to feed us in all ways—one Chicago classic over which we remembered another.

—**SCOTT SIMON**,
host of NPR's Saturday *Weekend Edition* and
special correspondent for *CBS Sunday Morning*

experimenting with longer fermented doughs and a reimagined deep-dish that was more balanced than its predecessors, with a serious dough bolstered by a Midwestern trifecta of corn oil, corn flour, and a coarse cornmeal undercarriage. It delivered that experience of getting a little bit of crust, cheese, sauce, and topping in every bite; the term I prefer using is Optimal Bite Ratio (OBR). This pizza wasn't a one-note boat anchor, and you didn't necessarily need a knife and fork (or a chainsaw) to eat it.

Then came the artisan pizzas. Guys like Jeff Lutzow, who had worked his way up in the kitchens at The Publican and Nico Osteria and quit his job to open Pizzeria Bebu, which changed the way we think about artisan pizza overnight. It was as if suddenly there was all of this kitchen talent out there, itching to do pizza rather than sautéed skate wing or sous vide short ribs. They were noticing what pizzerias in New York City were doing with longer fermentation times and higher hydration levels, and were making their own versions using Midwestern ingredients, and in some cases, flour and whole grains from our part of the country as well. Robert Garvey is another example. A transplanted New Yorker who grew up with a slice-a-day habit in Queens, he spent twenty years perfecting his dough and now treats each pie like it's his first: gently working out the three-day fermented dough with his fingers like he's playing a sonata, stretching it, and topping it with all manner of locally sourced ingredients—fennel he's pickled and roasted, sausage he's made, or even cured meats like duck prosciutto he's had shipped up from Smoking Goose Meatery in Indianapolis.

If these artisan and deep-dish pies laid the foundation for the third wave, the pandemic kick-started it like pouring lighter fluid on a Ravinia picnic's citronella candle.

Fifty percent of this book constitutes new listings. Most of these are places that have opened since early 2020. I also decided to focus this book more on the city. I realize if you're coming to Chicago for a couple days, you're not going to want to drive out to Warrenville to try Al's, or go all the way to Libertyville to sample the deep-dish at Pizza Italia, when there are several closer to downtown that are just as good. Since the first book has more of a big picture Chicagoland reach—which translates to a lot more tavern-style pies—this book takes a look at some places where the pizza might be overlooked: restaurants like Avec or Bungalow by Middle Brow that have great menus but also memorable pizzas. Those places deserve to be in any guide to Chicago pizza as much as a stalwart like Pat's or Villa Nova.

And speaking of the suburbs, yes, Villa Nova is back, along with the other "Suburban Stars" as I'm calling them, because even if you're only planning on visiting the city while you're in town, a lot of people come back home to visit family or they invariably wind up going to the suburbs to see things like the Frank Lloyd Wright homes in Oak Park or the Bahá'í Temple in Wilmette—I wanted them to have options as well, since finding independently owned pizzerias in the suburbs is like trying to remember a Bears winning season other than 1985. A few are new additions; others are classics that should not be missed and are worth the drive.

The other exciting thing that's happened in this third wave is the sheer number of new options in unexpected places: Detroit-style in an Edgebrook bar, Sicilian and tavern-style in a Bridgeport collective, weekly pop-ups in a Logan Square Indian-ish restaurant, outdoor ovens burning wood and charring pies year-round on the South Side. There are Michelin-starred chefs drilling down on Sicilian slices, producing pizza as good as anything in Williamsburg, and unemployed cooks pursuing their passion for the deep, caramelized pan pizzas started by Burt Katz fifty years ago. I hustled at the end of 2020 to capture all of it, first tasting, then shooting photos, and finally digging into the backstories to learn more about why these passionate cooks are turning to pizza now. For the pizzerias making a return appearance in this book, I've fleshed out their stories even more this time, adding context and perspective as to why they continue to make this their livelihood, and learning how they've managed to stay successful.

I also wanted to talk about some of the other important elements related to pizzas these days. With so many fantastic, personal microbreweries in town (a renaissance all its own), I asked local beer writer Josh Noel to dive into the various beers being produced locally and see which styles he'd recommend with different types of pizza. I also have been paying attention to the growing chorus of demand for gluten-free options. We launched Pizza City USA Tours in 2018—offering multiple tours every weekend from May through October—and the requests for gluten-free have steadily increased since then. I've provided a pretty comprehensive list at the end of the book of places where you can find some great gluten-free options.

Finally, the first-ever Chicago Pizza Family Tree! Illustrator Rich Lo really captured my vision, as I've struggled for years to try to explain the various styles on offer here. Each picture in that tree, by the way, is from an actual restaurant I visited.

Unlike the first book, this time around I've decided not to do a ranking of "Top 5" anything. I've got list fatigue, and besides, all of these places have been screened and tasted, so you can be assured they're all worth checking out. One important addition in this book is the expansion of the by-the-slice chapter. Not everybody listed in that chapter is making a New York–style pizza per se, but several great pizzas are now available by the slice, whether they're squares, rectangles, or triangular wedges. For that reason, several places might be listed twice in the book—under a Sicilian category, but also under the slice category. I wanted to give readers a quick and easy resource for nabbing a slice in the city without having to commit to a full pie, as I often did while eating my way through New York, at whole pie–only places like Lucali, Pizza Loves Emily, and John's of Bleecker Street.

I've also included a short story about the birth of the Pizza Puff. A Chicago original, this six-ounce snack was created here in the mid-1970s (as a response by hot dog stands that were experiencing competition from that second wave of pizza prodigiousness) by the family of an Iranian Assyrian immigrant who was in the tamale business. Most kids in Chicago take them for granted, but I loved this story of hard work and innovation, and how it led to the creation of a pizza treat now found in more than forty states—still run by the same family, now in the fourth generation.

Since businesses can pivot in the course of a few days, tracking their updates on Instagram became a necessary sport in 2020. For that reason, we've included the Instagram handle for every place listed here—assuming they're on Instagram—as an easy way to check their hours and location.

I hope you get as much enjoyment and inspiration from this book as I had assembling it. As we toast the fiftieth anniversary of several local icons, let's also celebrate the mom-and-pops in every neighborhood, relying on their stand mixers, hoping their ovens don't need a replacement part, and praying their drivers get the pizzas to you still warm. OBR always . . .

PIZZA BASICS

ILLUSTRATION BY RICH LO

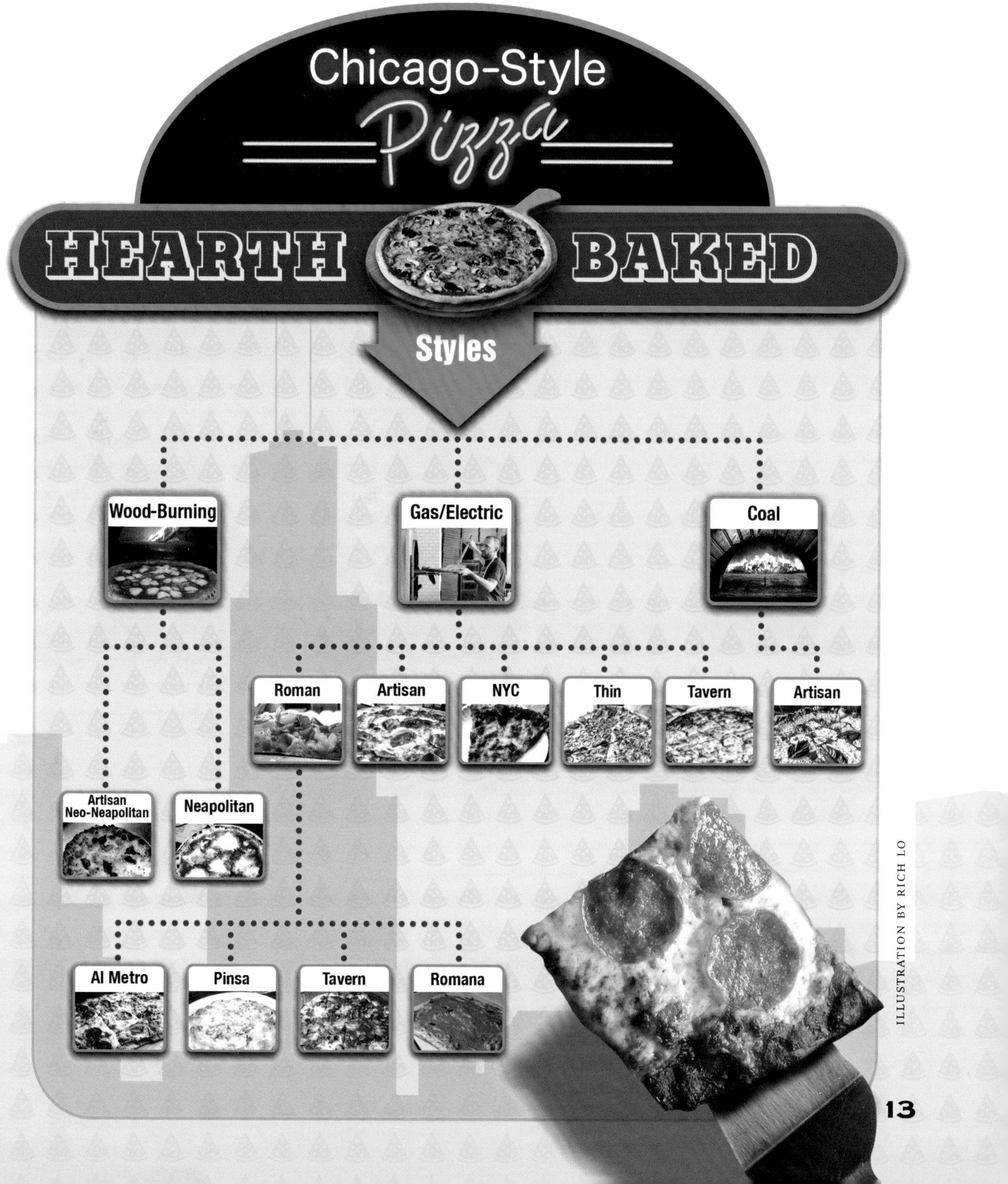

ILLUSTRATION BY RICH LO

1 WHAT IS CHICAGO-STYLE PIZZA?

When we started Pizza City USA Tours in 2018, we had a simple goal in mind: let guests experience four different styles of pizza in about three hours, while sharing local pizza history, mixed in with some Chicago history for good measure. We didn't want it to be a master class, but more like a casual hang with your buddy from college who just happened to be from Chicago. We're now up to four different tours every weekend and host a lot of private tours as well. You can find more info at www.pizzacityusa.com. One of the most important things I stress when training our doughcents is to emphasize the ten different styles of pizza we offer in Chicago: thin, Neapolitan, tavern-style (aka Chicago thin), NYC slices, artisan, deep-dish, stuffed, Roman, Sicilian, and Detroit. I think our variety, and the deep bench that's been fortified since the pandemic, has made the city an even stronger pizza city. But invariably, our guests want to know what does "Chicago-style" really mean?

Deep-dish, right? Well, sort of. That's one-third of the answer.

Nancy's stuffed pie

HOW DEEP IS YOUR SLICE?

Deep-dish was created here at a place called The Pizzeria (née Riccardo's) in 1943. Partners Ike Sewell and Ric Riccardo wanted to offer something a little different from the competition. Sewell wanted to have a Mexican restaurant, since he missed that from his native Texas. Riccardo convinced him to do pizza instead. Deep-dish was Sewell's answer to the thin "tavern-style" pizzas locals had been used to up to then. As a former University of Texas football player, Sewell believed the "bigger is better" mantra and, frankly, those puny squares weren't substantial enough for his Texas-sized appetite. Riccardo, and more likely Rudy Malnati Sr., their general manager, helped develop a pizza made in a deeper pan, built in reverse: dough, then cheese, followed by toppings, and finally a reduced, chunky tomato sauce.

The owners changed its name to Pizzeria Uno in 1955, when they opened Pizzeria Due just down the block. Riccardo had passed away the year before, and so Sewell, now the sole owner, sold franchises to a Boston-based company in 1978 and the brand began expanding in Massachusetts. After Sewell died in 1990, his widow sold the two Chicago pizzerias plus an adjacent Mexican restaurant, Su Casa, to the same Boston-based corporation. There are still just the two pizzerias in Chicago; the rest are scattered throughout Massachusetts and along the East Coast. The building at Ohio and Wabash may have given birth to deep-dish pizza, but the company that owns the brand abandoned the city more than thirty years ago (with a bankruptcy in 2010 for good measure).

Deep-dish Russo sausage from Labriola

The ironic thing about deep-dish is that despite its relative youth (compared to Chicago thin) and more limited exposure, at least historically in Chicagoland, it has, like a Japanese tsunami, completely obliterated any cogent discussion of Chicago's most ubiquitous pizza style. Chicagoans don't help their cause when they automatically default to a defensive crouch whenever a tweet or a late-night comedian or a Packers PR rep makes an offhand comment. In late 2020, Jimmy Fallon asked Barack Obama which pizza style he preferred, New York or Chicago? It would have been so cool if Obama would have asked for clarification: "Are you talking about tavern-style thin, deep, or stuffed, Jimmy?" He should know better! He and his family frequented Italian Fiesta on Forty-Seventh Street when they lived in Hyde Park—it was one of Michelle's favorites from growing up. But as long as people keep assuming "Chicago-style = deep-dish," there's going to be a perception problem. For the record, Obama chose a New York slice in what can only be described as a very political answer: preceded by a lot of love for his adopted home, but in the end, the simple logic of foldable portability won out.

It was so long ago that I can't remember the date, but pizza was a central character in the story.

I had just moved to Chicago and really did not know anyone. A couple of friends in New York mentioned that there was a great guy that I should meet in Chicago. Although I was too embarrassed to call him myself, as luck would have it, I ran into the guy at a party a few weeks later.

He asked me out the following weekend for dinner. The funny thing is that he kept asking me what kind of food I liked. I said that I was open to all kinds of food. He kept asking about my food preference and then he asked—how about pizza? Over time I would learn that this was one of the few foods John enjoyed. We had a lovely first date at Gino's East and got married about two years later. Although we are now divorced, we still enjoy pizza together with our daughter, Victoria. Thin crust for me; deep-dish for John.

—**DESIRÉE ROGERS**, CEO, Black Opal Beauty, and former White House social secretary during the Obama administration

THIN HAS ALWAYS BEEN IN

Tavern-style, or "Chicago thin" as it's frequently referred to, is our oldest and most prolific type of pizza. Midwesterners know what I'm talking about. Residents of Minnesota, Michigan, Wisconsin, and downstate Illinois are familiar with "bar pies." They started, not surprisingly, in the taverns in small towns and neighborhoods of Chicago, during Prohibition. Bartenders realized pretty quickly they only had customers for a short time before they made their way home for dinner. If they could give them something salty to eat, besides peanuts, they could get them to order more beers. Enter the bar pie. By making thin pizzas in their makeshift ovens, and cutting them into small squares—better to fit on a cocktail napkin—they could pass them around the bar for free. Customers would have a square or two, maybe the same number of beers, then head home for dinner. Tavern-style pies were always intended as a snack, not a meal.

"The square-cut pizza wound up being a staple of many classic Chicago taverns," said Tim Samuelson, cultural historian at the Chicago Cultural Center. "You can hold it in one hand and hold your drink in the other, which also marks the big difference with New York pizza, where you have to do this elaborate folding."

The workhorses like Vito & Nick's and Home Run Inn have roots that stem back to the 1920s. Like a lot of bars back then, they morphed into full-fledged pizzerias once the sons or sons-in-law came back from the war. (Home Run Inn was a tavern in the '30s, but became a pizzeria in 1947.)

One important element to point out: there is definitely a preference for a sweeter sauce on the South and Southwest Sides of the city. I've noticed this in the African American community when it comes to barbecue sauce. I've never been a fan of the Midwestern preference for sugar in sauces, since sugar burns and usually turns the sauce a darker color (it also overwhelms the tasty, savory notes in food). Also, I'm just not a fan of extra sweetness. But have a pizza at Triano's on South Archer Avenue or Arrenello's in Tinley Park ("That's-a-Some-Sweet-Pizza" they proclaim on their website) and you'll know right away there's sugar involved. Most places will use a little bit of sugar to balance the acidity of the tomatoes, but an all-out sweet sauce is definitely something preferred by Sox fans and regulars at the Glenwoodie Golf Club.

Tavern-thin from Salerno's

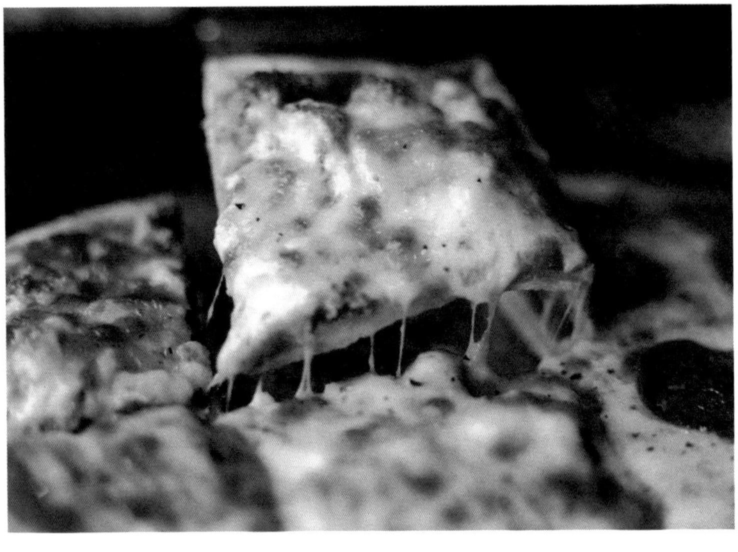

Every neighborhood and suburb in the region from the 1930s onward made this "Chicago thin" style of pizza. Eventually, entire pies are ordered and brought home so the kids can have some as well. Meanwhile, a handful of places in River North are offering deep-dish in the forties and fifties, with one more added in the sixties. Getting deep-dish is very much the Chicago equivalent of a NYC trip to Times Square until the 1970s.

I'M STUFFED

The year 1971 is the turning point. Rocco Palese, the owner of Nancy's in Harwood Heights, is itching to do something different from all the deep-dish places opening up. Nearly thirty years after Ike Sewell, Ric Riccardo, and Rudy Malnati decided to shift course from the sea of thin tavern pizzas to create a deep-dish, Rocco starts making a "stuffed pizza," based on an Easter pie from Italy that was traditionally stuffed with ricotta, salami, and eggs and eaten to commemorate the end of Lent. I get more into this in chapter 6, but suffice it to say that stuffed becomes the hottest pizza in town in 1974, when *Chicago* magazine bestows its "Best Pizza" award on Nancy's. Meanwhile, that same year, two former Nancy's employees open Giordano's on the South Side with essentially the same recipe.

In March 1977, *Chicago* magazine put Giordano's on its cover, with the headline "Discovery: Chicago's Best Pan Pizza." The eight-page article by Phyllis Magida, who had assembled an eight-member tasting panel—likely including Carla Kelson, the magazine's restaurants editor, and Dennis Ray Wheaton, the magazine's restaurant critic at the time—unanimously chose Giordano's as the city's best pizza. How times have changed. For all of you FanDuel oddsmakers, here was the ranking of the city's eight best pizzas from 1977, in descending order: Giordano's, Gino's East, Nancy's, Pizzeria Uno, Pizzeria Due, Pequod's, Gino's, Lou Malnati's (ouch). Note that #1 and #3 are stuffed pies, while #6 is a deep pan with a caramelized edge. Ironically, just a year later, Ike Sewell would start selling Uno's franchises on the East Coast. Judges liked Giordano's "high, double-crusted, oozing 14-inch souffle-like pizza . . .

substance without clumsiness . . . leaves a warm glow; beautiful, huge and oozing, the Cecil B. DeMille of pizza." I'm convinced the tasters were stoned when they did their eating. I found this excerpt particularly telling, a snapshot of how professional eaters regarded our homegrown pizza forty-plus years ago:

> *Deep-dish pizza is a ritual food, we concluded—a hassle-free, old clothes, complete, easy meal . . . Perhaps the quality that made it special was the sitting together, the waiting to be served; or maybe it was the atavistic eating together that is done with the hands; or possibly it was just we all shared it equally and together. But whatever this amorphous gestalt was, we concluded, thick-crust, deep-dish, Chicago-style pizza makes you feel better after eating it—and happier, and more mellow about whomever you happen to share it with.*

The one thing stuffed pizza has in common with deep-dish is the pan. But unlike its deep cousin, stuffed pies feature a second layer of dough across the top of the pie, just like if you were making a fruit pie with a double crust. The top layer isn't as thick as the bottom, has a few vent holes cut into it, and it holds up all the tomato sauce. The founder of Nancy's didn't like the ingredients stewing in the sauce, so this was a way to separate them, ensuring they could be tasted individually. I wasn't able to confirm this, but I'm pretty sure Rocco Palese was one of those kids who didn't want his food touching.

Moral of the story—when someone asks you, "What is Chicago-style pizza?" you tell them this:

It is three styles.

1. Square-cut, thin and crispy tavern pizzas are the most prevalent and have the longest history.
2. Deep-dish started downtown as a tourist attraction and is now a special occasion pizza—Lou Malnati's has dominated the category since the 1970s.
3. Stuffed is an offshoot of deep-dish, with a pie-like second layer of top crust, and while Giordano's has seventy locations across the country, serving as a de facto Chicago pizza ambassador, it's rarely eaten by locals within the city limits.

ILLUSTRATION BY DAN BRANSFIELD FROM CITIESBYTHESLICE.COM

To put it in terms my New York City friends would understand: stuffed pizza is to Chicago as Sbarro is to New York. Even though it was founded in Brooklyn in 1956, are you really going to tell me it represents your city's dominant pizza style?

As for deep-dish: if you're going to judge my city by Uno's, then I'll judge NYC pizza by Grimaldi's. Yes, there used to be just one beneath the Brooklyn Bridge, but now there are more than forty around the United States, including joints in Idaho, Texas, and Wisconsin. I rest my case. Now go toss another garbage bag onto the sidewalk and get in line for a Cronut.

NO STANDEES

2 METHODOLOGY

WHO DIED AND CROWNED ME the expert on pizza? I get this question frequently, and I'm happy to make my case here. Let's forget, for a moment, my professional credentials. I could probably just say I've been covering food professionally in Chicago full-time since 1995 and leave it at that. I've also eaten pizzas at some of the touchstones in America—Bianco (Phoenix), Frank Pepe's (New Haven), A16 and Delfina (San Francisco), Mozza (Los Angeles), and Lucali, Scarr's, L'Industrie, and Patsy's (NYC). But the thing that truly qualifies me more than anyone else is the fact that I wasn't born in Chicago.

Stay with me.

One of the unfortunate things pizza does is it creates bias. Midway through my research, I diagnosed a common ailment that affects thousands of people, which most likely includes you or someone you know. That malady is the Pizza I Grew Up Eating (PIGUE) Syndrome. The result of countless birthday parties, special events, and high school sleepovers, PIGUE somehow attaches itself to the frontal cortex. Few of us have fully developed palates when we're young, so it's difficult to assess food accurately in your preteen and teenage years.

The author leading a Pizza City USA tour, covering four styles in three hours

The pizza I had as a kid in St. Cloud, Minnesota, was Shakey's (born in Sacramento, 1954). It was our go-to destination after Little League games (followed by Dairy Queen), and it served as a de facto birthday headquarters for me and many of my friends. Do I think Shakey's has the best pizza in the world? Of course not—it's chain food mediocrity along the lines of Pizza Hut, Domino's, and Little Caesar's. I'm wise enough to know that there are plenty of pizzas out there far superior to the processed-cheese-and-sweet-tomato-sauce-on-cardboard that defined my childhood pizza eating experience.

PIGUE Syndrome, however, hits Chicagoans especially hard. I can now tell where someone is from based solely on the kind of pizza they love. You like Armand's? I'm guessing you grew up near Elmwood Park. More of an Aurelio's person? Even if you don't insist it comes out of the "old" oven, there's a pretty good chance you grew up in Homewood or Flossmoor. Still think Barnaby's has the best thin crust in the world? Here's some news for you: not only are you from the North Shore but that cornmeal crust is a myth—they only sprinkle cornmeal (as many other smart places do) underneath the pizza to keep the crust from sticking to the bottom of the oven.

But I get it. PIGUE affects everyone (the term I've seen used by East Coast writers, perhaps first used by the *New York Times*'s Sam Sifton, is the Pizza Cognition Theory). It doesn't matter if the dough is tough or flavorless, the mozzarella is pre-shredded from a giant bag, or the sausage comes in frozen. No one—not even a professional eater who attempts to judge on a level playing field—is going to change their mind. Which leads me back to my thesis on why I'm the most qualified person to tackle this subject.

I didn't grow up here, but I've lived in Chicago for nearly thirty years. I have no childhood memories from any of these legendary joints, but I moved here in my twenties, just as my palate started to grow up, and shortly thereafter began eating professionally. I became wise enough to know the difference between a place that made its own gyros (Parthenon) and one that didn't, despite its outsized reputation (sorry, Chuck Wagon). I still had plenty to learn, of course, and still do, but I like to think I don't carry biases around like those misguided souls who still think Gene & Jude's makes the best hot dogs.

In *Pizza City, USA*, I stuck to a strict rule: every pizza ordered would be half-sausage, half-pepperoni. Mainly because while pepperoni is the most popular topping in America, sausage beats it by a long shot in Chicago. Partly that has to do with the fact that the Union Stockyards were based here for decades. Companies like

Swift and Armour started here, and Italian immigrants found raw "bulk" sausage much easier to come by than pepperoni. Generations of kids here grew up on sausage pies, occasionally topped with giardiniera, our favorite condiment of briny and spicy chilies, carrots, celery, cauliflower, and sometimes olives, which usually finds its way onto Italian beef sandwiches.

This time around, I was also including restaurants and non-pizzerias like Avec and Table, Donkey & Stick, as well as pop-ups relying on local produce, and bread bakers more attuned to the crumb and crust on their pies. With talented chefs behind many of these new entries, I couldn't just limit orders to pepperoni and sausage. If the pizza place specialized in a Neapolitan-style with a fancier wood-burning oven and listed a Margherita, then that's what I'd order as a baseline, judging just the crust, tomato sauce, and mozzarella (but mostly crust). But if they had a wild mushroom special (Avec) or a pickled fennel situation (Sauce and Bread Kitchen), that's what I'd have to order.

I made a point to call ahead before visiting each establishment to ask what their specialty was, to ensure I was trying the proper pizza at each place. In several instances, menus listed multiple styles—thin, extra thin, double-dough, deep-dish, and stuffed—so I'd ask the person on the phone taking the order what the restaurant was known for. A few times they'd offer up a personal favorite from the menu, which didn't influence me at all. In several cases, a restaurant ended up in more than one category, such as thin crust *and* by-the-slice or New York–style. Paulie Gee's Logan Square, for example, is now listed

My husband and I were newlyweds and we . . . well, *he*, volunteered to coach a Little League team made up of boys from the Jane Addams' Homes. I became the Team Mama (or so I was called). The kids had never played baseball before, and my husband spent two afternoons a week readying them for their first game, while I looked on from the dugout. The motivation to win? Bragging rights and (maybe more importantly) pizza at Uno's! My husband has not met many pizzas he's disliked, so he was highly motivated too.

Well, *they won*! So, we took them, covered with sweat and diamond dirt, to Uno's off Michigan Avenue. What we didn't know was that the children had never had deep-dish pizza before. We watched them try to navigate their way around the pizzas—trying to pick up slices, grabbing knives and forks, trying to see how long their wads of cheese could stretch—it was a fun night! We had many more of those pizza nights—sometimes celebrating wins, sometimes easing losses. It was a way to connect with them. Even now, as men, my husband still meets some of them over pizza, because there isn't a better way to catch up . . . not in Chicago!

—**HEATHER HEADLEY**,
Tony and Grammy Award–winning singer, actress, and Northwestern University alumna

three separate times in the book: artisan (wood-fired), Detroit-style, and NYC slice (at its new Wicker Park location).

Some legendary spots are not included here. There is no Giordano's, Uno, Due, or Gino's East. Heresy? Disrespect? Possibly. Sure, there's a reason they've been in business for so long, but one could argue that's as much a result of tourists, out-of-town media, and private equity as it is true staying power based on quality and consistency. Uno and Due have been owned by a Boston-based corporation since the early nineties and have neither preserved nor improved the recipe; they went through Chapter 11 bankruptcy in 2010, emerging with a very different company based mostly on the East Coast.

Giordano's has been sold twice—the first time in 1988, when the founding brothers sold to former employee John Apostolou, whose kids ran it until 2011. That year, Victory Park Capital Advisors, a Chicago-based private equity firm, became the second buyer, acquiring the company through a bankruptcy auction.

Gino's East has grown to encompass ten locations, including Nashville and LA—although their headquarters is still in Chicago. They've been around since 1966, but I think they've also strayed from the original experience. When my friend Adam and I visited the Superior Street flagship for my anonymous tasting at lunch, we were not allowed to order ahead, and thus had to wait a full sixty-five minutes before our preposterously heavy, yellow-crusted pizza was set before us. I'm not the only one who thinks something is amiss. Brian Tondryk, grandson of Fred Bartoli, one of the founders of Gino's East, decided to open his own place several years ago—Bartoli's—because he was so annoyed with what had happened to his grandfather's pizza legacy (which should really be attributed to Alice Mae Redmond, the cook Bartoli and his partners hired away from Due's when they opened Gino's East).

As for the Chicago Pizza and Oven Grinder Co., which I'm asked about on nearly every Pizza City USA tour, I greatly respect the building's history, its connection to the St. Valentine's Day Massacre and Al Capone, and its rebirth from a devastating fire in the early seventies, but I'll just say this: melted cheese in a soggy bread bowl is not pizza. Thank u, next.

As always, I'm looking primarily at the crust (which is why bread bakers always have a slight edge), vibrancy of the sauce, the sausage (raw, pinched-and-pressed with just enough fennel) and pepperoni quality, application and mouthfeel of cheese(s), and overall taste—with crust weighing most heavily in the equation. Ratio is certainly a factor: the term I came up with is Optimal Bite Ratio (OBR). If the crust was good but overwhelmed by too much cheese and toppings that express moisture and result in sogginess, then points were deducted. Conversely, that didn't mean I wanted a mouthful of bare baked crust in every bite, the pizza equivalent of biting into the end of a Parkway Tavern po'boy that's all bread, no shrimp.

HUGE GALDONES

Guests on a Pizza City USA tour at Pizzeria Bebu

Finally, I always visited anonymously, without warning, and oftentimes alone, although on occasion I went with a friend or relative who was game. I always paid with my own credit card (essentially spending my book advance on pizzas) and, after leaving, would occasionally but not always post a picture and some commentary on Instagram, where I post both @stevedolinsky as well as @pizzacityusa. If you're curious about where I ate in New York City, check out #StevesNYCPizza. I've got a lot more summaries written about pizzerias visited on the pizzacityusa.com site, under the tab ABOUT and then OTHER CITIES.

3 GLOSSARY OF PIZZA TERMINOLOGY

Some of the following terms are industry standards. Others I created myself after realizing there were no other words to describe what I intended to say. It's a short list, but if you scan it quickly you'll gain a better understanding of my descriptions of individual places and pizzas, as I tend to use them frequently while describing pizzas in this book.

"00" The type of Italian flour usually used by hardcore *pizzaiolos* when making a Neapolitan pizza. The Caputo brand is the most widely used and considered a gold standard.

Associazione Vera Pizza Napoletana (AVPN) A governing body based in Italy—the Neapolitan Pizza Association—founded in Naples in 1984. Its mission is to promote and protect "true Neapolitan pizza" ("verace pizza Napoletana") around the world. It bestows the AVPN designation to *pizzaiolos* and restaurants that abide by a number of strict guidelines regarding the type of flour, tomatoes, and cheese, as well as the length of fermentation, type of oven, and other quality controls. Some highlights from the eleven pages of rules include:

Dough: The dough must be made using wheat flour type "00," water (71.6 degrees Fahrenheit with a ph of 6–7), sea salt, and compressed or natural yeast, and allowed to rise twice for a total of about eight hours.

Jeff Lutzow of Pizzeria Bebu

HUGE GALDONES

Fresh Tomatoes: Fresh San Marzano dell'Agro Sarnese-Nocerino DOP, Pomodorini di Corbara (Corbarino), Pomodorino del piennolo del Vesuvio DOP, and fresh or industrially prepared Roma tomatoes ("pomodoro lungo tipo Roma") can be used.

Canned Tomatoes: Pomodoro pelato San Marzano dell'Agro Sarnese-Nocerino DOP are acceptable canned peeled tomatoes. They should be strained, broken up, and homogenized by hand. Peeled tomatoes that are genetically modified or altered to increase desired traits, resistance to herbicides, or increased crops are unacceptable.

Cheese: Only the following cheeses are acceptable: certified mozzarella *di bufala* Campana DOP, mozzarella S.T.G., *fior di latte dell'appennino meridionale* DOP, and other certified *fior di latte*.

Cooking: The pizza must be cooked for no more than 60 to 90 seconds in a (oak, ash, beech, or maple) wood-fired oven that has reached 905 degrees Fahrenheit.

avalanche That depressing sight when you pull a pizza fresh from the oven, then remove a slice, and, as you pull it away from the pie, all the toppings slide off the crust. Term first documented by First We Feast. Also interchangeable with **mud slide**, depending on the severity of the slide.

beehive Refers to the shape of the brick wood-burning oven that is typically the focal point for a serious pizza operation. This includes a large igloo-shaped bottom where the wood burns and the pizzas cook, as well as a long, slender vent to guide smoke out of the building.

char The blackened spots that dot a pizza, usually from excessive hot spots in the oven. Charring is typically more prevalent on Neapolitan pies. New Haven, Connecticut, pizzas (especially Modern Apizza) tend to feature a lot of charring since they have coal ovens.

char dome A small dome, anywhere from a half-inch to an inch or so in diameter, which appears on the surface of artisan and Neapolitan pizzas. Char domes are blackened and filled with air pockets.

cheese lava The runny, oozing mass of mozzarella that typically spills out of an over-stuffed deep-dish, or (more likely) a stuffed pizza, when a slice is moved to a plate.

cheese pull Think of the Instagram-worthy shot of the mozzarella pulling away from the slice as you remove it from the main pie. Some pulls are flaccid and runny; others sturdy and majestic. Either way, a decent pull means the kitchen isn't skimping on mozzarella. Too much cheese pull, however, might mean an imbalance when it comes to OBR and a serious impediment to lactose intolerant eaters.

cornicione **(cor-nee-CHO-nay)** The outer lip or heel, or puffy perimeter, of a Neapolitan pizza. The *cornicione* should be slightly misshapen and jagged but also chewy and filled with tiny air pockets.

crumb The interior part of the pizza, usually referring to the part inside the heel or *cornicione*. The longer the yeast has to eat the sugars creating carbon dioxide inside the dough, the more riddled with air pockets the inside becomes. This adds lift, but also textural contrast and chewability. Also referred to as "hole structure" or, in bread baker's parlance, "open crumb structure."

crust The outermost part of the pizza. The barrier, the first thing you touch on the edge of a pizza and the first part of the pizza that your mouth encounters. Usually colored a deep brown, or in cases like some New Haven, Connecticut, pizzas, charred to black.

crust orphans Also referred to as "dough bones" or "pizza bones," these are the discarded pieces of heel or *cornicione* left over after someone eats only the part of a slice of pizza with cheese and/or sauce on it. They are usually a result of the crust not having enough flavor on its own. Once the cheese and/or sauce-covered parts of the slice are finished, these resulting "bones" are not pleasant enough to eat on their own. They can also be a result of pizza eaters not wanting to fill up on crust, in order to save room for more of the pizza's interior.

cup-and-char Refers to a type of old-school pepperoni with a natural casing. In the 1940s and '50s, all pepperoni had a natural casing, and when the small discs of pepperoni were baked, they would curl up, forming a cup shape (sometimes called a pepperoni chalice), holding the rendered grease inside each one. The edges of the cup would get charred in the baking of the pizza, resulting in tiny cups that were crisp on the edge but somewhat softer inside. In the '70s and '80s, manufacturers and pizzerias wanted the pepperoni to lay flat on the pizza, so this old style became less popular. Today, manufacturers like Ezzo Sausage in Columbus, Ohio, and Rosa Grande (Hormel) are bringing back the cup-and-char style, which has been popularized at joints like Prince Street Pizza in NYC.

docker Also referred to as a dough docker or roller docker, this hand-held tool has a small cylinder at the end (think of a mini steamroller like you'd see smoothing out blacktop) that has small squat pins or spikes on it. Bakers roll it across their doughs before baking to get rid of air pockets and prevent undesired rising or blistering in the middle of the pizza.

doming The act of using a pizza peel to raise a pizza in a wood-burning oven up to the highest point of the dome, where the hottest temperatures are. This quickly sears and bakes the top of the pizza, creating a little extra char and caramelization.

DOP Stands for *Denominazione di Origine Protetta*, a guarantee from the AVPN that cheese meets certain explicit standards related to origin, production, and aging.

fermentation The process of letting the dough rest to allow the yeast and bacteria inside the dough to convert carbohydrates to carbon dioxide, which causes gas bubbles to form. This has a leavening effect on dough, and the process causes a strong aromatic sensation that is usually pleasing. Every *pizzaiolo* has a different method for where and how long they ferment their dough. Some do a cold ferment in a cooler, while others leave the dough out at room temperature. It all depends on the ambient temperature where the pizzas are made.

***fior di latte* (fee-OR de LAH-tay)** Fresh mozzarella made from pasteurized or unpasteurized cow's milk rather than water buffalo milk (*bufala*), which is what a Neapolitan purist would typically use. It's usually less expensive than *bufala* and more widely used in America.

frico Term for the crispy cheese edge that forms around the perimeter of a square or rectangular Detroit-style pizza. Historically, it would be Wisconsin brick cheese, placed up along the edge of the raw dough, touching the upper, inner wall of the pan. The cheese melts down between dough and pan, caramelizing and turning black during the bake. *Frico* has since been adopted by other styles, such as deep pan pizzas in Chicago—Burt Katz famously employed a *frico* on his deep pans at Burt's in the '70s in Morton Grove, and the technique has spread to many other pizzerias, such as Apollonia in Los Angeles, where they are minor works of art.

leavening During fermentation, gas bubbles expand inside the dough, making it increase in size.

leopard spotting The tiny black char spots that line the perimeter of a nicely fermented Neapolitan or artisan pizza. Usually attained from baking in a hot, wood-fired oven.

lip The outer ring, or perimeter, of the pizza, frequently referred to as the "heel." Also known as a *cornicione* when talking about a Neapolitan pie.

mozzarella *di bufala* (BOO-fah-la) Fresh mozzarella made from the milk of the water buffalo. When true mozzarella is made in the Italian style, it usually calls for this kind of milk. Domestic producers in the United States often substitute *fior di latte*, or cow's milk. It is the crème de la crème for making Neapolitan pizza. It is usually offered on select menus for an additional cost, since most of it is imported from Italy. It has a richer, fuller fat flavor than standard whole milk or even fresh mozzarella.

Optimal Bite Ratio (OBR) My term for the perfect combination of dough, cheese, sauce, and toppings in each bite. Balance is key, either elevating a pie to the best-in-class or sinking it into the realm of forgettable pizzas. By extension, the term can also be applied to sandwiches, tacos, and Thai curries.

oven spring The suddenly rapid increase in the dough's expansion after it has been launched into the oven. The effect stops once the temperature of the dough reaches 140 degrees Fahrenheit (that's when the yeast dies). Contributes to additional open crumb structure.

peel The long-handled tool, usually with a metal or wooden head slightly wider than a pizza, used to move the pizza in and out of the oven as well as to reposition it while baking, which ensures even cooking. Typically, wooden peels are used to launch pizzas into the oven, while metal peels are used to move pizzas around and then remove them from the oven.

PIGUE Syndrome "Pizza I Grew Up Eating" is an affliction, a crippling bias that forces normally sane people to support the notion that the pizza they grew up with is somehow the best on the planet. Occurs most frequently in the Chicago suburbs. Also referred to as the "Pizza Cognition Theory."

pizzaiolo A person responsible for making pizza—from the dough to the sauce and on through the baking process. The word is usually used to refer to a person with extensive training who has mastered the Neapolitan pie.

proofing Term used by bakers for the final rise of shaped dough before baking. It refers to a specific resting period within the fermentation process.

San Marzano The tomato variety of choice not only for Neapolitan aficionados but also for many artisan cooks and *pizzaiolos*.

sheeter A machine with two opposing rollers that you can set to a desired thickness. It is used to pass balls of dough through, pressing them out into flat, wide sheets. While convenient and good for eliminating any chance that an inexperienced cook will mess up a dough by inexpertly hand-tossing or rolling out with a pin, sheeters tend to force all the air out of the dough, resulting in a tougher crust. Used mainly for tavern-style and thin, uniform pizzas.

tip sag The droop that occurs when you pick up a standard wedge slice by the heel, folding to maintain tension, and the tip of the slice still droops, forcing you to either hold the slice higher in order to steer it into your mouth, or fold the floppy tip over against itself, forming a sort of oblong rectangle so that you must then decide which end to start on.

undercarriage The area beneath the pizza that you usually can't see, unless you lift up a slice. It's the only part of the pizza that's in direct contact with the oven's surface. Also referred to as the "skirt" or the "bottom."

VPN A designation awarded to qualifying pizzerias by the Naples-based Associazione Verace Pizza Napoletana, also called Vera Pizza Napoletana.

PIZZA STYLES

4 TAVERN-STYLE (CHICAGO-STYLE THIN)

ASK DIE-HARD CHICAGOANS how they define "Chicago pizza" and they'll respond with a unanimous "thin" rather than "thick." So why is it that out-of-towners think Chicago is a deep-dish town? Blame it on the media, I guess, and those giant Giordano's billboards. Maybe it's because Pizzeria Uno debuted here in 1943 or because tourists come in droves to see, taste, and poke around what they think makes Chicago famous. But no amount of advertising or tourism hype can change the fact that *most* Chicagoans like their pizza thin.

Maybe a little history can explain this great pizza misconception. Chicago is the city that works, and immigrants who originally built the roads, bridges, and skyscrapers loved to end the workday at the neighborhood tavern for a beer. Savvy bar owners realized they could make ultra-thin pizzas for cheap, cut their pies into tiny squares (known as the "party cut"), and then pass the bite-sized snacks around the bar. Interestingly enough, "bar pies," as they're known on the East Coast and in New York City, tend to be baked first in a shallow pan, then finished directly on the stone or steel hearth; they're always cut into wedges, according to NYC pizza guru Adam Kuban.

The goal for Chicago's early tavern owners was to get something salty into the customers' mouths so they'd order more beer. The plan worked. This practice launched the Chicago tavern-style pizza, also known as Chicago-style thin, which shows up at legendary places like Marie's, Vito & Nick's, and Pat's, not to mention suburban haunts like Barnaby's and Armand's.

Chicago thin at Salerno's

In line with this backstory, Chicago historian Tim Samuelson says that one of the reasons thin, square-cut pizzas came about was because "you can pop the whole piece in your mouth at once. The corners—you've got a lot of nice pieces in there. That built-in crusty handle is missing from the middle. But you rarely see a pizza platter with any remaining pizza going back to the kitchen."

In other words, those middle pieces have no crust on their borders; they're flabby and cheesy all the way around. The pie's corner pieces have actual hard crust on the sides—your "crusty handle"—which makes it easier to hold a pizza slice. Chicagoans actually have two camps of pizza eaters when it comes to tavern pies: Edges and Middles (I'm an Edger).

The late film critic Roger Ebert was also a fan of Chicago thin pizza. Ebert, who grew up downstate, attended the University of Illinois at Urbana-Champaign, and lived for many years in Chicago, was always a fan of tavern-style pies. He and his on-camera co-host, Gene Siskel, were fond of Father & Son on Milwaukee Avenue, but in the early 1990s, Ebert declared Pat's to be his personal favorite. The restaurant's business nearly doubled overnight.

There are entire swaths of the city that claim true Chicago pizza is thin and not a thick casserole. My eating research led me to actually identify five different categories of thin pizza in Chicago: thin, Chicago-style thin (or tavern-style), Neapolitan, New York–style slices, and artisan. After all my research, I theorize that tavern-style is what Chicagoans mean by "thin." Unfortunately, some old-school favorites like Pete's (b. 1955) and J. B. Alberto's (b. 1965) fell flat. In other cases, places I'd heard great reviews of, like Green Street Local and John's Pizzeria on Western Avenue, remained closed during the pandemic, especially at the end of 2020, when I was doing a lot of my final tasting, so I was unable to try for myself.

Much of *Pizza City, USA* was dedicated to this style. From gems like Chester's Tavern and Orsi's Pizza in Summit to blink-and-you'll-miss-it Bije's on West

I grew up in Berwyn, so my parents would order Salerno's every Saturday night. Then we moved to St. Charles and switched to Armand's, which is still my favorite today. Those are a couple of real Chicagoland classics, but those Saturday nights when we knew we were getting some delicious pizza for dinner were always a highlight of the weekend as a kid. I do also enjoy the Chicago deep-dish—Art of Pizza and Pequod's are my definite favorites in that category, no offense to Lou.

—**WAYNE RANDAZZO**,
play-by-play announcer, New York Mets

Pinch-and-press sausage pie at Vito & Nick's

Irving Park Road, a solid 25 percent of that first book is focused on tavern-style. The problem with places like those two—they're just too far away if you're only in Chicago for a couple of days. For that reason, I focused this chapter more on a few gems within the city; a few more are listed in chapter 15 ("Suburban Stars"). If you really want a fuller picture of tavern-style options in and around Chicago, by all means order my first book, *Pizza City, USA*, from the publisher!

I'm also including a basic recipe here from the guys at Pizza Fried Chicken Ice Cream in Bridgeport. In 2020, they reverse-engineered the fabulous tavern-style pizza from Pat's in Lincoln Park. I realize most people don't have a dough sheeter at home, and keeping the rolled-out dough in your refrigerator for five days may not be practical, but I hope it will give you a taste of what they've been able to create at their fabulous ode to Chicago-style thin pizza. At the very least, their recipe will give you a new appreciation for it the next time you visit them.

FLO & SANTOS

1310 S. Wabash Avenue
312-566-9817
www.floandsantos.com
@floandsantos

Touting "pizza & pierogi," and with a giant signboard listing the number of Polish vodkas they carry, this South Loop neighborhood joint clearly has more than just pizza on the menu. A number of sandwiches and salads also star here, although their Polish ingredients—like smoked kielbasa and sauerkraut—can also be used as pizza toppings. I never really thought of it until I visited, but that combo is so perfect for Chicago—a city where fennel-laced sausage and pickled giardiniera cover thousands of pizzas. Why not substitute Polish smoked sausage and briny sauerkraut? We are a city, after all, with a massive Polish population. Flo & Santos typically has a "Farmers' Market" pizza as a special, but, as per my original pizza quest rules, I opted for their half-sausage (Italian rather than Polish) and half-pepperoni pie.

The crust here is your classic tavern-style, which I'd define as a supremely thin layer of dough that's just enough to hold the toppings. I would have preferred a slightly crisper crust, as there was no crunch, just chew. Whole milk mozzarella is generously applied, though a tad too heavily in the center, where it overwhelms the ingredients. The toppings themselves are tasty, especially the generous crumbles of sausage. The sauce is pleasant, but not necessarily remarkable—kind of like an older Tame Impala song, it's great the first time you hear it but doesn't get stuck in your head.

Overall, it's a tasty pizza that I'd have no problem crushing with a hungry friend. If you want a place to watch the game, eat some pizza, and drink a nice craft beer (or sip Polish vodka), there are few better options in the South Loop. And if your picky uncle from the burbs doesn't feel like pizza, he'll be content with some of the hearty menu's other plentiful options.

GEO'S PIZZA

2849 N. Harlem Avenue
773-237-4450
www.geospizzachicago.com

DON'T PLAN ON GETTING too comfortable waiting for your pizza at Geo's. The beloved Montclare joint has a couple of wooden benches in the tight front room, adorned with maps, pictures of both Wrigley and Comiskey (sorry, I forget which corporate sponsor currently has naming rights), some military pictures, and a Hawks sign. The kitchen is about ten times as large as the front room, and the old clothespins used to hold tickets are straight out of another era. You just know the old guys in the kitchen speak Chicago-ese (Da Bears, saaasage, etc.).

Geo's is located directly in the middle of Chicago's second Italian wave. After families fled Little Italy and Taylor Street following the expansion of the UIC campus and the Eisenhower Expressway in the 1950s and '60s, most resettled up and down Harlem Avenue, which divides the city limits from towns like Harwood Heights, Elmwood Park, and Norridge. You can throw a stone in any direction and still hit a pasta shop, bakery, or mom-and-pop grocery store. Ironically, only a year before Geo's opened in 1972, Nancy's had started making its stuffed pizza just two and a half miles north, at Lawrence and Harlem Avenues.

They sell tavern-style thin and deep-dish, but the people who recommended it encouraged me to go with the Chicago thin. I loved how the zippy sauce is drawn all the way to the edge, balanced between acid and sweetness, although I think if they had left any part of the crust bare, it wouldn't be nearly as enjoyable uncovered. Sausage boulders are textbook, exactly what I want in pizza topping: jagged, generous, and kissed with enough fennel to remind you it's there in every bite. The cheese—applied generously without being overbearing—is mottled brown in spots from the heat, like a dalmatian. My sausage and giardiniera served as a delicious reminder of how well fattiness plays against briny crunch.

I'm not a fan of delivery or carry-out pizzas—I've gone on the record several times about how they rob the pizza (and its maker) of proper appreciation. But there is no other option here. I'd suggest just eating it on the tailgate of your car. Don't forget to bring cash (there's an ATM in the Walgreen's across the street), as they don't take plastic. My kinda town, Chicago is . . .

HOME RUN INN

4254 W. Thirty-First Street
773-247-9696

10900 S. Western Avenue
773-432-9696

6221 S. Archer Avenue
773-581-9696

www.homeruninnpizza.com
@homeruninn

Home Run Inn has five suburban locations: Berwyn, Bolingbrook, Darien, Hillside, and Melrose Park.

At first, I was extremely pessimistic about Home Run Inn—especially considering that it's from a mini-chain with eight locations in the region and a massive frozen pizza line (well respected among industry peers, by the way). They also used to sponsor the White Sox, and anytime there's a pizza at a stadium, it's usually not of the greatest quality. Choosing to visit Home Run Inn Pizza's original location, which launched in 1947, I figured the pizza might have a chance of rising above mediocrity—despite the higher-than-normal price tag. It did.

But first, a little history. Mary and Vincent Grittani opened the tavern in 1923, directly across the street from Piotrowski Park. Twenty years later, their daughter, Laura, married Nick Perrino. When Nick returned from World War II, he decided to go into business with his mother-in-law, Mary, and began serving pizza in 1947. After a home run (or perhaps just an errant baseball) came crashing through the tavern's window one day, they decided to rename the place the Home Run Inn. The main dining room used to be a collection of Everywhere, USA: a big screen, a small bar with neon beer ads, and a long brick wall. The row of Tiffany lamps hovering over the wooden booths was a nice touch, right out of the 1970s Chicago neighborhood pizzeria design playbook. You felt as if you were in your friend's basement, Elton John blaring, Atari on the TV. But the entire building needed a rehab, as it was falling apart, and so the owners (still part of the original family who started it) decided to gut the interior, bringing everything up to code and then some, while keeping some of those old lamps around for nostalgia (I miss the original decor).

My pizza arrived resting on a proprietary pan, which features a series of protruding, stubby dimples that elevate the pizza to allow airflow underneath and prevent the bottom from getting soft or soggy.

Even though this pizza is classified as "thin," there is a slightly raised lip—the result of pinching the dough before baking, like the crimping pie bakers do with their crusts—that gives it a slightly elevated perimeter. I loved the crunch, both on the sides and from underneath. As I bit into the lip, the dough had an almost malty character.

This is pizza to be eaten while drinking beers. And despite the raised edge, make no mistake, the interior is as thin as can be. Generously applied homemade sausage is assertive without being overwhelming; you can taste the fennel without it dominating each bite. The mozzarella and tomato sauce combine in a very pleasant way. The result is not too sweet, not too acidic.

There's no doubt Home Run Inn is a South Side institution. Oddly enough, they tried opening a large store on the North Side a couple of years ago, just a few blocks from Wrigley Field, and it didn't make it. North Side loyalties, perhaps? I can't imagine why someone wouldn't want to crush one of these pizzas. But maybe some brands are just better known in their neighborhoods. They've expanded to the South and the West, likely following their regulars, who've moved from the city to the suburbs. OK, so I was wrong about this going in, and I'm glad to see that having eight locations doesn't necessarily mean skimping on quality.

ITALIAN FIESTA PIZZERIA

1919 E. Seventy-First Street
8058 S. Halsted Street
1306 E. Forty-Seventh Street
773-684-2222

Also in suburbs:
Dolton
15425 S. Cottage Grove
708-849-9204

New Lenox
2021 Calistoga Drive
815-462-5555

italianfiestapizzeria.com

"CHICAGO-STYLE PIZZA is a thin, crispy crust," said Patti Tubbs, third-generation owner of Italian Fiesta Pizzeria. Tubbs's grandparents, Phillip and Connie DeCarlo, started the business in 1944, originally located at Sixty-Seventh and Dorchester, just south of the University of Chicago. The restaurant moved to Seventy-First and Euclid, in the South Shore neighborhood, in the 1950s. Their son, Frank DeCarlo, worked in the restaurant, where he met Joan, a waitress at the pizzeria who eventually became his wife. The DeCarlos had three daughters, Patti, Connie, and Kathy, who have all been involved in the family business. Patti and her mom took over in 1993, after Frank passed away.

Tubbs just shrugs her shoulders when asked why she thinks the world outside of Chicago considers it a deep-dish town. "I didn't even know what it was until I was in my twenties," she said.

The neighborhood has changed since the 1950s. Following the Great Migration, African Americans settled in Kenwood, Bronzeville, and South Shore, as most of the Jewish and Italian residents moved farther south or to the North Side. Today, nearly all of Tubbs's employees at the South Side restaurants are Black, serving their community. Michelle Obama grew up on Italian Fiesta's tavern-style, square-cut pies, which were reportedly a reward for getting good grades. She carried on the tradition with her own family, since the Obamas' Hyde Park home was only minutes away from the pizzeria's Forty-Seventh Street location.

Tubbs won't share a lot of details about their pizza, but after I visited to record my podcast, I did notice a wall of flour bags from Minnesota and, based on their website information, there is butter in the dough. Proofing time is short. They'll pass the freshly mixed dough through a machine that turns it into balls, then a short time later they're run through a dough sheeter as orders come in. A deep-red tomato sauce, slightly thick and with no sugar added, is ladled evenly across the dough, which is maybe an eighth of an inch thick. They'll leave about half an inch uncovered along the edge, so that you get a crusty handle; Tubbs never eats interior pieces, only edges.

The most popular topping is sausage, and since this is Chicago, it's a mass of raw sausage, seasoned with fennel and other undisclosed spices. A cook makes quick work of it, holding a palm-sized ball in his left hand, while rhythmically pinching off pieces no larger than a golf ball, pressing them onto the sauce-covered pie. I also choose hot giardiniera, so a bucket of briny, oily pickled chilies, olives, and celery is scattered around the sausage. Finally, two huge handfuls of whole milk mozzarella shredded in-house are evenly distributed around the pizza, completely engulfing the sausage pieces and other toppings like an avalanche in the Alps. I make a comment to Tubbs about how much cheese they use per pie, and she nonchalantly tells me they go through forty-five to fifty *thousand* pounds of cheese each month.

The pies bake on a steel deck for about fifteen minutes at 500 degrees, emerging slightly browned across the top (Tubbs prefers hers a little on the well-done side) and even though the sausage has been buried beneath that milky blanket, it's still fully cooked, albeit without the crispier nooks and crannies I've enjoyed at shops where they place the sausage on top of the pie. Not a complaint, just an observation.

As the establishment approaches eighty years in business, the fifth generation is now expressing interest in going into the family business. I have no doubt they'll be feeding "Chicago-style pizza" to several generations to come.

PAT'S PIZZA
WE DELIVER
BI-8 0168
CHICKEN RIBS SHRIMP

PAT'S PIZZA

2679 N. Lincoln Avenue
773-248-0168
www.patspizzachicago.com
@patspizzachicago

HOW MANY ITALIANS do you know who go by the name "Pat"? For Nick Pianetto Sr., it was a nickname with lasting consequences. Pianetto grew up next door to an Irish family in Chicago. He'd play with the neighbor's son—they had tragically lost another son, Patty. The mother began calling little Nick "Pat" as a way to remember her late son. The name stuck—so much so, that when Pianetto signed his marriage license, his new wife, Jean, asked, "Who's Nick?"

Pianetto was a truck driver and thought it would be a good idea to start a pizza joint so Jean would have something to do while he was on the road. They started at 3114 N. Sheffield, across the street from the Vic Theater (there's a great old black-and-white picture on the wall of Nick's son—Nick Jr.—with a scowl on his face and the facade of the Vic just behind him).

Nick Jr. stayed on the North Side and eventually took over the business, while his brother, Sam, took a branch of the business and went south. There is another Pat's on South Clark Street near the Loop, still run by the extended family, although I prefer the pizza at the North Side location. There's a cousin named Nick, plus a grandson; even the family dog's name is Nikko.

Nick Pianetto Jr. at the original Pat's on Sheffield

But the legend that is Pat's has always been about its thin crust. Pianetto Sr. may have started things in 1950, but his son steered the pizza's construction in a slightly different direction to where it is today. The style had always been a square-cut, thin pie, but Nick Jr. insisted the pizzas measure no thicker than seven sheets of paper (he used the ordering slips as a guide). In order to achieve this, he asked the company that produced his dough sheeter to come out and re-drill the holes, so he could roll his dough even thinner than normal—certainly thinner than anyone in town. They told him he was crazy, but he persisted. He also required his cooks to place those sheeted circles of dough between large pieces of paper, placed into the cooler and left in tall speed racks for at least four to five days, in order to dry them out. After nearly a week, you can see splotches of moisture that have leached out of the dough onto the paper, like a greasy Rorschach test.

Pizzas are baked in a giant relic: an antique Faulds oven with a series

Gina Pianetto cutting a sausage-giardiniera pie

HUGE GALDONES

Pat's pepperoni

of steel, rotating decks that could house a Mini Cooper. In this case, you wouldn't want a stone deck, because the porousness of the stone would pull out additional moisture. Since the dough is already pretty dry by the time it hits the 500-degree oven, a stone deck would not only be overkill, it would likely render the dough inedible.

When the pie arrives at your table on a stainless-steel disc, you can tell immediately how thin it is. Almost caramelized on the edge, the pizza is nicely browned and blackened all over its undercarriage. The cheese is baked until it's nice and golden. I highly recommend trying a sausage-giardiniera pie. The sausage renders its fat into the pie upon baking, while the briny chilies, carrots, and celery offer a crunchy and spicy contrast. You definitely won't be needing any dried chili flakes. My friend Lawrence, from New York City, whom I brought here on a visit, instinctively reached for the canister of flakes; I had to literally block his hand like I was Li Mu Bai in *Crouching Tiger, Hidden Dragon* and ask him to try it first. He relented.

The sauce is hardly notable, but I like how it goes all the way to the edge. The crust is truly where Pat's excels: so perfectly crispy, almost like eating a salty cracker dipped in cheesy tomato sauce. You can actually hear it when you bite into the crust, which is rare among thin crust competitors in the city.

PIZZA FRIED CHICKEN ICE CREAM

960 W. Thirty-First Street
773-565-4192
www.pfcic.com
@pizzachickenicecream

IN 2019, childhood friends Bradley Shorten and Billy Federighi (along with Billy's fiancée, Cecily Rodriguez) were producing impressive, artisan pies under the @eatfreepizza handle on Instagram. The pizzas were reminiscent of the creative approaches at Pizzeria Bebu and Robert's Pizza and Dough Company, with crispy edges and chewy interiors. Those lucky enough to score one would usually join the founders on their front stoop, cracking open a beer, courtesy of a friendly sponsor. That weekly pop-up grew somewhat organically into a permanent space in Bridgeport—part of what I refer to as the "Bridgeport Collective," including Won Kim's juicy, Korean-inspired fried chicken next door at Kimski and with Logan Square's Pretty Cool Ice Cream on offer as well.

After a few successful months of making exquisite Sicilian pies and slices (and getting a nod from *Esquire* as one of the notable "Best New Restaurants" in the country) they pivoted . . . to tavern-style.

But in late 2020 and early 2021, they were limited to producing only one style of pizza at a time, due to the fact that their deck ovens could only recover so much heat after baking a particular type of pie. "The minute we get a better oven, we'll do them simultaneously," Federighi told me at the end of 2020.

That day has come, and now PFCIC is producing one of the city's best tavern-style pizzas, all thanks to a Pizza City USA tour they took back in 2018. "We were inspired by Pat's," said Shorten. "It was so much thinner and crispier than the kind I had growing up [at Vito & Nick's]."

Just like Pat's, they ball the dough and sheet it almost immediately, placing the large, thin discs between sheets of paper and then keeping them in the cooler for six days. "We want them to get as bone-dry as possible," said Federighi. "Also, it's a lot easier to have someone else come in just to top and bake them. They don't have to make or stretch the dough."

Another nod to Pat's is the application of a thin dusting of bread crumbs beneath the crust. Pies are topped evenly with a thin sauce that has a slight kick from chilies, rather than the sugary notes often found on the South Side. They top their tavern pies with a blend of low-moisture mozzarella and provolone, just before launching onto the stone deck of the oven. Baked at 550 for about ten to twelve minutes, they get finished with some shredded Pecorino just before serving; slices are light, crispy, and irresistible—whether you grew up on the style or not. Each small square fits into the palm of your hand, like an oversized cheesy postage stamp, its bottom riddled with charred splotches.

"We could snack on it all day and never get tired of it," said Federighi.

Me too.

SALERNO'S PIZZA OF CHICAGO

1201 W. Grand Avenue
312-666-3444
www.salernospizza.com
@salernoschicago

Salerno's Pizza also has three suburban locations: Bolingbrook, Oak Park, and Lyons.

THIS FAMILY-FRIENDLY restaurant in West Town has been around since 1966—they have a few other locations in the suburbs, too. Pizzas take about twenty-five minutes but are worth the wait. Normally, smaller pizzas are cut into wedges, but if you get a twelve-inch or larger pie, it's cut into squares, tavern-style. I'd ask before ordering, just to be sure.

The crust here differs from many of the usual tavern-style pizzas in that it has dimension and some cracker-like qualities, a result of baking directly on the steel decks in the rotating, gas-fired oven. In other words, it's not one solid mass throughout, and you can actually chew it. The crust perfectly absorbs the zesty tomato sauce and cheesy topping, which, incidentally, covers the entire pizza like a yellow shield. The pepperoni has a slight bite to it, but the mild, homemade sausage is the star. Even though I had tasted six pizzas previous to this one—on the very same day—I still managed to eat a full three pieces, which says a lot.

VITO & NICK'S PIZZERIA

8433 S. Pulaski Road
773-735-2050
www.vitoandnicks.com
@vito_and_nicks

THERE'S A REASON Vito & Nick's has been in business since 1920, and it's not just the nostalgia on the walls. PBR and Old Style are on tap, the vinyl booths are still turquoise, and the Formica tabletops have the worn patina of a faded era—definitely pre–*Mad Men*. Families in Hawks T-shirts, grandparents celebrating birthdays, and countless softball teams have made Vito & Nick's their go-to pizza joint for generations, and I can see why.

In 1920, Vito and Mary Barraco—Sicilian immigrants who met and married on the West Side—opened their first tavern, located at 2708 W. Congress in Lawndale. That address no longer exists, since the Eisenhower Expressway expansion. In 1932, they moved southwest, opening Vito's Tavern at Eightieth and Halsted, in what is now the Gresham neighborhood. Seven years later, they relocated five blocks west, at Seventy-Ninth and Carpenter, so there was space for more tables, a bar, and an expanded menu, which at that point included Italian sausage and beef sandwiches.

Their son Nick joined the business in 1945 after returning from the war with an English bride, Mary. A year later, Nick, Vito, and Mary began making pizzas. Vito's granddaughter, Rose Barraco George, is the matriarch and third generation in charge today, greeting many of the regulars by name, which is easy to do, since she lives upstairs.

The pizza crust is ultra-thin, still bearing the blistered burn marks from the hot spots in the giant, industrial-strength Blodgett ovens. There is a thin sheath of

Mary and Vito Barraco with their two kids

Staff photo from the 1950s

seasoning scattered across the bottom edge, too, redolent of black pepper and oregano. The harmony (yes, I said harmony) between the mozzarella, chunky sausage (made outside, but to their specs), and the zesty yet thin tomato sauce makes this pie a pleasure to eat; thankfully, they haven't gotten lazy like so many others who simply pile on the cheese and call it a day. This is pizza with balance (think OBR), not overkill, and since it's so thin, you could easily polish off a large and a few PBRs with a friend and still have change left for the jukebox. When Frank Pinello came to Chicago to tape the Chicago episode of *The Pizza Show* for Vice, we chose to meet here because it's just SO Chicago. We easily crushed a large sausage-giardiniera before we left.

Four of the rituals, unique to Vito & Nick's, that are worth keeping an eye out for when you visit:

Note the pizza maker stationed next to the dough sheeter. He'll cut a perfect circle directly on the wooden peel without the aid of a cardboard cut-out.

Watch the guy adding toppings, because most orders will be for sausage, and he'll likely first wet a softball-sized piece of sausage with a bit of tomato sauce, then proceed to pinch and press equal amounts of it directly onto the pie, as fast as a robot welding joints on a car assembly line, each one as wide as a quarter.

Check out the oven guy. After he launches a pie into the oven, directly onto the deck, he'll bang the wooden peel once against a metal counter, which catches the

attention of the guy next to the dough sheeter, and then he flicks it, underhanded, in one motion so the pizza guy can catch it in the air. The whole process takes about three seconds.

Finally, watch them cut the pie. Most places use giant mezzalunas, which look like swords from *Game of Thrones*, to help them cut parallel then perpendicular lines, but everything is a throwback here, so you'll see the guy eyeball the lines with a simple old-school pizza cutter, finishing the job in about five seconds.

Note for pizza historians: Rose is quick to point out that the business is not related to Barraco's, a well-known mini-chain on Chicago's South and Southwest Sides. According to Rose, her grandfather sponsored his nephew (also named Vito Barraco) to emigrate from Italy in the 1940s. He worked at Vito & Nick's and learned the business. Years later, the younger Vito and his wife, Pauline, left to open their own place—Barraco's Pizza—on Ninety-Fifth Street in Evergreen Park. The company went on to open several more pizza establishments. I'm guessing no one bothered to ask a lawyer to look at any paperwork, because even today, you can find both Vito & Nick's frozen pizza and a Vito & Nick's II in Hickory Hills (different website), and at the very bottom of Vito & Nick's website, it says "Not affiliated or associated with Vito and Nicks II in Mokena IL or any licensee or franchisee." Just stick to the original and you'll be fine.

RECIPE

CHICAGO-STYLE THIN

BILLY FEDERIGHI AND BRADLEY SHORTEN,
PIZZA FRIED CHICKEN ICE CREAM

YIELD: TWO FIFTEEN-INCH ROUND PIZZAS

Here's a simple recipe for a Chicago tavern-style pizza. You'll notice that all the ingredients for the dough are given by weight. We can't stress this enough—get yourself a digital scale for the kitchen! Measuring by volume isn't as accurate. Plus, you'll later use the scale to weigh your dough balls. You should also invest in a pizza stone or, better yet, baking steel. It's the only way you can get a nice crispy bottom.

INGREDIENTS

DOUGH

525 grams of bread flour
300 grams of water
80 grams of extra virgin olive oil
1 gram of instant yeast
14 grams of salt

SAUCE

28-ounce can of tomatoes (crushed or tomato puree)
2 cloves of garlic, grated or diced
1 tablespoon of olive oil
1 stem of basil, torn into pieces
½ tsp. of salt
1 pinch red pepper flakes

CHEESE

1 pound whole milk low-moisture mozzarella (shredded)*
¼ pound provolone (shredded)*
For both cheeses, buy them whole and shred them yourself.

FOR ASSEMBLY

salt
dried oregano
Parmesan or Pecorino cheese

TO MAKE THE DOUGH

1 To mix the dough by hand, combine your flour, yeast, and salt in a large bowl or a twelve-quart Cambro container (this can be found online or at a restaurant supply store) and give them a good stir to make sure they are well incorporated. Next, add the water and oil. Sometimes people add the oil after the water is mixed in, but I find it's harder to incorporate it after the fact and it sort of sits on the surface of the dough. Stir everything with your hand in the bowl (or Cambro) until the water and oil are absorbed by the dough. Once it is, you can dump the dough out onto your countertop and then proceed to knead the dough for about ten to fifteen minutes. It should look very smooth.

If you are using a stand mixer, combine the flour, yeast, and salt into the bowl and run it with the dough hook attachment for about thirty seconds to make sure the dry ingredients are well incorporated. Next, add the water and oil and run it on its first speed for about ten minutes. Once the dough is mixed, dump it onto the countertop.

2 Cover the dough with a clean, moist dishtowel. Let it sit for about fifteen minutes.

3 After fifteen minutes, the dough should be relaxed. With a dough scraper, cut your dough in half. Use your scale to weigh out two 385-gram clumps of dough. There will be a little dough left over, don't worry.

4 Next you need to ball your dough. Honestly, it's a lot easier to look this up online and watch a video than it would be for me to explain. So find some balling videos on YouTube.

5 Once you've successfully balled your dough, lightly flour the balls and put them in an airtight container. We use dough boxes, but Tupperware will work just fine. Make sure there's a little extra room because your dough will expand a bit.

6 Now put the dough into your refrigerator for at least twenty-four hours and up to three days. The reason we do this is to slow down the fermentation, which will give you a better texture and, more importantly, a better flavor.

Recipe continues

TO MAKE THE SAUCE

The sauce can be made ahead of time, just like the dough. Tomato sauce gets better with time, so it's best to make it early. This is a simple sauce, but it'll be nice and bright tasting.

Combine your tomatoes, garlic, olive oil, basil, red pepper flakes, and salt in a medium container. Give it a good stir and taste. Add more salt if needed. Store your sauce in the fridge until you're ready to bake your pizza.

TO ASSEMBLE THE PIZZA

When you're ready to bake your pizzas, insert a pizza stone or steel toward the top of your oven and set it to 500 degrees (or even a bit higher if your oven allows). Let it heat up while you prep everything else.

Remove the dough from the fridge and put it on the countertop covered by a clean towel. Let it rest for at least an hour, if not two. You want it to relax and come to room temperature.

Once your dough is ready, take one dough ball and roll it out with a rolling pin. We use a sheeter machine at our shop, but most people will not have one at home. A rolling pin will work just fine. Roll the dough until it's round and roughly fifteen inches across. For this amount of dough, it should be fairly thin.

Now it's time to build the pie. You're going to need a wooden pizza peel that's lightly floured (you can also use cornmeal). Put your dough on top of the peel and give it a little jiggle to make sure it's not sticking. Top your pizza dough with several spoonfuls of your tomato sauce. Use the back of the spoon to work the sauce around the pizza. Take the sauce almost to the edge but leave approximately a half inch of crust. Take a pinch of dried oregano and sprinkle it over your sauce. Do the same with a pinch of salt.

Cover the sauce with two handfuls of your cheese mixture. Work the cheese from the middle to the edge of the pizza with your fingers. Once again, leave yourself about a half inch of crust. Grate some Parmesan or Pecorino over the top of the cheese. This will add a nice salty, nutty flavor.

Slide the pizza onto your pizza stone or steel. Make sure to jiggle it before you do this, just to make sure it hasn't stuck to the peel. Let it bake for about eight to ten minutes. The crust should be nice and golden brown and the cheese should be melted and have some good coloring.

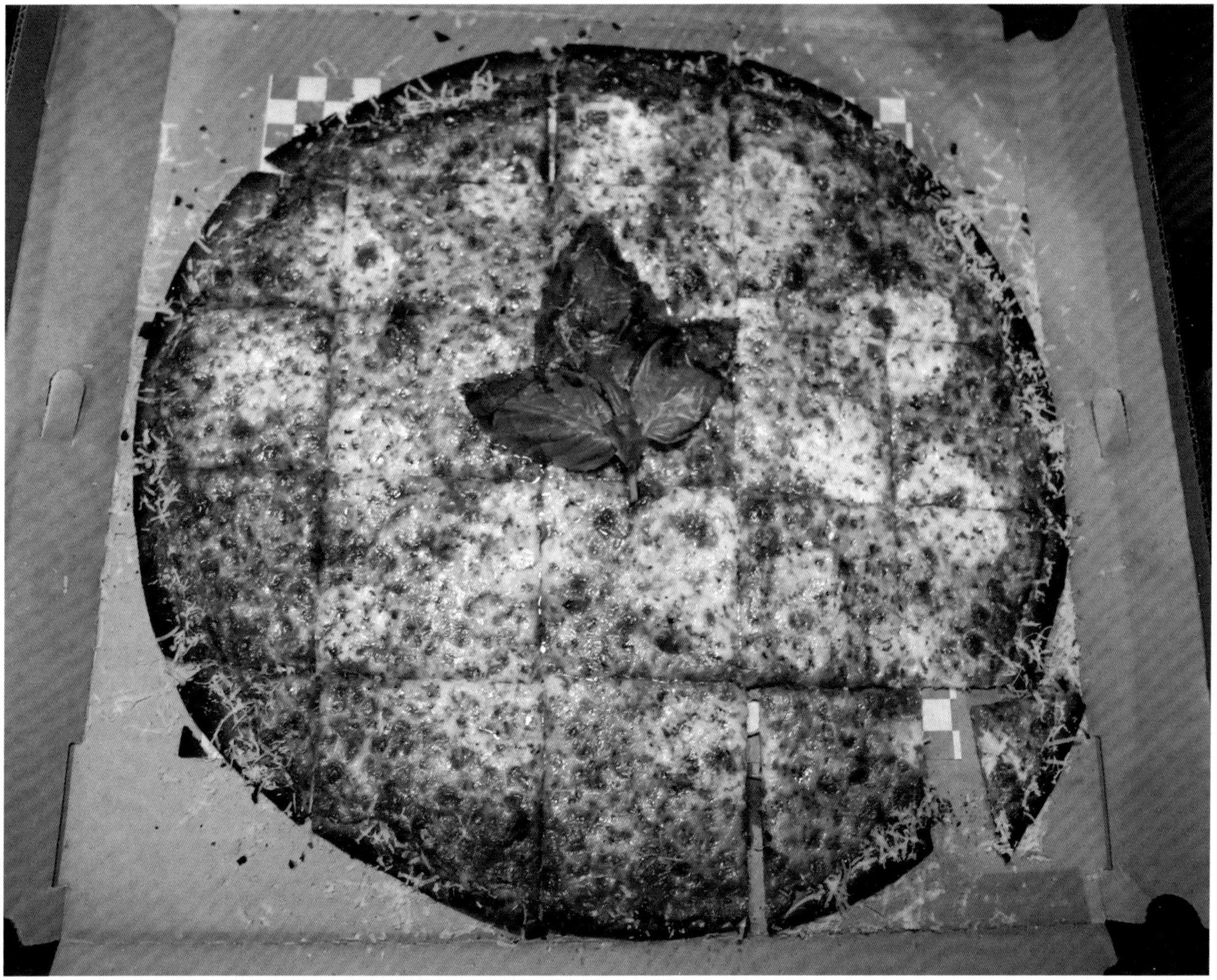

Remove the pizza with the peel and drop it onto a cooling rack. If you don't have one, that's fine, just drop it onto a cutting board. But if you do, the rack will keep the bottom of the pizza nice and crispy. After a minute or two on the rack, move the pizza to a cutting board and cut into squares. That is very important. This is Chicago tavern-style—it needs to be squares. Enjoy!

5 DEEP-DISH AND DEEP PAN

WHEN IT COMES TO assigning credit where credit is due, Chicago historian Tim Samuelson begs to differ with the often-told story about deep-dish's evolution. "I take every opportunity to remind folks that Ike Sewell really didn't come up with what's served at Pizzeria Uno," he said. "It was Ric Riccardo all the way. Ike was a great guy and early partner. But develop the actual pizza? Ain't so—even if there's a bronze plaque saying this at Wabash and Ohio. If Ike was alive to speak for himself, he'd readily agree. All of the other stories are a big lumbering freight train of fake history." One reason Samuelson knows this to be true is a conversation he had with Chicago literary lion Studs Terkel in October 2008, just two weeks before he died.

The author, historian, and Pulitzer Prize winner told him, "Ric invented the fucking pizza, for God's sake."

A big Texan who played for the University of Texas football team, Sewell was initially interested in opening a Mexican restaurant, allegedly because he missed the food from growing up and complained about not having any good options nearby (this was forty years before Rick Bayless came to town). But he was also an executive with the Fleischmann's liquor company, which meant he could not own a restaurant with a liquor license.

Deep pan slice removal at Pequod's

"Riccardo opened the business at 29 East Ohio as the sole owner," said Peter Regas, a pizza historian who broke the story about Lombardi's in New York City *not* being the first pizzeria in America. He has done a similar, ah-hem, deep dive on the origins of Chicago pizza.

"I think a lot of the stories Sewell told were fabrications," said Regas. "We know he was probably covering up the fact he had an ownership stake in the business." Regas says even though the business, which cycled through various names—The Pizzeria, Riccardo Pizzeria, Pizzeria Una, Pizzeria Uno—was solely owned by Riccardo in December 1943, by February 1944, Sewell became a 50 percent owner, most likely because Riccardo needed alcohol at the bar, and due to the rationing during the war, it was hard to come by. How did Sewell manage to get his name on the license if he was still at Fleischmann's?

"Basically, his wife [Florence Davis] was on the license and she used her maiden name. When Sewell retires from Fleischmann's in 1966 he says his wife is in the partnership and he's taking a more active role," said Regas.

In the mid-1940s, Riccardo and Sewell hired a bartender named Lou Malnati, who had recently moved to Chicago from Italy. He had joined the Marines and was stationed at a recruiting office in Chicago. Lou's father, Adolpho ("Rudy") Malnati was managing the restaurant by this time.

People weren't used to paying for pizza. It had always been a freebie in the neighborhood taverns, after all, passed around and eaten on cocktail napkins as a snack. So in order to get people to come to the downstairs bar at Riccardo's, they initially tried to lure customers with the promise of free pizza. The Pizzeria's location in River North meant deep-dish was primarily a treat for tourists and for locals who had to make a special trip downtown. In 1949, "they'd put dough in the pan and then either cheese with sauce or sausage with sauce. They didn't marry the two typically," said Marc Malnati, Lou's son and now president of the company that bears his father's name. "My dad got back in the kitchen and he was quite the cook," said Malnati.

Regas says the pizzas in the mid- to late 1940s weren't all that deep. "The pizza essentially grew over time," he said. "I think in the '50s, Rudy said they could cook a pizza in twenty minutes. Years later that rose to thirty minutes or more." That theory is consistent with the story I heard from the family behind Louisa's, in Crestwood (featured in chapter 15). The pizzas there—based on recipes and methods

Louise DeGenero learned working at Due's for more than twenty years—were more akin to a grandma-style in terms of height, but made in a deep, circular pan rather than a rectangular sheet pan.

Problems at Uno began after Riccardo's death in 1954. "There's a stipulation clause in the agreement that says when a partner dies, that partner's estate gets their original investment back and profits from that year," said Regas. "They [Riccardo's estate, including his ex-wife] got paid off and then Sewell and Florence owned the entire business."

There were fights with lawyers in 1955 and 1957. Riccardo's family held a grudge against the Sewells, and Regas says it comes down to Riccardo not hiring the right lawyer to draw up the initial agreement.

Less than a year after Riccardo's death, Sewell, with the aid of managers Rudy and Lou Malnati, opened a second location—Pizzeria Due—just a few doors north along Wabash. Shortly thereafter, Rudy got hit by a cab and required surgery; his health took a turn for the worse. "My dad [Lou] was the one closing Uno, closing Due, closing Su Casa six nights a week," said Marc Malnati. "Sewell would come in once in a while to drink with friends."

Uno and Due offered the only deep-dish pizza anywhere in the country at the time, and they maintained a monopoly on this pizza style for at least twenty years in Chicago. Regas says, based on early pictures, that the deep-dish we know today, with its high side walls, was most likely part of an evolution. Those black-and-white pictures from the late 1940s and '50s remind him of a pizza that's more like an East Coast grandma.

In 1963, James Stolfe began serving deep-dish pizza in Bridgeport, the first of its kind far from downtown, at Connie's Pizza near Chinatown. The company

November 1954. My dad is from Israel, doing his residency at Mt. Sinai Hospital; my mother works in the emergency room as a nurse. They met there. Within a week they basically decided they were gonna get married. About two months later they're at Pizzeria Uno, on the one time that their schedules aligned where they were both off. It was there, at the table, that he informed her—he didn't ask her to get married—he informed my mother that he was going to talk to her father, Herman Smolovitz, my grandfather, and ask for her hand. They etched into the wood their names, Ben and Marsha. My brothers and I have gone there to look for it, but no luck. According to my mother, my dad was eating the pizza with a knife and a fork, and the waiter said, "You must not be from Chicago, because I don't know what you're doing eating like that."

It is at Pizzeria Uno that the Emanuel journey in Chicago begins.

—**RAHM EMANUEL**,
former Chicago mayor and chief of staff under President Obama

Building a deep-dish pizza at Bartoli's

is known for an "Original Pan" as well as a deep-dish, but I think the latter has far too much dough for its own good. They should just rebrand the "Original Pan" as deep-dish and no one would be the wiser. One thing Connie's pioneered, however, was pizza delivery. Their trucks were outfitted with propane heaters, at first to roam around the South Side, eventually heading to the lakefront. There's no question the first deep-dish delivery was courtesy of a tricked-out, Connie's-branded vehicle.

In the mid-1960s, Alice Mae Redmond, a cook at Due, was moonlighting at Gino's on Rush. "They caught her," said Regas. Sewell and Malnati asked her to choose—Due's or Gino's? In 1966, cabbies Sam Levine and Fred Bartoli, along with their friend George Loverde, put Redmond in charge of the kitchen at Gino's East, while her daughters continued working at Uno. The original Gino's East at 633 N. Wells Street is now a condo building. Their flagship eventually moved just east of Michigan Avenue on Superior Street. Uno and Due became incubators for the city's nascent deep-dish scene. Other employees would leave to go open their own places—like Louisa's in Crestwood—or just move to other existing pizzerias to build out their deep-dish program.

By 1970, Lou Malnati was forty years old, and went to Sewell with some pressing questions: What's going to happen to the business when you and/or my dad is gone? Is there anything here for me? Do I have a chance to get in?

"He said, 'I love you like a son, Lou, but my plan is to sell it,'" said Marc Malnati. "I guess he felt like my dad wasn't bankable or wouldn't be able to get a loan to buy it, but my dad wound up leaving." Fourteen months later, he'd open his namesake—Lou Malnati's—in Lincolnwood. The business celebrates its fiftieth anniversary in 2021 with more than fifty locations in Illinois, Arizona, and Wisconsin. I've got more of that story in chapter 15 ("Suburban Stars").

Nearly a decade later, Sewell would sell a few franchises to a Boston-based Popeye's Fried Chicken owner. After Sewell's death in 1990, his widow, Florence, sold the remaining buildings to the same group in Boston. The Uno's corporation established itself there, where it remains today, overseeing some 150 locations worldwide. As the Uno's franchise grew, its original name morphed into the more universally accepted Uno Pizzeria & Grill, and it never really made much of a lasting impact in Chicago. Even today, as tourist throngs wait outside for a chance to try their deep-dish, I can't help but think they're just lining the pockets of an East Coast company that hasn't sunk as much goodwill into the community here as it has in Boston .

To put it bluntly, the company that made deep-dish famous (and continues to promote it around the world) hasn't been a Chicago company for decades. And yet, if you randomly ask visitors walking down Michigan Avenue where they're going for dinner, I'll bet you more than 75 percent will tell you Giordano's, Gino's East, Uno's, or Due's. Ask anyone standing outside one of these four businesses on a Friday or Saturday night where they're from and my guess is not one of them will hail from Chicago. Being so close to the majority of the city's hotels has its benefits.

This is not to say that deep-dish or its close relative, pan pizza, can't be an enjoyable, albeit occasional, indulgence. Classic deep-dish usually begins with a circular steel pan, greased with corn or vegetable oil. A pliable, somewhat oily dough is smashed into the pan, until it covers both the bottom and interior walls. Some restaurants will make a butter crust, which emerges from the oven with an almost pastry-like crispness. As much as I find myself putting it down, I do still appreciate the buttery crust at Pizano's and Lou's. Note: if you do order a sausage from Lou's, specify "crumbled," otherwise you'll get a solid mass of a sausage frisbee pressed on top of the crust. Also, if you order a deep-dish to go, *always* ask for it uncut unless you want a soggy bottom by the time you get it home. I can appreciate the boulders of fennel-laced sausage and hunks of juicy tomatoes at La Barra. I can easily polish off two thick slices from Bartoli's, even though I know it's like eating the equivalent of a block of mozzarella. There is a delicious harmony between the brightly acidic, charred, and naturally sweet tomatoes and the rich layer of Wisconsin mozzarella that rest above a buttery, short-dough crust from the likes of Pequod's or Labriola. I dare any naysayer to take two bites and proclaim otherwise.

There is some disagreement about the differences between pan and deep-dish. My theory is "all deeps are pans; not all pans are deep." To me, pan implies baking in a rectangular pan—what some might refer to as Sicilian, or, if you live in New York, grandma-style. In Detroit, they make their pizzas in a high-sided

Deep-dish from Pizano's

square pan, which is technically a deep-dish. In Chicago, the hair-splitters might point out the dough recipe is slightly different between pan and deep; one could argue a deep has more crispness and richness in the dough—a direct result of the butter or oil—while pan implies a broad spectrum of doughs, but most Chicago deep pans also have oil in them. The bottom-up architecture, however, should remain the same: dough, then cheese, then toppings, and finally, sauce. The big difference between pan and deep-dish has more to do with the interior walls. On a classic deep-dish, the dough is pressed up along the walls, forming a fortress or barrier. On a deep pan, like at Pequod's or Labriola, the dough is simply allowed to go to the edge of the circular, deep pan and is not pressed and pinched any higher.

This allows someone like Burt Katz or Rich Labriola to place slices of mozzarella on top and up against the walls, so that as it bakes, the cheese caramelizes and chars, just like with a Detroit-style pie. Did Detroit influence Katz in the '70s? Possibly. Did Katz influence Labriola? You bet.

Having several homegrown businesses all laser-focused on making deep-dish is one of Chicago's unique characteristics. It makes the city a true Pizza City, because it shows that, while we have plenty of the styles that are well known in New York, we also have styles that are homegrown. Sure, you can find deep-dish at an Uno's franchise anywhere in the country, but that's about as unique as a Burger King or Arby's. A friend from New York City, who has eaten in some of the best restaurants in the world, asked me where to get deep-dish when he's in Chicago, since it's something he cannot find at home. It's not an unusual request. Professional food reporters and critics I know, who come to town for two to three days of concentrated, focused grazing, often sheepishly ask me where to go to try a deep-dish, knowing it's like asking a friend in Philly where to grab a cheesesteak. I'm excited to add Milly's Pizza in the Pan to this book. Opened during the pandemic, Milly's is making a pie inspired by the owner's fond memories of Burt's Pizza. It's not made in cast iron, but it's still a pizza worth seeking out from its quirky location in a shared kitchen space in Logan Square.

I have local friends and colleagues, too, who will order a deep-dish pizza—in a moment of laziness or if the thought of Grubhub seems overwhelming. It's just sometimes easier to go the deep-dish route, mainly because there are so many convenient locations not more than ten minutes from most downtown businesses and hotels. If you live in one of the neighborhoods, however, chances are your deep-dish will come from Lou Malnati's, since they're about as ubiquitous as Walgreen's. But when people ask me for deep-dish recommendations in the city, I usually send them to one of the places listed in this chapter.

If the spirit moves you, you can also try your hand at making your own deep-dish at home. Rich Labriola was kind enough to share his recipe with me at the end of this chapter, and while it will require some effort, I think you'll find the payoff worth it. You will, obviously, need to buy a pan. I'm partial to the widely available pans made by Lloyd or American Metalcraft.

BARTOLI'S PIZZERIA

1955 W. Addison Street
773-248-0455

658 N. Ashland Avenue
312-929-4133

www.bartolispizza.com
@bartolispizza

COURTESY BARTOLI'S

HERE'S THE THING about deep-dish: each person really only needs about one slice, so don't feel any shame ordering a small pizza for four or five people. Also, at Bartoli's and most similarly established places, expect a thirty- to forty-minute baking time (we always call ahead), but often the wait is worth it.

Brian Tondryk's grandfather, Fred Bartoli, was partners with Sam Levine at the very first Gino's East. They had originally hired Alice Mae Redmond, a former cook at Uno, to make the deep-dish at their store on North Wells Street. In my opinion, Gino's no longer belongs to the upper echelon of deep-pie slingers. As I've done with Uno's, I would again blame corporate bean counters. Tondryk had missed the flavors of his childhood and spent the better part of a year trying to re-create and rebuild that original recipe. His efforts paid off.

Bartoli's bakes one of my favorite pies in the city. High sides show heft, but don't take a side-view-only approach and misjudge. It's only about a quarter-inch thick at the bottom, where a gooey, melted mozzarella layer supports huge pieces of impressively meaty, well-seasoned sausage that would be right at home on a South Side Italian nonna's table. There are enormous hunks of juicy tomatoes, blistered from the oven, exploding with bright acidity and sweetness. The highlight is the buttery-crispy crust, which is reminiscent of the crust on its best days at Lou's and Pizano's.

Even though my pizza quest took me to several places on the day I revisited Bartoli's, I had no problem polishing off a full slice here.

CONNIE'S PIZZA

2373 S. Archer Avenue
312-266-6437

Connie's Pizza at
McCormick Place
2301 S. Lake Shore Drive

Midway Airport, Concourse B

www.conniespizza.com
@conniespizza

Having sold their pizzas at the United Center, Taste of Chicago, Lollapalooza, and your local frozen food aisle, Connie's is familiar to many Chicagoans, mainly via their deep-dish and "Original Pan" pizzas. The thicker, heavier deep-dish is the style they typically sell outside of the restaurant and at special events. It's also what they ship all over the United States. But when you dine in their massive Bridgeport restaurant, with its soaring ceilings and decorative industrial belt system that looks like a gear factory from the dawn of the Industrial Age, you see a few differences right away.

The size difference, for one thing. With nineteen ounces of dough, the "Original Pan" has a great ratio of crust to toppings. At twenty-seven ounces of dough for the deep-dish, it's a little unwieldy, at least for this eater. The deep-dish has slightly higher sides and more crust to eat through. That means the "Original Pan"—while technically cooked in the same black, anodized aluminum pan—is just slightly shorter on the edges. It makes a difference. With less dough to chew through, the OBR is definitely better.

In the 1950s, Ray and Connie DeGrazia had a small store in Bridgeport, selling sandwiches and bakery-style pizza slices at 638 W. Twenty-Sixth Street. James Stolfe was one of the neighborhood kids who stopped by for a slice or a snack after school. But he also liked to hang out at the pool hall, wearing his hair greased back and

James Stolfe pulling a deep-dish from the rotating deck oven at Connie's

his sleeves rolled up. With the help of a friend, he got set up on a date with Patricia Sue, a girl who had already faced a number of struggles in her young life. Her dad had contracted tuberculosis in prison and she had to drop out of school to care for her ailing mother. She was well aware of the rougher elements of her neighborhood and knew the importance of a strong family. When James asked her out, "she said I'll go out with you, but I'm not looking for a guy who hangs out on the corner, looking for a good time. I'm dating for a husband," said her son, Michael Stolfe.

James's whole mindset changed. He got a job with the city doing surveying. Having a paycheck and a pension was fine, but he figured a more stable job would involve selling food like Italian beef, hot dogs, or pizza. As he got to know the DeGrazias, he learned Connie was getting too old to run the business and wanted to sell. He and a friend from work bought the entire store in 1963, leaving intact the etched "Connie's" on the front window.

It didn't take long before his business partner got tired of the routine. They'd work their city jobs until 2 p.m., then go open the store at 4 p.m. and close at midnight. Stolfe relished it; his partner, not so much. Stolfe bought out his partner a year later by trading him his 1962 Oldsmobile Starfire for his half of the business.

Unlike the rectangular sheet pan pizzas Connie DeGrazia was selling before him, Stolfe decided to make a deeper pan pizza. They'd rub the anodized aluminum pans with olive oil and onion powder (to promote browning), then press the dough up high along the sides. Unlike other deep-dish operators in town, they applied the sauce first, then the ingredients, and finally, a blend of whole milk and part-skim mozzarella, which is chopped into large chunks for a slower melt. By adding it last, it caramelizes and browns into pleasant little freckles of crispness. "The dough is the superstar though," said Stolfe. Those sides of their "Original Pan" are so high, the pies almost look like Dutch baby pancakes from Walker Bros.

One hot summer night in the mid-1960s, when air conditioning was still considered a luxury, James Stolfe was sitting on the stoop when he saw a rush of people gather around the ice cream man, flocking to his truck. This was his "light bulb" moment. What if he delivered too? "He was one of the first guys to trick out a car, put a propane oven in back to keep the pizzas hot," said Michael. "He'd send trucks down Lowe, Thirty-First Street, and Halsted, and people would be sitting outside, see the name and number, and order a pizza because they didn't want to cook."

Suddenly, they were doing a hundred deliveries a night.

But the thing that really turned business around for Stolfe was moving the business a few blocks away to Twenty-Sixth and Normal in 1976 (the space is now a Chinese noodle company). "Once people knew there was a place to go before or after a Sox game, that really helped," said Michael Stolfe.

By 1980, they were doing 1,500 deliveries a night with forty trucks. They moved into the current space on Archer Avenue in 1985.

Stolfe ran Connie's without incident for twenty years, but in the 1980s, the mob paid him a visit, and some of the same neighborhood toughs whom he knew growing up were now demanding protection money.

At the corruption trial of Frank Calabrese Sr. in 2007, Stolfe testified he made "extortion payments" to Calabrese Sr. and the Chicago Outfit for twenty years, beginning in the 1980s, of roughly $1,000 per month. "He didn't want to take the shortcuts. He worked hard his whole life," said Michael. "But it's neighborhood rules. He figured it would keep him from having to worry about it."

Michael Stolfe is now president of the company, which also has an FDA-licensed facility adjacent to the Bridgeport restaurant, producing frozen pizzas for shipment to more than twenty states.

Both the "Original Pan" and deep-dish are served on special metal pizza pans that have holes cut into them, allowing for air circulation, which keeps the evenly tanned, slightly dimpled undercarriage crisp and prevents sogginess.

Fontanini Italian Meats produces Connie's sausage of choice, while the restaurant uses a simple Wisconsin mozzarella blend to present a cheesy blanket of sorts. They do make their sauce in-house, adding touches of sugar, basil, and oregano as they see fit.

The thing about the crust here, on both the "Original Pan" and deep-dish, is that while the outside is a tad crispy, the inside resembles a focaccia, with tiny air pockets and a fluffy, pleasant chew. Depending on how busy the restaurant is, pies emerge with a decent browning across the top—the result of even baking and a cook paying attention. The Margarita brand pepperoni is mild but intriguing; it's got a coarse grind, smaller diameter, and thicker cut. Had it been placed on top of the pizza, the discs would curl up and char, but since they're snuggled beneath the cheesy blanket, they simply render their fat out into the sauce and bottom dough while remaining chewably soft. Do what

the locals do though, and go with either a sausage or a spinach, and call it a day.

I can't promise this, but after a conversation with Michael Stolfe for this book, I have a feeling they might retire the "Original Pan" pizza in name only. Since that pie has a better ratio of crust to toppings, and since tourists want so desperately to try a deep-dish when they're in town but might balk at the larger dough amount, they might change the name to "Deep-Dish," and offer just that one deep pie instead of two. At some point in the 1970s, consultants suggested James Stolfe offer a deep-dish rather than just his "Original Pan," despite the fact both pizzas are exactly the same. The only difference is eight ounces more dough in the deep-dish. It was purely for marketing purposes, so they could be carried in stores and at stadiums. But I think if they retire the twenty-seven-ounce dough version, no one will complain too much.

LABRIOLA

535 N. Michigan Avenue
312-955-3100
www.labriolacafe.com/chicago
@labriolachicago

Labriola has a café and bakery in Oak Brook, but they do not serve deep-dish, only Neapolitan. They do run La Barra in Oak Brook, however, where they sell tavern, artisan, and deep-dish.

HUGE GALDONES

Rich Labriola's downtown location, just off Michigan Avenue, has struggled with its identity ever since it opened. After going through countless tweaks and menu exorcisms, he has opened pizza concepts in the suburbs (La Barra) and still maintains the original Labriola Café in Oak Brook (although they only make Neapolitan pizzas at that location). His Michigan Avenue restaurant is well within the tourist strike zone, which means deep-dish is a must. Sit at a table during lunch on any given day, and I'll bet 80 percent of the tables are ordering one. Since 2018, we've kicked off our weekly Friday night and Saturday afternoon Pizza City USA tours from here.

As my twelve-inch deep-dish with sausage is placed in front of me, I like what I see: generous, chunky icebergs of fresh tomato lightly seasoned with dried oregano; fragrant, juicy, jagged-edged pieces of sausage (from Russo in suburban Alsip) intermingled with fennel and Calabrian chilies, nestled within a wide base of melted Grande mozzarella; and then—the best surprise of all.

As I lift out my first piece, I see that outer edge, just like at Pequod's—a caramelized, darkened, thin layer of cheese clinging to the perimeter, all the way around the equator. Detroiters will recognize it immediately, like the Bat signal; it signifies a crispy, cheesy edge. Underneath, I notice how firm the dough is; as I cut into it with my knife, I realize it is actually crispy all the way around, and so I pick up the rest of my piece with my hands, and summarily devour it. The ratio! Unlike so many dough-heavy pies at Pequod's, they figured out the OBR.

I bet it was hard for Labriola to temper his ambition in a high-profile restaurant with his name on it. After burning through some chefs and a lot of sleepless nights—forever trying to figure out if tourists *really* wanted extruded pasta and handmade cavatelli—turns out all they want is a good pizza. Here, in the shadow of the former Tribune Tower and across the street from a gigantic Nordstrom store, he and his staff have cracked the code: they offer a deep-dish pizza that both tourists *and* picky locals like me actually crave.

MILLY'S PIZZA IN THE PAN

1801 N. Spaulding Avenue
224-656-4732
www.millyspizzachi.com
@millys_pizza_in_the_pan

Wednesday through Sunday, pickup or delivery only

Over at the Envision Unlimited shared kitchen space in Logan Square, just a block or so north of the 606, Robert Maleski took his sixteen years of kitchen experience and taught himself how to make a deep pan pizza. He said he was inspired by the one he had at Burt's in Morton Grove a couple of years ago, after the namesake had sadly passed away, but still, the experience led him to create Milly's Pizza in the Pan once the pandemic got under way.

"It's got a *frico* crust around the edge; it's salty, it's crispy, it's crunchy," Maleski said.

Thick slices of mozzarella are blanketed over his wet dough, covered generously with a tomato sauce as red and vibrant as a runway model's lipstick, then baked in a convection oven. After a few minutes, he removes it, tops it with ingredients like peppers, onions, or mushrooms, then bakes it a second time. Finally, after another ten minutes or so, the pepperoni or sausage goes on and it gets a third and final bake. The result, after about twenty-five minutes of total baking, is a darkened *frico* cheese crust along the upper perimeter. Fans of Labriola, Pequod's, and yes, even Burt's, will appreciate the contrast of textures.

"It's not as thick as Detroit, it's not as deep as deep-dish, it's kind of somewhere in the middle," said Maleski, who has to be one of the most humble pizza makers in the city.

MY PI PIZZA

2010 N. Damen Avenue
773-394-6900
www.mypiepizza.com
@mypipizzachicago

Larry Aronson with a prized challah

RICH ARONSON comes from a long line of bakers. He can trace his family's history back four generations, to Bialystok, where his ancestors studied their craft. In the 1950s, his dad, Larry, had fallen in love with this new type of pizza in Chicago called "deep-dish." It was only available at one place—Pizzeria Uno—then in 1955 it showed up again at Pizzeria Due. Since Aronson Sr. had always been a tinkerer in the kitchen, he began experimenting with his own version of that deep-dish, even while studying business at Northwestern University. Eventually, prodded by friends, he opened My Pi (it was, after all, *his* version of that famous pie downtown at Uno) near Loyola's campus on the far North Side in the summer of 1971, just five months after Lou Malnati opened his namesake in Lincolnwood, and only weeks after the Union Stockyards had closed for good.

Few people know this, but My Pi was the first Chicago deep-dish available outside of Illinois. At one point they were in nine states. I remember having it as a kid in Minneapolis in the 1970s. But a trademark dispute cost them too much money in legal fees, and so Aronson folded the out-of-town operations, retrenching to just one store in Lincoln Park. Eventually, that Clark Street shop closed, but by then, Aronson's son, Rich, had decided to take over. Just like his great-grandparents, Rich had the bug; he attended culinary school, worked at a white tablecloth restaurant in Evanston for a while, then eventually gave in to the pull of the family business. He reestablished My Pi in a tiny Bucktown strip mall next to a tanning salon, a Korean nail shop, and a 7-Eleven, sharing a space with his other concept, Lil' Guys Sandwiches.

The construction of the My Pi deep-dish is a bit different than at other shops in town: the dough is an even thickness across the bottom and then rises up on the sides a good one- to one-and-a-half inches. Wisconsin mozzarella covers the bottom layer, insulating the crust from becoming soggy from rendered sausage fat or tomato juices. Then comes the pepperoni or raw sausage, and finally, the tomatoes. But unlike thin tomato sauces elsewhere, this topping is a forest of tomato chunks, roasted and slightly blistered, releasing their sweetness as they combine with dried oregano and a hint of garlic. The secret weapon is actually the spice packet

Larry developed many years ago. He was concerned that someone ordering a vegetarian cheese or spinach pie wouldn't have the benefit of the same spices found in their popular sausage, namely fennel. So he devised a secret recipe—still unknown to Rich, it's apparently in the will—that mimics the flavors of sausage. The other surprise with this pizza is its portability. It travels well and you can easily lift a piece out and not need to eat it with a knife and fork. You can thank four generations of baking know-how for that one.

Even after visiting several other pizza places on this particular day, I had a hard time stopping after one slice. This is a wonderful pie that I think pizza lovers can agree on, and unlike a lot of deep pizzas in Chicago, the ones coming from My Pi get the OBR just right.

Rich Aronson showing off how his deep slices don't need a knife and fork

NUEVA ITALY PIZZERIA

7109 N. Clark Street
773-770-8296
www.nuevaitalypizzamenu.com
@nuevaitalypizzeria

YOU CAN GET a thin pizza at this Rogers Park takeout joint (that's apparently what *Chicago* magazine prefers), but Nueva acknowledges that they are best known for their butter crust deep-dish.

Located on a dingy stretch of Clark Street, a few blocks south of Evanston and tucked among Mexican grocery stores, Nigerian restaurants, and discount shops, Nueva is mostly takeout and delivery. The stack of white carryout boxes, piled all the way to the ceiling behind the front counter, is a pretty good indicator. Yet, even though they lay claim to only three tables, the woman working the counter couldn't have been nicer when my party of four showed up on a Friday night and wanted to eat in. She put two tables together, fetched us plates, silverware, and water, and then took our order for a nine-inch pizza, which would yield only four pieces. (We had to hit three other places that night.)

What arrived was truly among the better deep-dish pies in the city. The butter crust is excellent, not unlike Lou's or Pizano's, with a flaky-rich crust on the outside, plenty of tiny air pockets inside, and the overall texture of a good focaccia. The outside lip is narrow and relatively squat, about two inches high—not insurmountable and not so thick as to throw off the OBR.

Large pieces of Greco sausage rest on the bottom layer of part-skim mozzarella and mix with the large, heaping chunks of fresh tomato that are scattered about like cumulus clouds covering most of the pepperoni and sausage. The undercarriage is wonderfully crisp, which is somewhat surprising since they serve the pizza on a flat plate set on top of a dimpled tray. Usually, the pizza is placed directly on the dimpled risers to allow for airflow beneath it—like a few of my favorite tavern-thin pizzas—yielding a crispier bottom. But look closer under the hood and check out those tiny holes, allowing for airflow into the nooks and crannies.

That's the difference between Nueva and so many other wanna-be deep-dish joints. This is a dough that's rested a bit, gone through a little fermentation, and, upon hitting a hot deck oven for thirty minutes, reveals itself to have more character than the factory pies coming out of the tourist traps downtown.

PEQUOD'S PIZZA

2207 N. Clybourn Avenue
773-327-1512
www.pequodspizza.com
@pequodspizza

8520 Fernald Avenue, Morton Grove
847-470-9161

PEQUOD'S MARKED THE final notch in the literary-themed trifecta of pizzerias run by the late Burt Katz. Remember [Dante's] Inferno, in Evanston? Or how about Gulliver's [Travels] in West Rogers Park? The trickiest of the three is Pequod's—named for the whaling ship in *Moby-Dick*—which Katz opened in Morton Grove in 1970. His calling card back then was a caramelized cheese perimeter around his deep "pans" (he didn't refer to them as deep-dish), achieved by not just placing mozzarella on top of the bottom layer of dough, but resting it up against the high, inner wall as well. Katz sold the business in 1987 to Keith Jackson, a pharmacist from Maywood who spent eighteen years behind the counter at a Sears pharmacy. Like so many pizza deals that have gone down the wrong way over the years, either attorneys weren't consulted or noncompetes were not discussed, because just a couple of years later, Katz came out of retirement to open Burt's Pizza practically around the corner.

"They had an arrangement, but I guess Burt said 'screw it,'" said Sean Asbra, who helped open the Lincoln Park Pequod's in 1991 and is now the general manager.

Both Pequod's and Burt's have that signature burnt cheese crust, or *frico*, similar to what you'd see on a standard Detroit-style pizza. In recent years, the only major change in the kitchen has been a shift to using low-moisture whole milk mozzarella. But I think the thing that separates Pequod's from Burt's is the amount of dough used in each pan.

"Ours is very thick," said Asbra, echoing a personal criticism I've had the last few times I've visited. There is oil in the dough to promote richness and a fluffy, focaccia-like interior. There's also a little extra oil in the bottom of the deep, circular pan to promote a crispy undercarriage. They're cooked more quickly than your usual deep-dish, however, at about 600 degrees for just twenty minutes on a Bakers Pride stone deck. Asbra says the cheese caramelizes on its own—there is no extra sugar added—and the dough itself goes through three different rises; the third being in the oven. I tell him I had heard you can order "easy dough" or "light dough" to compensate for that hefty lower half of the pie. He confirms this. I would think since a smaller amount of dough wouldn't rise as much, the ratio would obviously be more palatable.

Another oddity is the choice of toppings at Pequod's. Unlike most Chicago deep-dish joints, where sausage is king, pepperoni is more in demand in Lincoln Park. Asbra says for their frozen orders (Goldbelly, etc.) they sell about a third more pepperoni than sausage.

The sauce—a blend of two different types of tomatoes—and the spice packet haven't changed in twenty-five years. Every pie is

finished with dried oregano and imported grated Romano cheese, a pair as familiar in Chicago as Ditka and Payton.

"It's been a weird ride," said Asbra. "I've been privileged to see us go from using one case of mushrooms every three days to twelve cases in one day."

Now with shipping all over the country, the cult of Pequod's expands. Every time one of those out-of-town "Best of" lists includes them, the lines are sure to follow. Asbra says they've always tried appealing to everyone, not giving anyone special treatment.

"I made A. J. Pierzynski and Theo Epstein wait for a table," he said. "We treat everybody the same here." I just wish that bite ratio was better on the bottom crust, and not have to make a special request, as an old Depeche Mode song would plaintively ask, to get the balance right.

PIZANO'S PIZZA & PASTA

61 E. Madison Street
312-236-1777

864 N. State Street
312-751-1766

800 N. Dearborn
(carryout and delivery only)
312-335-8833

2106 S. Indiana
312-842-0777

1808 N. Waukegan Road,
Glenview
847-486-1777

www.pizanoschicago.com
@pizanospizzachi

It's not exactly Borg vs. McEnroe or Jordan vs. Bird, but the competition between Pizano's and Lou Malnati's is definitely the only significant matchup that has deep-dish-worthy historical roots. What makes the faceoff even more intriguing is the fact that the owner and founder of Pizano's is a Malnati himself.

Rudy Malnati Jr.'s father—Rudy, né Adolpho—was one of the architects and original creators of deep-dish pizza, along with Ike Sewell and Ric Riccardo in 1943. Malnati Sr. had a son with his first wife, named Lou. Lou would attempt to buy Uno and Due from Sewell years later, only to be rebuffed; he quit to open his namesake in Lincolnwood in 1971. But Rudy Sr. wound up remarried to a woman named Donna Marie, with whom he had another son—Rudy Jr. Using the same recipe they had at Uno's, Rudy Jr.—with help from his mom—opened Pizano's in 1991 on North State Street in the Gold Coast. Almost instantly, bragging rights over which version was the true original emerged.

"We just carried on the tradition of our family," said Malnati Jr. "There's a little competition there between us [and Malnati's] and obviously trying to stay ahead of each other. One time they'll get voted number one. The next time I'll get voted number one. We pass the torch back and forth."

One of the reasons there's as much parity between the two pizzas as there is in the cheesesteaks between Philly's Pat's and Geno's is the recipe upon which they're based. Considering Lou and Rudy Jr. had the same dad, who was there at the birth of deep-dish, their recipes reflect one another. Both doughs contain olive oil. Tomatoes are chunky and cooked on top of the pizza. The sausage recipe certainly tastes the same, and there's no denying the similarities between the creamy, rich, full-fat mozzarella blend from Wisconsin that blankets the top. Pizano's does have a slightly thinner bottom, though it's not any crispier than Lou's.

"Our pizza will come out sometimes where it's got the flavor of the oil, so it's like steak. You

start eating, you can't stop," said Rudy Jr. I've never heard the steak comparison before. Perhaps it's an umami thing, since the pizzas are typically finished with a fine grating of salty Pecorino.

Both companies also offer a thin pizza now, but Pizano's has drifted further away from tradition than Lou's, following the occasional trend by offering Hawaiian pizzas with canned pineapple and Canadian bacon. The pizza that's drifted the furthest (and perhaps one of the reasons it did not make the cut in either of my books) is the one currently being sold by Uno's. Rudy Jr. says those original recipes from the 1940s have not been preserved over the course of franchising. A request for comment from Uno's corporate office was not returned.

If you had the time, and inclination, doing a side-by-side comparison between Lou's and Pizano's would be a fun exercise. I'd make things even more interesting and throw in a Gino's East pie (since they poached Alice Mae Redmond from Uno to run their kitchen in the 1960s) and also Louisa's in Crestwood, since Louise used to be a waitress at Due's in the 1950s. Tasting all four of these pizzas in rapid succession would surely give you a 35,000-foot perspective of Chicago's deep-dish evolution.

RECIPE

DEEP-DISH

RICH LABRIOLA

YIELD: ONE TWELVE-INCH ROUND, DEEP-DISH PIZZA

Rich Labriola is a baker by trade. After he sold his commercial bakery in the early aughts, he started messing around with pizza. This deep-dish recipe is the result of a collaboration with his opening chef at La Barra in Oak Brook. He brought the recipe to Michigan Avenue in 2014. You'll need a high-sided pizza pan, which you can buy from Chicago Metallic. The cooks at the restaurant typically pinch and press the raw, bulk sausage directly onto the cheese, before the sauce is applied.

INGREDIENTS

DOUGH

390 grams of all-purpose flour
208 grams of water
1 teaspoon salt
1 teaspoon sugar
1 tablespoon toasted corn flour
2 teaspoons instant dry yeast
5 teaspoons corn oil
5 teaspoons olive oil

SAUCE

2 large cans (about 6.4 lbs each) of Saporito Filetto tomatoes, ***drained for at least three hours***
2 teaspoons granulated garlic
16 ounces of Thin Pizza Sauce (*see recipe*)

FOR ASSEMBLY

4 tablespoons olive oil (to brush the pan)
handful of coarse cornmeal
24 ounces whole milk mozzarella, sliced into twelve pieces
9 ounces bulk fennel sausage, with 2 teaspoons of Calabrian chiles or red chili flakes and 1 teaspoon black pepper added
3 tablespoons dried oregano
3 tablespoons grated Pecorino Romano cheese

TO MAKE THE DOUGH

Mix flour, water, salt, sugar, corn flour, and yeast together until incorporated. Then add corn oil and olive oil to combine. Let sit for two and a half hours, then form into a ball and refrigerate overnight.

Next day, form a twenty-one-ounce ball. Brush the inside of a twelve-inch deep-dish pan with a few tablespoons of olive oil. Sprinkle a generous but even amount of coarse cornmeal around the bottom and sides of the pan. Press out the dough on a floured surface and then place it into the pan and let proof, covered, for an hour.

Flatten dough to the edge of the pan and let sit for another twenty to thirty minutes. Push the dough down evenly across the pan to the edge. Do not push dough up the edge of the pan. Cover with plastic wrap for another sixty to ninety minutes.

THIN PIZZA SAUCE

1 large can (about 6.56 lb) Stanislaus 7/11 ground tomatoes
⅔ can (about 4.40 lb) Stanislaus Full-Red Extra Heavy tomato puree
2 ounces sugar
3 ounces salt
½ ounce black pepper
½ ounce dried basil
1.5 ounces dried oregano
pinch of cayenne
4 ounces *mirepoix* (5 onions, 2 carrots, 2 sticks of celery, small dice)
up to 1 quart water

1 Combine and blend first three ingredients (tomatoes, tomato puree, and sugar) by hand.

2 Combine next five ingredients (salt and spices) and add to tomato mixture.

3 Sweat the diced onions, celery, and carrots until the onions are translucent and the carrots are soft.

4 Puree veggies, using some of the water if necessary, to make them smooth.

5 Add vegetables to the tomato mixture and adjust the thickness with water.

TO MAKE THE SAUCE

Mix the sauce and thin pizza sauce thoroughly by hand with a spoon (do not use blender) until fully incorporated.

TO ASSEMBLE THE PIZZA

Once dough has been resting in the pan for at least one-and-a-third to two hours, flattened out, top evenly with slices of mozzarella, so the cheese completely covers the dough. Be sure to overlap slightly. This serves as a sort of barrier against the sauce. Allow just a little bit of the cheese—maybe a half-inch or so—to touch the inner wall of the pan. This part will melt and drop down along the side of the pizza, caramelizing into a crispy cheese *frico* once baked.

On top of the cheese, pinch and press the raw sausage with the chilies and black pepper into small dollops. They should be about the size of a thumb when placed on the pizza.

Finally, add generous dollops of the sauce, being sure to cover most of the cheese. Sprinkle on the dried oregano and then the Pecorino Romano, evenly across the top.

Place into a preheated 525-degree oven (or 500 degrees, if your oven doesn't go that high), preferably on top of a preheated pizza stone. Bake for thirty-five to forty minutes, until the pizza bubbles and the edges of the cheese touching the walls of the pan have blackened.

Use a large spatula to scrape and separate the pizza from the inner walls, then, with the spatula beneath the pizza, lift and remove to a cutting board to slice into pieces with a large knife (most circular pizza cutters are too small to handle the job).

6 STUFFED

I DON'T WANT TO MAKE THIS ALL ABOUT GIORDANO'S, but we have to address the nine-hundred-pound gorilla in the room. With seventy restaurants in nine states, fifty of which are in Illinois, the brand has stores as far west as Las Vegas, and east to Ohio and Florida. Ironically, they manage to sell a significant amount of tavern-style thin pizza, which makes up about 40 percent of their business. The rest is stuffed. "It's all about the cheese pull; it's indulgent," said Tod Barber, Giordano's vice president of operations. "When you have the tourists in town, they think about that one trip they had to Chicago as a kid, and they want the deep-dish."

So let's pause there for a second. True, a stuffed pizza is made in a traditional deep-dish pan. But stuffed and deep-dish are different styles. In a deep-dish, the slices of cheese across the bottom dough meld with the ingredients and the tomato sauce while baking. In a stuffed pie, the sauce is segregated above a second layer of thin dough (the top crust) so that you can taste the independent flavors. That cheese resting on the bottom layer of dough is typically shredded mozzarella, and by adding a pound or more to a medium pizza, you'll get those dramatic cheese pulls for your Instagram feed. Even Giordano's trademarked facade says "Chicago's Famous Stuffed Pizza," not deep-dish. So let's be clear: a stuffed pizza is not a deep-dish. Or to be more Yoda about it, "All stuffed pizzas are deep-dish; not all deep-dishes are stuffed."

Stuffed pie from Suparossa

Italian-born brothers Efren and Joseph Boglio founded Giordano's in early 1974, after having worked for Rocco Palese at Nancy's (a lot more on this in the Nancy's story in this chapter), which opened in 1971, making the city's first "stuffed" pizza. Giordano's Restaurant and Pizzeria started at 6253 South California Avenue. According to Barber, the Boglio brothers had worked at some local pizzerias but didn't necessarily like what they were serving. They apparently left to open Giordano's to honor their mother, a native of Torino, Italy. Giordano was her maiden name. Their big break came in March 1977, when *Chicago* magazine put a photo of their pizza on its cover and anointed it the "Best Pan Pizza" in town. That was three years after Nancy's—the restaurant where the Boglio brothers used to work—was recognized with the same honor.

The pizza, as I'll explain more in the Nancy's story, consists of two distinct doughs: one on the bottom that is connected to a circular wall of dough lining the deep pan, like a Trump fever dream racing around the border; the other, a thinner "top crust" dough that rests over the cheese and ingredients, punctured with a few vent holes, then topped with an even amount of tomato sauce. Excess dough outside the pan is cut off with a dough scraper.

Giordano's was eventually bought by a former employee, John Apostolou, in 1988. His kids helped run it for about twenty years, until they filed for bankruptcy. In 2011, Chicago-based private equity firm Victory Park Capital Advisors bought the company, including all of its trademarks and non–real estate assets, through a bankruptcy auction. Since then, Giordano's growth has been primarily focused in the Midwest, although there are restaurants in Florida, Arizona, and Nevada.

So from an Italian immigrant's idea in 1971 that led to a dispute, left unchallenged by IP attorneys, on through a Greek family's franchise expansion and eventual bankruptcy, rescued by private equity, this behemoth, with its massive commissary near O'Hare, has become the face of Chicago deep-dish pizza to a large chunk of the nation. Remember that the next time you talk shit about Chicago pizza.

But the stuffed trend didn't end there. Several pizzerias saw their success, and rabid media attention, and have since added stuffed as an option. In fact, chances are pretty good if the restaurant or pizzeria you're visiting makes a traditional deep-dish, they'll also offer a stuffed version. A great example in the city is The Art of Pizza. They used to make a pretty good deep-dish, and the *Tribune* deemed it the #1 version in Chicago . . . in 2001. But now they offer thin, pan, and stuffed; not only whole pies but also by the slice. I hate to say it, but it tasted a lot better when we were all freaking out about our computers during the buildup to Y2K.

If you have the wherewithal—and a deep pan—Nancy's was kind enough to share their stuffed pizza recipe at the end of this chapter. If you attempt it, be sure to tag us at @pizzacityusa. Good luck!

Growing up in New York City, pizza was not just a favored delicacy. It was a way of life. There was at least one pizzeria every few blocks. My hangout was Ralph's, on the corner of Twentieth Street and First Avenue, down the block from my junior high. Every day, I'd plunk some change down on the metal counter and repeat the same order: "Slice and a coke." When the dough-flipping pizza chef pulled the pie out of the oven, piping hot, I'd fold my slice over, turn it upside down to drain the rush of oil, and eat it sandwich-style.

When I came to Chicago as a college student in the early '70s, it was culture shock. You could find pizza, but not as readily, and certainly not New York–style. I found it deeply offensive.

Then I heard from a friend about a neighborhood joint on the Southwest Side with a whole new approach. At Giordano's, they really took the idea of pizza pie seriously. It WAS a pie: mounds and mounds of cheese, layered so thick you had to eat it with a fork and knife. It was decadent, outrageous, and irresistible.

As word spread, folks would line up outside on California Avenue for a seat. My wife, Susan, and I had some of our first dates there; the hour-long wait was a perfect chance to get to know one another.

After a while, success necessitated that Giordano's move to larger digs and then franchises that became global, making their sinfully layered pie synonymous with Chicago-style pizza.

Which pizza do I like more, New York or Chicago? After years in politics, let me answer this way: it depends on in which town I'm asked!

—**DAVID AXELROD**, former senior advisor to President Barack Obama; director, University of Chicago Institute of Politics; and senior political commentator for CNN

ANGELO'S STUFFED PIZZA

4850 S. Pulaski Road
773-927-9355
www.angelosstuffedpizza.com
@angelosstuffedpizza

SINCE 1992, THIS Archer Heights family favorite has been located next door to Zaragoza—one of my all-time favorite joints, where they honor the goat in all its glory, especially in their *birria*, a hearty Mexican stew. I must have completely missed Angelo's Stuffed the last time I was in this Southwest Side neighborhood. By the way, it's a convenient stop if you're flying into or out of Midway Airport, and it's best to call ahead with your order, since their stuffed pies take anywhere from forty-five minutes to an hour, depending on how busy they are.

The room has the requisite four TVs, all tuned to whatever Bulls or Blackhawks game is on, and the menu is probably too ambitious for its own good. With "stuffed" in your title, why offer fried appetizers, pastas, burgers, and entrées like chicken Parmesan? Regardless, my majestic pie arrives showered in Romano cheese and dried parsley; the cheese pull (a combo of low-moisture and whole milk mozzarella) is impressive. Unlike most other stuffed versions, this one doesn't ooze a river of cheese lava.

Just above that bottom crust, and nestled amid the cheese, are large icebergs of Battaglia sausage on one side and mild pepperoni discs on the other. Both could use more assertive seasoning, as most of the pie consists of dough and cheese. The outer perimeter of crust—at least two to three inches high—has a nice, even browning, like a retiree in Boca, and the chew is pleasant, although I would have liked mine baked just another five minutes longer. The homemade sauce is the star here. It rests above that top layer of dough, and it's good enough to serve with pasta or meatballs—vibrant, with bright acidity and a freshness that only comes from a product made in-house, each day.

NANCY'S

1000 W. Washington
(now the only city location)

Nineteen locations in suburbs and downstate

Twenty-eight locations total (including in Georgia, Missouri, and North Carolina)

www.nancyspizza.com
@nancyspizza

Rocco and Nancy Palese, circa 1971

THE STORY BEHIND why Chicago became known as ground zero for stuffed pizza, and why that style has superseded traditional deep-dish and the more ubiquitous tavern-style in the eyes—and stomachs—of tourists around the world, really comes down to three words: marketing, muscle, and money.

It begins in 1969, when Rocco Palese moved to Chicago and got a job at a local pizza joint on the Northwest Side. He wound up buying another place, called Guy's, just down the street at 4350 West Armitage, in the Hermosa neighborhood, in 1971. Like most pizzerias then, they were serving tavern-style thin. "My dad wanted to be completely different from everyone else," said Marisa Palese. "His friends said 'you gotta do a deep-dish.'"

The only problem was, in 1971, as the second wave of pizza was sweeping over the city, there were already a number of deep competitors. Lou Malnati's had opened on St. Patrick's Day that year. Larry Aronson opened My Pi on Loyola's North Side campus in August, and Burt Katz had just started making

his caramelized deep pan pizza at Pequod's in Morton Grove.

"Rocco was an innovator, he wanted to do his own thing," said Dave Howey, the president of the company that now franchises Nancy's Pizza. "He said, 'I gotta do something different.'"

Marisa Palese says her father remembered how his relatives back in Italy had often made a savory Easter pie as a celebratory dish to break Lent. "It was like a cake, with ricotta, eggs, salami, and cheese inside," she said. They would finish these pies with a sprinkle of sugar on top and an egg wash so they'd glisten. A fourteen-year-old at the time, Marisa remembers her father's first attempt included just sautéed spinach and garlic, nestled among shredded mozzarella. A second, thinner layer of dough was placed on top of the ingredients, and finally, a lake of tomato sauce would cover that upper layer, sprinkled with Romano cheese and some dried oregano. The pizzas were baked for forty-five minutes.

Rocco may have been one of those people who don't like their food touching on the plate. "The deep-dish, it bakes like a stew. He wanted to separate those flavors so you taste the sauce," said Howey. "A stuffed pizza has the distinctiveness. We're not stewing everything in tomatoes."

This "stuffed pizza" operated under the radar for the better part of two years. In 1973, Rocco bought Stella Alpina's and eventually sold it to two of his employees—Jose (aka Joseph) and his brother, Efren Boglio. The brothers ended up closing Stella Alpina's the next year, while Rocco had already moved on to a place called Mario's, located near the intersection of Lawrence and Harlem Avenues in Harwood Heights. It was there that he changed the restaurant's name to Nancy's, an anglicized homage to his wife, Anunziata. The Boglio brothers once again came back to work for Palese at Nancy's, but in 1974, told him they were going to move back to Argentina and said their farewells.

Around the same time, two important things happened to Rocco. First, *Chicago* magazine named his stuffed pizza the best in the city. The second was his chance meeting with Howey, an eighteen-year-old pre-med student from Loyola, who would later become a partner, and just four years later, open his first Nancy's in suburban Oak Lawn. Little did they know then that this chance encounter would keep the company afloat for the next fifty years.

It was a magical time for Palese, as he presided over his thirty-five-seat restaurant on the Northwest Side in 1974. "Rocco would walk around the dining room pouring wine for guests," said Howey. Never one to trust lawyers—and still not fluent in English—he would ask the young college student to read over leases with him at the table, sending out an appetizer platter as payment.

"I was getting a lot of mail and calls from people in Norridge and Harwood Heights about this pizza place," said Vicki Giammona, a former colleague of mine at ABC7 who used to write restaurant reviews for the *Suburban Sun-Times* in the early '70s. "We went to check it out, and it was amazing. Like nothing we had ever seen before," she said. "It was like walking into your aunt's house. Rocco was there, Nancy was hiding out in the kitchen—just the sweetest, shyest lady."

Giammona had grown up in Austin, on the city's West Side, a child of a Sicilian family who grew up on thin, square-cut pizzas in the '50s and '60s, mixed in with an occasional sheet pan pizza made by her grandmother. An admitted deep-dish fan, she says the original stuffed pizza she tasted in the '70s was nothing like the monstrosities being pushed onto tourists these days.

"It was filling, but it wasn't heavy," she said. "It was just put together so well. If you think about

Marisa and Rocco Palese, circa 1971

lasagna—with the layering, the different flavors—you don't eat a full pan, you eat a square. Same thing here. The topping was thin; it wasn't like two deep-dishes on top of each other."

Giammona recalls spinach being the flavor she most frequently had, rather than sausage or pepperoni.

The Paleses' success allowed them to expand to more than 130 seats. Around this time, in late 1974, they heard from one of their suppliers about a similar concept on the South Side, along Fifty-Fifth Street. "One of our vendors said there's a place called Giordano's buying the same ingredients as us, selling the same stuffed pizza," said Marisa. "They [the Boglio brothers] never went back to Argentina. They took our story and copied it. They were not from Torino [as they claim on the company's website]."

"The brothers went from Turin to Argentina and then to the U.S.," said Tod Barber, the vice president of operations for Giordano's. He said the brothers did work in a local pizzeria in Chicago, but couldn't specify which one. "They didn't like the pizza they were making, so they took Mama Giordano's recipe for an Easter pie and tweaked it," he said.

The brothers opened the first Giordano's on the South Side in 1974, and started expanding with the help of investors, including the Apostolou family, who still maintain a seat on the company's board.

Giammona, who eventually left her job at the *Suburban Sun-Times* to become a news producer at ABC7, retired in 2011, the same year, coincidentally, Giordano's was bought by Victory Park Capital Advisors, an investment firm in Chicago. Even now, nearly fifty years later, she vividly remembers what that time was like for the Palese family.

"It was quite upsetting. They felt betrayed," she said. "Because they were immigrants, they felt they didn't have any recourse."

One of the other problems for the Paleses was their lack of marketing know-how. All of their business was word-of-mouth, Giammona said. "These other guys were more street smart. They were savvier; they had more help to expand. They [the Paleses] didn't expect anybody to behave like that."

It didn't help that Rocco turned to less-than-ideal business partners to help grow his business. "That backfired," said Giammona. "They were going to help him and then they just ripped them off. They got bad advice."

Still, the original recipe was known only to Rocco, who always

maintained a separate spice room in each store. "When I opened Oak Lawn, he'd have special cups for measuring spices," said Howey. "When the Boglio brothers worked there, they never knew the recipe. That's why the difference [between Nancy's and Giordano's] is night and day. They make their dough in a commissary with chemicals to retard fermentation, since it travels all over the country. Ours rests in a cooler overnight; it's more of a bread dough," said Howey, who stresses none of the employees in

any of the Nancy's locations are privy to the exact recipe for the sauce or the dough. For their part, Barber says there are no preservatives used in the food at Giordano's, but they do manage a large commissary near O'Hare Airport.

Howey's company now has more than two dozen locations, scattered around the state, as well as in Georgia and North Carolina. In 2019, they opened a flagship location in the West Loop, with his three sons—David, Adam, and Alex—and daughter Kayla, a Culinary Institute of America grad. Few pizzerias can claim a former cook from Thomas Keller's Bouchon in Napa Valley as a staff member. But for all of his daughter's skill and culinary acumen, the recipe for the stuffed pizza has remained pretty much the same. Ingredients, including a gigantic handful of shredded mozzarella, are scattered atop a firm bottom dough that also lines the interior walls of a deep pan. A much lighter top crust, as thin as a hand wipe, is gently placed over the top, the excess cut away with the aid of a dough scraper rubbed along the outer perimeter. A few vents are cut into the top layer, while the outer edge gets a drizzle of olive oil. Finally, ladles of dark, slightly chunky tomato sauce are spread across the top, all the way to the edges. Baked in a conveyor oven, the pizzas are dusted with grated Pecorino and dried oregano just before serving. You can definitely taste the separation of the sauce versus the other ingredients. The question is, how many slices can you eat before it's nap time?

SUPAROSSA

4256 N. Central Avenue
773-736-5828
(carryout and delivery only)
www.suparossa.com
@suparossachicago

7319 W. Lawrence Avenue,
Harwood Heights
708-867-4641
@suparossa

The Suparossa Hospitality Group has pared down their portfolio from a few years ago. They now run just the two pizza operations (carryout and delivery only) as well as a gastropub connected to the Central Avenue location called Legno.

Like so many pizza shops in town, Suparossa offers multiple styles, namely thin, pan or deep, and stuffed. The stuffed was the style I tried for my first book, and since that's what they're known for, I figured I'd stick with it this time around. Though I find the extra top layer of dough unnecessary (it makes the pizza look more heavily fortified than a castle in *Game of Thrones*), I begrudgingly tried it for the sake of the quest. Honestly, by this point in my research, I have about as much energy and enthusiasm for a stuffed pizza as I do for haggling over my cell phone bill charges with AT&T.

But this recipe has a lot more appeal than the usual stuffed cheese casseroles I've tried around the region. Yes, there are those high sides holding a potential lava flow of whole milk mozzarella, but once you bite into it, there is actually some flakiness, not the usual wet cardboard. The top layer is as thin as the *Trib*'s business section, holding up a lake of fresh, vibrant tomato sauce that I'd be happy to have mingling with some pasta.

On my first visit, back in 2016, I noted how, buried beneath the top layer of dough, lived some of the juiciest, most flavorful boulders of sausage—made in-house. But this time around, I opted for spinach instead. What a joy to see some vibrant green beneath that cheesy lava flow!

The standard construction for a stuffed pizza, from the bottom crust up, goes like this: cheese, ingredients, maybe some more cheese, top layer of thin dough, and sauce. But that sauce, which the owners readily admit has sugar in addition to the oregano and other proprietary spices, somehow manages not to overwhelm. It adds a lovely, sweet acidity to the richness from the cheese and the meats. Having the combo of spinach and cheese would have been the perfect substitute for my vegetarian friends, if any of them would have

had the courage to have accompanied me on my visit.

This is a one-slice-per-person endeavor; knife and fork recommended. It's the modus operandi that makes East Coast pizza snobs laugh at Chicago through their greasy, flaccid, yeast-crusted glasses, but for a certain segment of the population, it's truly a thing of beauty, reminding them of their childhood on the city's Northwest Side.

RECIPE

STUFFED

DAVE HOWEY, NANCY'S PIZZA

YIELD: THREE TEN-INCH ROUND STUFFED PIZZAS

To make a really good stuffed pizza you have to have patience and discipline. Why? Because to get this just right, you have to plan ahead and be willing to make your sauce and dough at least one day ahead of your planned cooking date. The dough needs time to rest after you mix and proof it and the sauce needs time for the flavors to meld.

INGREDIENTS

DOUGH

2.5 pounds bread flour
1 packet dry Red Star active yeast
17 fluid ounces lukewarm water (filtered if possible)
6.5 ounces vegetable oil
1.5 teaspoons sea salt or kosher salt
2 teaspoons sugar

SAUCE

56 ounces crushed peeled tomatoes
6 ounces water (ideally, filtered)
2 tablespoons sugar
1 teaspoon dry basil
1 teaspoon black pepper
2 teaspoons sea salt or kosher salt
1 teaspoon garlic powder
3 tablespoons finely chopped fresh parsley

FOR ASSEMBLY

1 stick (quarter pound) softened salted butter
3 ounces grated Parmesan cheese
1 teaspoon dry oregano
1 ounce extra virgin olive oil
12 ounces shredded mozzarella
other ingredients that you enjoy

TO MAKE THE DOUGH

First empty the packet of dry active yeast and the sugar into the lukewarm water. (Water temperature should be approximately 100 to 110 degrees Fahrenheit.) Mix it well and let rest for ten minutes to fully activate.

While the yeast is activating, add the flour, salt, and vegetable oil to your mixing bowl. It is best to use a stand mixer with the dough hook for this step.

Once the water mixture is ready, add the full amount to the bowl with the flour and begin mixing on a low speed for a total of eight to ten minutes or until the dough comes together in a ball. (Nothing should remain stuck to the side of your bowl.)

Once the mixing is complete, cover the dough with plastic wrap and set aside in a warm area to rise for about sixty minutes or until the dough doubles in size.

Once the dough has risen, divide the large dough ball into four equal pieces, wrap each one in plastic wrap, and store the four wrapped dough balls in the refrigerator overnight.

You cannot use the dough the day you make it. It must rest in your refrigerator for one full day and is good for up to two days from the day you mixed it.

TO MAKE THE SAUCE

Mix all of the sauce ingredients in a large mixing bowl with a whisk. Mix well, cover the bowl with plastic wrap, and place in your refrigerator.

You cannot use the sauce the same day you mix it. It takes time for the spices and herbs to infuse the tomatoes with their flavor.

Recipe continues

TO ASSEMBLE THE PIZZAS

Now you can make your pizzas. You will need three cake pans that are ten inches across and one inch deep. Move your oven shelf to the middle position and set your oven to 450 degrees.

If you are going to make all three pizzas at one time, get your pans out and generously spread one third of the softened butter completely over the bottom and up the sides of the pans. (It should be pretty thick.)

Remove the plastic wrap from one of the four dough pieces and roll it into a ball with your hands; then use a rolling pin to roll the dough into a round piece of dough, twelve inches across (it will be thick). You are rolling the dough to twelve inches so there is enough to cover the entire bottom and up the sides of your ten-inch pizza pan plus up the one-inch sides.

Once rolled, place the dough into the pans and gently press the dough up the sides of the pan, making sure there are no bubbles under the dough or holes in the dough. Make sure all the dough fits into the pan and the dough on the sides is pulled all the way up the sides so the top layer of dough can connect to it.

Once the dough is in place, quickly add your ingredients. (*This recipe will show you how to make a cheese stuffed pizza. If you add additional ingredients you will have to decrease the amount of cheese to fit everything into the pan.*)

So, for this cheese-stuffed pizza, add twelve ounces of shredded mozzarella cheese into the pan on top of the dough. Spread the cheese across the inside of the pan, making it level across the pizza.

Once all your ingredients are added, cover the ingredients with a paper-thin piece of dough that you have rolled out and cover the entire top of the pizza. (The amount of dough for this part is approximately one third of the fourth dough portion from the original batch of dough.)

With your fingers, crimp the thin top layer of dough completely around the edge of the pizza to connect it to the bottom dough on the sides of the pan.

Before adding the pizza sauce, tear 4 small holes in the top layer of dough to create some vents for steam to escape during the cooking time.

Now add fourteen ounces of pizza sauce to evenly cover the entire top layer of dough. Be very careful not to get the sauce anywhere near the edge of the metal pan. Any sauce touching the pan will burn and turn black during cooking.

Once the sauce is applied, gently drizzle about a quarter ounce of extra virgin olive oil around the sauce, just enough to add droplets around it.

Bake at 450 degrees for about thirty minutes. Because every home oven cooks a bit differently, carefully check the pizza and make sure the middle internal temperature of the cooked pizza is at least 160 degrees before removing it from the oven.

After removing the pizzas, sprinkle grated Parmesan and a little oregano over the top of the hot pizza.

Once the pizzas are cooked, let them rest for about ten minutes before you cut into this unique Chicago delicacy. Enjoy!

7 NEAPOLITAN

It's not exactly a secret society like Skull and Bones, but the fraternity of *pizzaiolos* who ply their trade beneath the mantle of Neapolitan pizza do refer to each other with reverence. In Chicago, Jonathan Goldsmith is the high priest of Neapolitan pizza at Spacca Napoli. A pioneer in his trade, he's the "dough whisperer," managing to transform flour and water into one of the city's most heavenly chews. Some of his former employees have opened their own Neapolitan pizza joints (a sort of Rick Bayless effect for the beehive oven set), assembling faithful re-creations, doming them just before serving, and in the process, expanding the Neapolitan-style pizza landscape. During the pandemic, Goldsmith has had to pivot somewhat, setting up a bank of electric PizzaMaster ovens in the dining room, ready to bake up pizzas for delivery or carryout, as most wood-fired pies do not travel well in a cardboard box. Even a VPN-certified shop has to take drastic measures once in a while.

What is a Neapolitan? In short, it's a pizza style originating from—you guessed it—Naples, Italy. There is actually an international governing body, the Associazione Vera Pizza Napoletana (AVPN), which attempts to preserve this tradition and ensure that restaurants claiming to serve the real thing abide by certain rules, such as the type of flour, cheese, and oven used in the restaurant. There is also an Association of Neapolitan Pizza Makers (APN), and, like the AVPN, their goal is to

Textbook cornicione *at Eataly*

make sure anyone claiming to sell a Neapolitan pizza is upholding tradition, but in the case of the APN, they certify only the pizza maker.

In short, these *pizzaiolos* must use "00" flour, which is highly refined. The water must have a certain pH level; sea salt and compressed solid yeast must be used; and there are rules regarding how many times the dough should rise and for how long. In addition, San Marzano tomatoes must be used for the sauce. Even the type of oven used to bake the pies is specified with somber authority. In this quote from their official guidelines, the Association of Neapolitan Pizza Makers describes what a pizza should look and taste like when it emerges from the oven:

Working the oven at Mozzarella Store, Pizza & Caffé

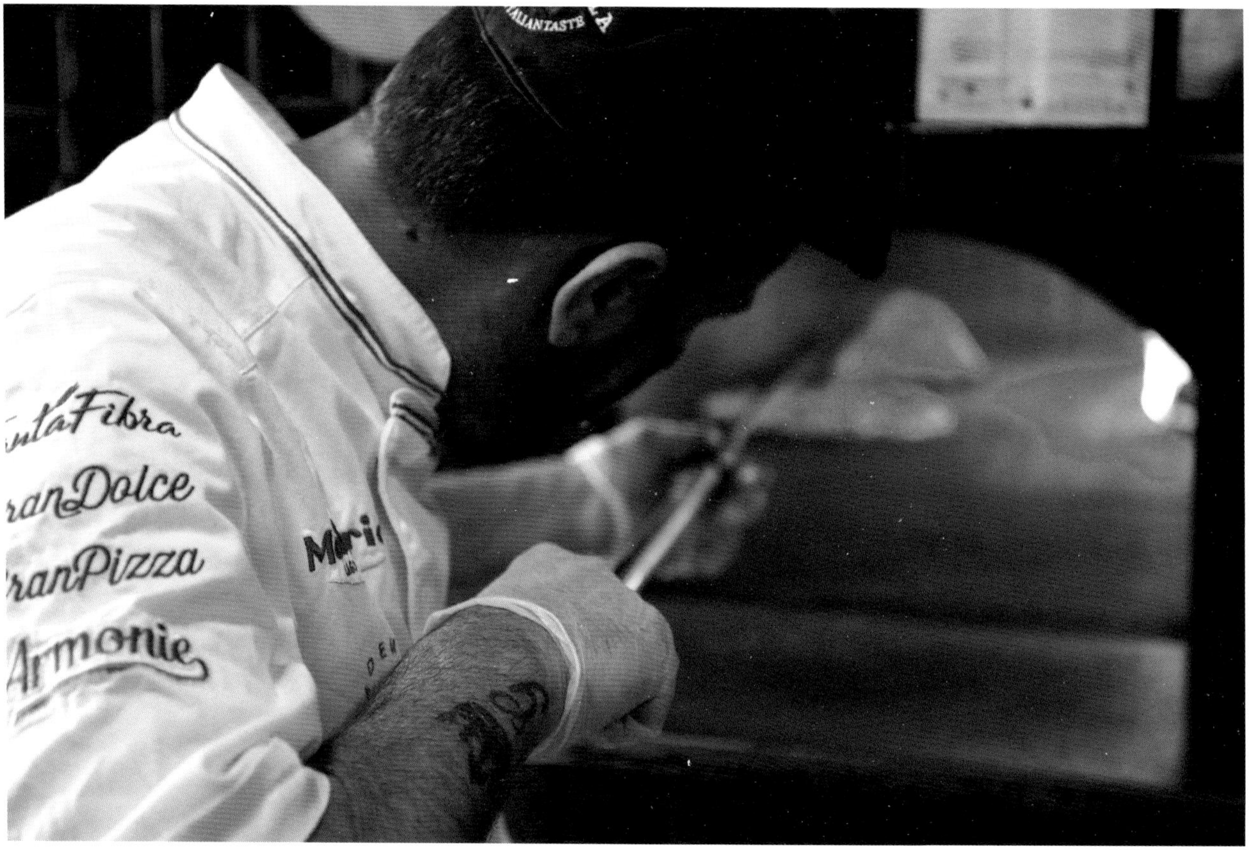

The consistency of the pizza should be soft, elastic, and easy to manipulate and fold. The center should be particularly soft to the touch and the taste and appearance of the pizza must be evidenced by the red color of the tomato. For the Pizza Marinara, the green of the oregano and the white of the garlic must be homogeneously spread, while, in the case of the Pizza Margherita, the white of the mozzarella should appear in evenly spread patches, in contrast with the green of the basil leaves, slightly darkened by the cooking process. The crust should possess the flavor of well-baked bread. The slightly acidic flavor of the densely enriched tomatoes, mixed with the characteristic aroma of the oregano, garlic or basil ensures that the pizza, as it comes out from the oven, delivers its characteristic aroma of a fresh and fragrant typical Mediterranean product.

There are nearly a dozen reputable Neapolitan pizza makers in the city now, and a few more in the suburbs. I'm happy to add a few new ones here, including the Mozzarella Store—a great suggestion if you're walking down Michigan Avenue and jonesing for *fior di latte*—and returning is Nella Grassano at her namesake in Hyde Park. Once the Obama Presidential Library opens, she'll be sitting pretty, but until then, University of Chicago students and faculty know the only Neapolitan option on the South Side is in their backyard. For the record, the six restaurants currently holding AVPN certificates in Chicagoland are: Coda di Volpe, Forno Rosso (Harlem Avenue and Randolph Street), Napolita (Wilmette), Parkers' (Downers Grove), and Spacca Napoli.

COCO PAZZO

300 W. Hubbard Street
312-836-0900
www.cocopazzochicago.com
@cocopazzochicago

WHEN BUSINESS LUNCHES eventually return to River North, no one will be more relieved to see a professional clientele sitting in chairs again, drinking glasses of Nebbiolo with their pastas, than Jack Weiss. The owner of Coco Pazzo for more than twenty years has seen it all, and he's one of the few remaining holdouts from an almost bygone era of long, lazy lunches served to suit-wearing attorneys, politicians, and brokers.

The Long Island native grew up fishing and crabbing, got a corporate job as an adult, but fell in love with the restaurant business after working in the West Village. His passion for food, wine, and hospitality has rubbed off on his family—his wife, Tamra, is the restaurant's wine director and his son works as a manager and host.

The secret to Coco Pazzo's Neapolitan pizza is also the centerpiece of its restaurant: a sixty-inch Renato wood-burning oven. The high-temperature oven burns a lot of wood, imparting the faintest hint of smokiness.

"We believe the oven is really conducive to cooking the pizza at the right temperature," said Weiss.

Weiss's team imports all of their ingredients directly from Italy, bringing cheese and tomatoes from San Marzano and "00" flour from Caputo. The true test of a Neapolitan pizza? A simple Margherita pie, perfected. Weiss calls this the "gold standard" of pizza, because it allows the ingredients to shine. Indeed, their pies emerge from the oven sufficiently blistered and puffy, and slightly tangy; the middle is ample, soft, and chewy. *Fior di latte* bursts with creaminess and the tomato sauce has that wonderful balance of sharp acidity that manages to be mellow, not off-putting.

Weiss also runs Coco Pazzo Café on East Ohio Street in Streeterville, a more casual spot for walk-ins since there are more hotels and shops in the area. The pizza there is thinner, more like a Roman tavern-style. But in River North, if you're looking for a little splurge and want to remember what it feels like to be coddled for an hour, go join the professionals supping on Hubbard Street. Even the dudes in suits can't resist these pizzas.

CODA DI VOLPE

3335 N. Southport Avenue
773-687-8568
www.cdvolpe.com
@cdvolpe_chi

BILLY LAWLESS HAS always, it seems, had a pretty good idea about what his customers want. On Michigan Avenue, he mastered the gastropub concept at The Gage, serving food that doesn't play dumb for the masses. Next door to The Gage, at Acanto, he created an Italian lounge with stellar cocktails and a better-than-expected Neapolitan pizza. At Coda di Volpe on Southport, he's struck a balance between an approachable neighborhood restaurant and a River North vibe.

Coda di Volpe patrons are two-deep at the bar on the Friday I decide to go check it out. High-backed booths, not unlike something from The Pump Room, line the middle of the dining room. The glorious white-and-gray-tiled pizza oven is impossible to miss, sitting next to a wall of chopped wood no less than eight feet tall. Like the Hope Diamond, it is proudly displayed (and guarded) behind a phalanx of cooks, all scurrying around, shifting and transferring blistered pies into and out of the oven's mouth.

There are just eight options on the menu, and these are the only Neapolitan pizzas in Chicago that come with your very own set of kitchen shears, with which you are left to cut the pie as you wish. Preserving the integrity of the pizza, in its whole form, is something a lot of *pizzaiolos* would probably like to do, rather than cut it prematurely. This small detail speaks volumes; maybe that's why it's one of only four pizzerias in the city with VPN certification.

The kitchen also understands OBR, as it manages to add just the right amount of tangy *fior di latte* and tomato sauce (which might be a tad too thin for some) without overwhelming the delicate, thin slices.

A pizza with high ambitions must have an impressive *cornicione*, and this one is no different. It's speckled and blistered with a generous amount of char (both on top and underneath), giving each bite a pleasant chew with the slightest hint of tang—a result of letting the dough rest enough to kick-start fermentation. Another plus is the appropriate seasoning and salt usage, so that the naked pieces of the lip that are left over actually retain flavor, and are not left to become crust orphans on your plate.

You can (and probably should) upgrade your cheese to mozzarella *di bufala*. The buffalo's milk has slightly more fat to it than a *fior di latte* or other fresh cow's milk mozzarella, and since it's applied sparingly and with an even hand, this small luxury is well worth it. I can't wait to go back and try the versions with pesto, roasted mushrooms, and fennel sausage.

EATALY

43 E. Ohio Street
312-521-8700
www.eataly.com/us_en/stores/chicago
@eatalychicago

THIS INTERNATIONAL CHAIN of Italian marketplaces, now with five locations in the United States, another in Toronto, and a gondola load across the globe, opened its gigantic, two-level ode to all things Italian in River North in 2013. Boasting a larger footprint than the New York City original in the Flatiron District, the sixty-thousand-square-foot behemoth in Chicago houses several stations and restaurants inside. Naturally, I visited La Pizza & La Pasta on Eataly's second floor.

The Margherita, cooked in a stunningly gorgeous gold tile–encrusted wood-burning oven, looks like a Neapolitan child's ideal pizza as it hits the table. The *pizzaiolos* are constantly in motion, like an army of ants, stretching dough, tearing on *fior di latte*, and launching the pizzas into one of the two beehive-shaped ovens. If I'm in the mood, and a little hangry after being on my feet while shopping around Michigan Avenue, the simple pleasure of the creamy fresh mozzarella nestled into the sauce of San Marzanos, experienced while chewing the pliable, leopard-spotted crust, is pure pleasure. They now offer a few dough options, such as rustic and gluten-free, but for my visit, I stuck to the standard "00" flour–based original.

Eataly actually outsources the pizza-making to a Napoli-based company called Rossopomodoro, which sends trainers to Chicago to supervise the *pizzaiolos*. The main *pizzaiolo* here—Simone—must have a cot behind the ovens, because I've never not seen him here. When does the man sleep? Just FYI, Eataly is only a block off the Michigan Avenue tourist corridor, so if it's a summer Saturday afternoon, ticket counts run high and the noise level increases; sometimes the staff gets harried and the kitchen is in the weeds. They should take a page from fellow Italian Carlo Petrini and slow down. Take their time and get each pie right. The pizza here can be very good, but the *pizzaiolos* not named Simone need to remember consistency is as important as anything else.

FORNO ROSSO PIZZERIA NAPOLETANA

1048 W. Randolph Street
312-243-6000

3719 N. Harlem Avenue
773-716-3000

www.fornorossopizzeria.com
@fornorosso

NICK NITTI WORKS a metal peel like Anthony Rizzo does a wooden bat. Years of muscle memory allow him to transform an inanimate object into a functional appendage, giving him a necessary tool to ply his trade. Nitti has been a student of Neapolitan pizza for some time, and when I interviewed him a few years ago for ABC7, I recall him telling me how he looked up to (and visited) gurus like Chris Bianco, in Phoenix, before deciding to open his own place in the Dunning neighborhood on Chicago's Northwest Side. His newer location, on West Randolph, is much more convenient for Neapolitan-loving pizza fans near downtown.

The *cornicione* here is majestic. Slightly charred from the heat of his wood-burning, beehive brick oven, the Margherita arrives amply blistered, covered in generous blobs of fresh mozzarella and a half-dozen fresh basil leaves. The tomato sauce is simple, fresh, and evenly applied, contributing to slices that miraculously hold their shape even when lifted. There's a reason that giant AVPN certification is mounted on the wall next to the kitchen—one of only six in the entire region. Both of Nitti's locations have the VPN certification. The view outside the floor-to-ceiling windows might be West Randolph, but close your eyes and chew, and you're in a Neapolitan daydream.

The bottom crust has a decent amount of char and the perimeter is soft yet chewy. Take a look inside that crust and you'll see air pockets, revealing a full day's worth of fermentation. This is a crust you want to finish off, and I'd be surprised if there were many crust orphans left on plates nearby.

One note: this is a fragile creation. Don't get it to go, or you'll miss the entire experience. Eat it as soon as it hits your table, or if you have to, crush it in the car!

GALLUCCI PIZZERIA NAPOLETANA

1551 N. Wells Street
312-888-3993

www.gallucchicago
@galluccichicago

THE FIRST THING I noticed upon walking into the old Dinotto space (rated my #2 overall Neapolitan in *Pizza City, USA*) was the new oven! Owner and *pizzaiolo* Gianni Gallucci is a former member of the U.S. Pizza Team and previous *pizzaiolo* at Forno Rosso in the West Loop. He and his brother have given the Old Town space new life with a series of giant graffiti-like religious-themed murals and that giant, gold-tiled Marra Forni oven that's as reflective as a disco ball.

Gallucci took top honors at the 2017 Caputo Cup (part of the annual Pizza & Pasta Northeast convention). He topped his winning pie with buffalo ricotta, *prosciutto di Parma*, red *piennolo del Vesuvio*, and summer black truffle. Here on Wells Street, he's making puffy, blistered pizzas speckled with white and black truffles and bursting with classic flavors highlighted by DOP tomatoes, imported cheese, and olive oil.

You won't find any neo-Neapolitan pies here. He's not interested in compromising flavors or using alternative ingredients to satisfy a range of peculiar tastes. Yes, the pies will be a little wet in the middle; yes, you'll need a knife and fork; no, you don't send them back to be cooked "well done." That would be like asking for ketchup on a hot dog. But if you're craving the flavors of fresh mozzarella you had on that trip to Naples back in college, or miss the chewy, leopard-spotted *corniciones* you first experienced in New York, then waiting the ninety seconds for one of Gallucci's pies to emerge from the oven is your ticket to nostalgia.

MOZZARELLA STORE, PIZZA & CAFFÉ

822 N. Michigan Avenue
312-285-2449
www.mozzarellastores.com
@mozzarellastores

NOT MANY PIZZA PLACES in town are making their own cheese, but at the Mozzarella Store, Pizza and Caffé just off Michigan Avenue, the Italian import is making stracciatella, mozzarella, and burrata fresh each day.

"In Italy we produce mozzarella fresh every day. We eat fresh every day, maximum after one week," said co-owner Giorgia Somma. "The flavor, it's completely different. There is more fat in our milk and this makes the mozzarella have a more strong flavor than other mozzarella."

Those warm, fresh balls of mozzarella are then transported about fifty feet to the pizza station.

"Our master *pizzaiolo* is Neapolitan and he has more than thirty years of experience in the restaurant," Somma said.

It's all pretty much textbook here: "00" flour for the dough, San Marzano tomato sauce, and homemade *fior di latte*. However, here the dough does get a longer rest than most Neapolitans.

"Our pizza has seventy-two hours of fermentation. The dough is so completely light you can eat two at the same time. You stay fantastic with your stomach," said Somma.

The 900-plus degree oven bakes them in about ninety seconds, resulting in a slightly wet middle.

"But this is good because it means the pizza is real Neapolitan," she said. "I eat with the hands, yeah, I eat with hands or you can close like a wallet."

NELLA PIZZA E PASTA

1125 E. Fifty-Fifth Street
773-643-0603
www.nellachicago.com
@nellapizzaepasta

A PIONEER OF SORTS in Chicago, Nella Grassano is the only female *pizzaiola* manning the oven in her own restaurant. She is as comfortable making a Neapolitan pizza—stretching the dough, building the pie, wielding a metal peel to maneuver it in a blazing wood-burning oven—as an alderman is taking a donation from a developer. The muscle memory acquired over a lifetime began when she was just six years old, watching her grandfather make pizzas, and has become second nature. The only reason Chicago is lucky enough to have her is that she met her husband while visiting the city many years ago, and never left.

She enchanted Chicagoans with her deft touch while working as the *pizzaiola* for Jonathan Goldsmith at Spacca Napoli between 2000 and 2010. The duo famously parted ways, with Grassano going to work first for Scott Harris's Francesca empire, then opening her own place on a congested stretch of Fullerton with historically very little foot traffic.

In late 2017, a dispute with her landlord (and some wooing from the University of Chicago) led her to a much larger space at the base of a new dorm on Fifty-Fifth Street in Hyde Park. Her skills, honed over a lifetime of trial and error, have been rewarded and praised by several local critics, and rightly so. What a pleasure it is devouring Nella's Margherita. I'm sure the ones topped with arugula or *prosciutto di Parma* are equally enjoyable, but whatever you order, just inhaling the smell of the dough, made from Caputo "00" flour, topped with imported *fior di latte*, and baked to exact specs in the wood-burning oven, is pleasure enough. Biting into the textbook delicious *cornicione* delivers one of the city's best Neapolitan-style pie experiences . . . *mmm*.

PANINO'S PIZZERIA

3702 N. Broadway Street (entrance on Waveland Avenue)
773-472-6200
www.paninospizzeria.com
@paninoschicago

They also have locations in Evanston and Park Ridge.

Each of Panino's suburban locations is a stand-alone restaurant and pizzeria. But the city location is really two different restaurants within one. On the Broadway side (facing an unremarkable strip mall), it's a standard-issue thin, deep-dish, and by-the-slice joint, with pies baked in electric ovens—although during the pandemic, all customers had to enter on the Waveland side. Over there, a completely different personality emerges as you see not only the warming boxes with slices ready to go, but also the majestic, red-tiled, wood-burning oven in the back, with "*master pizzaiolo*" spelled out in white tiles, indicating they take the pizzas a tad more seriously here.

As you look around the room, you'll see lots of articles mounted on the walls, touting the success of owners Gino and Lenny Rago. As members of the U.S. Pizza Team, they've built a steady record of wins in regional competitions. The only problem with that is they don't reflect a consistency at their restaurants—like, say, an article from the *Tribune* or *Chicago* magazine might recognize. There are no "Best of . . ." mentions in stories from local publications. Their competitive honors reward creativity and on-the-fly adaptation to making pizzas in convention halls and serving a panel of judges. I wish the Ragos well in these endeavors, but I also wish they'd focus their efforts a bit. The menu on Broadway features thin, deep, Sicilian, grandma, and Neapolitan. But this is not Tony's in San Francisco, it's Northalsted/Boystown, where a decent slice will suffice. The thins and deeps in the warming boxes up front have little appeal. Here, you want to sample the thin, puffy Neapolitans (and grandmas, which I discuss in chapter 8).

The key is their mother starter, a strain of yeast that is recycled and reused, integrated and fed with more water and flour, then kneaded and aged—left to ferment and develop serious air pockets within the dough.

After the pizza—topped with healthy blobs of fresh mozzarella, zesty tomato sauce with a few basil leaves, and a drizzle of olive oil—is scorched and baked in the Italian-made oven, it emerges with beautifully charred edges as well as blackened splotches above and below. There is a great chew, with wonderful texture, and a homey, misshapen *cornicione*. The Neapolitans definitely don't travel as well as the thin or deep slices, but you can reheat them in a large skillet and still appreciate the work that went into them.

The Margheritas are nicely charred and I love how the middle is just thick enough to withstand the blobs of mozzarella and fresh tomato sauce. And that chew! One of the hallmarks of a great pizza—and a compliment to the *pizzaiolo*—is being able to thoroughly enjoy the entire slice, from the point all the way to the *cornicione*. I doubt there will be many crust orphans left behind after a visit to one of the city's truly great Neapolitan pizza shops.

SAPORI NAPOLETANI

6050 N. Northwest Highway
773-628-7894
www.saporinapoletani.com
@sapori_napoletani

It's tough to spot Sapori, which is situated directly in the middle of a tidy strip mall that runs along busy Northwest Highway (which is really just a city street, despite the name). After passing an engraving and embossing shop as well as a transmission repair shop and a dentist's office, you'll finally find it in the middle of the mall.

Here, Antonio Vitiello, a Naples native who lived there for twenty-five years, plies his trade, making every pizza and firing each one himself. Vitiello even built his own large, beehive oven; wood-fired, of course, it gets up to about 700 degrees, turning the crusts into blistered beauties. San Marzano tomatoes, *fior di latte* cheese, and a few large basil leaves come together so well here, and despite the fact that he adds a bit more cheese than the usual suspects in town (creating a slight pool of liquid in the center), his version—hewing more closely to the Naples original—is still complex and not overwhelmed by any one ingredient.

He lets the dough rest at least a day, but more often than not it will be forty-eight hours. With more than a dozen options on the menu, I was tempted to taste something different, maybe a daily special with mozzarella, potato, and rosemary, or a fantastic-sounding pizza with caciocavallo cheese and spicy soppressata. Considering how perfect his *cornicione* is, with its occasional blister domes, leopard spotting, and misshapen edges, I know I'll be back to try more.

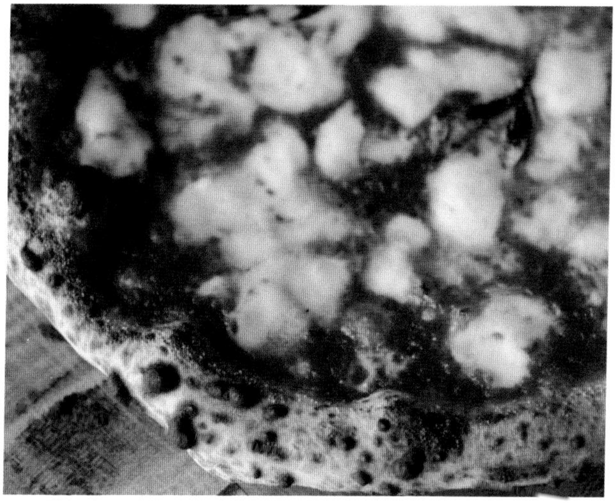

SPACCA NAPOLI PIZZERIA

1769 W. Sunnyside Avenue
773-878-2420
www.spaccanapolipizzeria.com
@spaccanapolichicago

JONATHAN GOLDSMITH has become not just a *pizzaiolo,* he has, over the past fifteen years, become one of Chicago's true ambassadors for Neapolitan pizza. He lectures on the subject of pizza making at trade shows and conventions, travels to Italy regularly, and has made the art and tradition of Neapolitan pizza his mission since he opened on a quiet stretch of Sunnyside Avenue in 2006.

If children dreamed of becoming a Neapolitan *pizzaiolo* when they grew up, like some kids fantasize about playing in the NBA or NFL, they'd have posters of Goldsmith up on their walls, elbow-deep in flour or poised at the mouth of his oven, peel in hand, ready to turn or dome a pie.

All of the hallmarks for a fine Neapolitan are here: "00" flour; the *fior di latte* cheese, which is oozing, creamy-sweet, and placed haphazardly about the hand-formed spheres; and the San Marzano tomatoes, crushed into part-sweet, part-acidic oblivion. The telltale crust—puffy and blistered—has a remarkable chew that comes from a long fermentation. Early on, when Spacca Napoli first opened, I felt that the pie centers were too thin and too wet (I know true Neapolitans adore this tomato-cheese puddle), and while I enjoyed the *cornicione,* I rarely praised the interior. Things have changed (Goldsmith admits the recipe has been tweaked), and those droopy interiors are a thing of the past. The dough these days is a little bit more structured, and the other

dozen or so pizzas offered all feature top-quality ingredients, such as arugula, imported prosciutto, homemade sausage, and rapini—a crunchy, green cruciferous vegetable that works exceptionally well when paired with rich, full-fat ingredients.

During the pandemic, Goldsmith added a bank of electric PizzaMaster ovens to the dining room to aid with to-go orders. I'm wishing him well of course, but I'm also looking forward to seeing a full dining room again with customers able to enjoy those pizzas just minutes after they emerge from his blazing oven.

8 SICILIAN, GRANDMA, AND SHEET PAN BAKERY SLICES

THE RECTANGULAR SLICE HAS BEEN ELUSIVE IN CHICAGO, a city with at least ten unique styles to brag about. Suffice it to say we are a city bathed and marinated in the three predominant styles I mentioned in chapters 4 through 6.

But for sheer pizza eating pleasure, it's hard to beat a proper Sicilian slice. New York ex-pats who've moved to the Midwest might lament the absence of classic slice shops, and many will admit they miss the squares as much as the triangular, foldable wedges. I've tried about seventy pizzerias in and around New York City over the past three years, and favorite spots include Mama's TOO! on the Upper West Side, L'Industrie in Williamsburg, and Philomena's in Queens. I can name my favorite Chicago Sicilians on one hand. A year ago, there would have been maybe one worth mentioning.

Nonetheless, before there was Prince Street Pizza in New York City's West Village, capturing people's attention with their cup-and-char pepperonis on Instagram (and more recently, their vile posts on social media), there were plenty of shops in Chicago selling rectangular slices, albeit not as memorable as the crispy-meets-spongy Sicilians on the East Coast. While there is no official pizza taxonomy, the best I could come up with in technical terms would be a sheet pan bakery-style slice, and it's done the trick for generations of Chicagoans.

Grandma-style pie from Panino's

Sicilian at Foxhole

Once the dough is mixed for a Sicilian pizza, it is often left to rest, rise, and ferment in the pan for at least a day or two (although I've been hearing about three- to five-day rests with a pit-stop in the freezer to absorb excess moisture, but that's a little too inside baseball for most).

For the last seventy years, D'Amato's has been baking both breads and pizzas in its gargantuan coal-fired oven (itself a relic from 1912). Known for their rectangular, bakery-style slices, topped with all manner of fennel-laced sausage or artichoke and olives, their pizzas tend to be softer underneath, with a spongy texture. The same is true at Sicilia Bakery on the Northwest Side—not to be confused with Sicilian Bakery, both of which are old-school joints selling sturdy slices always good for a last-minute reheat and a quick lunch. Pompei in Little Italy does an admirable job, producing a thin, crispy undercarriage flecked with cornmeal, but the middle and undercarriage is where many of these old guards struggle. None have the hallmarks of a classic East Coast Sicilian: the focaccia-esque interior contrasted with a crispy, sturdy skirt, riddled with tiny craters, the result of an oiled (or Crisco-rubbed) pan and an overnight (or much longer) ferment.

Anthony Scardino, who goes by the moniker "Professor Pizza" and makes one of the only grandma-style pizzas in Chicago, says many bakeries rely on aluminum sheet pans, even after years of use; while the pans may become coated in a scorched black layer, resembling a steel pan, they are still just made of aluminum and cannot produce that crispy undercarriage no matter how much oil is spread out first. As legendary pizza maker John Arena told me, after I took a generous bite of his gorgeous five-day Sicilian at Metro Pizza in Las Vegas, the result of decades of R & D from his early days in New York, a great Sicilian should "look like a brick, but eat like a feather." In Elmwood Park, even gelato stalwart Massa Cafe Italiano is getting into the game, now selling frozen Sicilian pizzas in four flavors. Just heat in a 425-degree oven for about twenty minutes, preferably on a preheated pizza stone, and you've got a thick, crispy-edged pie with a typical crater-riddled undercarriage.

A couple of years ago, when chef Todd Stein was running things, Nonna's started making a spicy Sicilian. Now that David Schwartz has taken over, he's tweaked the recipe a bit, still using Greco pepperoni and Grande mozzarella, but now he's making a homemade sauce with more punch, acidity, and bite than the previous iteration. Pleasantly chewy, it has a respectable undercarriage, though still not what you'd find on the East Coast.

One of the best old-school Sicilian options is made each day at Freddy's Pizza, where Joe Quercia not only makes the region's best gelato but also crafts several styles of pizza. His Sicilian could feed a small Italian army, with its thick crust and sturdy undercarriage, but it's more Midwest than East Coast, as it lacks the contrast of soft interior-to-crispy skirt from places like L & B Spumoni Gardens in Brooklyn. It's filling, for sure, but I'm looking for more nuance in my slices.

When it comes to pizzerias with a house style, Sicilian just hasn't caught on here yet. But several new options are challenging that assessment and creating craveable slices as good as anything in New York City.

Over the past year, I've been tinkering at home with a pan pizza I've come to know as Stevie's Squares. It's a cross between a focaccia-like Detroit and a standard grandma. Lots of oil, a two-day cold ferment, and some seriously strained and reduced tomatoes. They have a strong Chicago accent with the addition of something I call "'ndujage": a combo of 'nduja and raw sausage. I also strain and finely chop giardiniera for the full effect. I hope you'll give the recipe a try. It's at the end of this chapter. Please tag me on Insta at either @pizzacityusa or @stevedolinsky and let me know how it turns out.

Sheet pan at D'Amato's

D'AMATO'S BAKERY

1124 W. Grand Avenue
312-733-5456
www.damatosbakerychicago.com
@damatosbakery1

You can't miss the "Cash Only" sign directly behind the cashier at this legendary West Town bakery. Generations have come here for the fantastic, crusty loaves baked in their coal-fired oven (grandfathered in after city regulations changed) from 1912. Patrons also flock here for the excellent sandwiches (hello, chicken Parm) and round focaccias, the latter embedded with black olives, artichokes, and plump tomatoes. Look farther down the case for the blackened rectangular sheet pans and you'll find a treasure trove of Sicilian gold: large rectangular slices of colorful pizzas, topped with all manner of onions, tomatoes, pepperoni, and anchovies.

The sausage slices are clearly the most popular, as they consume most of the real estate. By Chicago standards, the sausage balls are mini (and sourced from elsewhere; they wouldn't disclose the producer). But no matter; you could put jawbreakers in their place and I'd still happily devour these slices.

D'Amato's takes a different approach to their assembly. While still raw, the dough is embedded with both cheese and sauce

(redolent with the plumpest, ripest tomatoes), and then left to rise a second time. This Sicilian tradition of adding toppings and cheese before the dough is fully proofed is still carried on at places like Buddy's in Detroit. Finally, it goes into the oven, where the cheese-sauce-topping mixture literally bakes into the soft, supple dough.

And that dough is what you come for. The undercarriage looks like the surface of Europa, with tiny craters and ridges that provide a caramelized texture, while the top is pillow-soft, as light as cotton candy but with a sturdy density that holds up the cheese and sauce so well. The edges are also what you need to try, with their blackened and charred exterior. It's a perfect crispy counterbalance to the softer interior. For that reason, make sure you ask for a corner or an edge piece, and if you're going to eat it right away, ask them to heat it up, directly on the oven stone, please. The other option is to take it home, preheat your pizza stone, and then finish it directly on the stone for about five minutes. I much prefer a crispier undercarriage.

I'm very disciplined when it comes to eating pizzas. Lord knows I've had more than most people in Chicago, and when I'm doing a crawl of three or four places in one day, I usually take just one to three bites, depending on quality. But in this case, I ate the whole damn slice. I dare you not to finish yours.

FOXHOLE

3335 N. Southport Avenue
773-687-8568
tinyurl.com/yaxx3nyf
@cdvolpe_chi
#thefoxholeatcdv

When you've conquered one thing, why not stretch your wings and see what else you can do with your talents, right? Jordan tried baseball, Bradshaw tried broadcasting. For chef Salvatore Lo Cascio, garnering a VPN Certificate for his Neapolitan pies at Coda di Volpe wasn't enough. The Sicilian native also wanted to share his childhood pizza with his regulars in Lakeview. But how do you carve out a separate personality from within the established restaurant at the corner of Southport and Henderson? Knock a wall out, of course.

Owner Billy Lawless (The Gage, Acanto) always seems to know what his customers want, just slightly before they start asking for it. By cutting a window out of the Henderson side of the building, he gives the neighbors a quick option to go, or to sit on the patio, while he keeps his energetic cook challenged and on his toes. It didn't hurt that Chicagoans seemed to want something besides tavern-thin and deep-dish with their Negronis, so Foxhole was born in the spring of 2020. There really isn't a separate identity on Instagram, mainly via the hashtag #thefoxholeatcdv.

Lo Cascio makes a focaccia-style dough with the telltale spongy-soft interior, crispy bottom, and crunchy sides. Its shallow height makes it appear more grandma than Sicilian, despite that long seventy-two-hour dough making process. Lo Cascio imports Mariani Italian flour, and since the end of 2020 has also been making a gluten-free Sicilian—practically unheard of in Chicago.

"I think people are going to go crazy for that," said Lo Cascio.

I absolutely love his sauce. Imported Pomodoros from Italy cooked between three and four hours. It's as simple as the plot of a Benigni film: tomatoes and salt finished with oregano. Toppings like sausage and spicy pepperoni are made in-house (who the hell makes their own pepperoni?) using pork from a farm in Indiana. His cheese is a blend of provolone and mozzarella.

The menu is tight. First choose a size: slice, half pan (serves six), or full pan (serves twelve). Then flavor: Margherita, sausage and red onion, or that spicy pepperoni. Even with a pie as seemingly simple as the Margherita—cheese, sauce, fresh basil—Lo Cascio's Sicilian instincts overrule taking the easy way out. He insists on finishing it with wild oregano, because "the flavor is closer to mine, so I feel like home."

The other key to the success of these slices is the trio of bakes. First, a five-minute naked bake in the pan—just the crust. Then a second bake with the toppings on for five minutes more; finally, removed from the pan and baked directly on the stone hearth of the oven for five minutes to properly crisp the undercarriage. It may be more labor- and time-intensive, but I wish more bakeries and pizzerias in town would take these extra steps to ensure a crispy bottom on their pan pizzas. I'm not worried about my dental work (yet) and have never longed for a soggy bottom. Crispy, crunchy, and chewy are a hell of a lot sexier.

LUDLOW LIQUORS

2959 N. California Avenue
773-754-7492
www.ludlow-liquors.com
@ludlowliquors

To make a reservation:
www.exploretock.com/ludlowliquors

PRE-PANDEMIC, Ludlow Liquors was a truly great neighborhood bar in Avondale, just a few blocks north of the Kennedy Expressway, where you could stop by for a handcrafted cocktail, a shot, or even a tasty, inexpensive bite to eat. Mickey Neely—formerly of Bungalow by Middle Brow, another stellar option for a circular artisan pie, which is now selling DIY pizza kits—has been tweaking his Sicilian pies ever since he took over the kitchen. I did a story on him for ABC7 at the end of 2019, when Neely would present them only on Monday nights.

"The oven we have necessitates doing a Sicilian-style. It's lower heat, longer bake, bigger rise in the dough," Neely told me then. "I want that bottom layer to be crispy, crunchy, fried."

During the pandemic, they shifted to a weekly model with pizzas available for pickup or dining (on the patio, depending on COVID rules) Wednesday through Saturday, usually indicated on their Instagram feed (although you order via Tock). He typically offers four flavors: cheese, pepperoni, a vegan option, plus a wild card, where he gets a bit more creative. You can also purchase whole nine-by-thirteen-inch pies, rather than slices, if you order ahead. The highlight is that undercarriage, which has a much crispier texture than any Sicilian in town. Some spots are as crunchy as peanut brittle. It's certainly a world of difference from the softer, bakery-style slices you find on the Northwest Side and along Taylor Street.

"It's ultimately baked three times: it's par-baked once, then topped, baked again, comes out, cut, baked a third time before the guest eats it," Neely said.

Each pizza comes with two ounces of ranch dressing and two ounces of red sauce. His crispy Sicilians are available for preorder only via Tock, but on Sundays, you can get them by the slice.

PANINO'S PIZZERIA

3702 N. Broadway Street (entrance on Waveland Avenue)
773-472-6200
www.paninospizzeria.com
@paninoschicago

They also have locations in Evanston and Park Ridge.

PANINO'S OBVIOUSLY ASPIRES to be more than just a slice joint. Located in one of the blandest strip malls in the city, there are two entrances—one on Broadway, facing the mall; the other on Waveland. As you walk in, you'll see warming boxes with the standard-issue thin wedges and deep-dish by the slice. Behind them, squint and you'll see a majestic, red-tiled, wood-burning oven with "*master pizzaiolo*" spelled out in white tiles, indicating they take the Neapolitan pizzas a tad more seriously here (and I discuss them in chapter 7, "Neapolitan").

The menu on Broadway features thin, deep, Sicilian, Neapolitan, and grandma-style. You want to focus on the thin, puffy Neapolitans and grandmas, a style seen about as frequently in Chicago as a street free of potholes.

Grandmas are big in New York City. A transplanted New Yorker even has a shop in Las Vegas—Good Pie—dedicated to them. Shorter and thinner than a traditional Sicilian, they don't have an overnight rise, so they tend to be denser, with less open crumb. Back in the day, grandma would make her dough in the morning and then top it and bake it for dinner that night, hence the term. Besides Panino's, the only other dedicated pizza maker doing grandma-style in Chicago is Anthony Scardino ("Professor Pizza"), also featured in this chapter.

The key is Panino's mother starter, a strain of yeast that is recycled and reused, integrated and fed with more water and flour, then kneaded and aged—left to ferment and develop serious air pockets within the dough.

While the grandma at Panino's is absolutely higher and thicker than anything I've seen on the East Coast, I'm not going to complain about it. Yes, it may look unwieldy and far too heavy to eat, but pull away a small square and see that open crumb. The fermentation allows the interior to gain air and lightness. The chew is pleasant, even more so with the slightly reduced and thick ruby-red tomato sauce. I opted for a sausage, and those crumbled pieces held up nicely below that blanket of mozzarella, releasing their fat into the bottom dough. This pizza takes about thirty-five minutes to make and could easily feed four hungry teenagers (and their parents), so plan accordingly. But it's not offered by the slice. If they'd only ditch their sub-par thin slices from those warming boxes to focus on offering a proper grandma slice like they do in NYC, I'd become a regular.

PIZZA FRIENDLY PIZZA

1039 N. Western Avenue
(enter through the alley)
773-395-2483
www.pizzafriendlypizza.com
@pizzafriendlypizza

One of the most exciting Sicilians to hit our deep-dish- and cracker-thin-loaded shores comes as the fruit of a collaboration between a Michelin-starred chef and a partner in a local hospitality group—both of whom were forced to make a pivot during the pandemic.

As executive chef of Oriole, Noah Sandoval garnered two Michelin stars in 2019. He's also a partner with Julia Momose at Kumiko and Kikko down the street, so his typical workday involves meticulous prepping of luxe ingredients such as Ossetra caviar or King crab, then donning chef's whites during service. Oriole underwent a major renovation in 2021, but at press time, still hadn't reopened. The chef has had a lot of free time on his hands.

Meanwhile, Bruce Finkelman and his company—16″ on Center—a partner at Oriole and operator of several bars and restaurants in town (Dusek's, Longman & Eagle, Moneygun) were looking to do something different with Bite, the tightly packed, nearly thirty-year-old café next to the Empty Bottle in Ukrainian Village. I met Finkelman years ago shooting a story at Longman, and in 2019, I curated a year's worth of local neighborhood pizzeria pop-ups at Revival Food Hall, which 16″ on Center runs, in an effort to promote my book and weekly pizza tours. Bite, he acknowledged, was "going to have some extreme difficulty" surviving in a post-COVID world.

Friendly chit-chat and late-night texts between Sandoval and Finkelman progressed pretty rapidly from a mundane discussion about a band playing at the Bottle the first week of March 2020 to a full-on freak-out six days later, talking about what they were going to do about their respective businesses with everything on lockdown.

"My initial thought was, let's open a pizza place," said Finkelman, who started giving it serious thought at the beginning of May. The follow-up questions from Sandoval struck Finkelman as intuitive. "We pretty much did the whole thing over text message," he said. "The way that he [Noah] went at this . . . the thought process of being proud of what he'd want to put out there; it was an amazing conversation."

Sandoval, a native of Richmond, Virginia, who was weaned on large, floppy slices, thought immediately of a style he had come to fall in love with later in life—Sicilian.

"We [with wife, Cara] decided that Prince Street [in New York City] was our favorite. It's unique. That was going to be it," he said. "But

CLAYTON HAUCK

I didn't know what I was doing. I made three pizzas for staff meal and I thought we'd just figure it out. I got to the point where I didn't want to put out just an average sheet pan pizza," he said.

Tackling a thick Sicilian, like the ones coming out of the ovens at Prince Street, coated in cup-and-char pepperoni and zesty tomato sauce with a soft chew, wasn't going to be easy, even for an accomplished chef who once earned a coveted star cooking a gluten-free menu at the late, lamented Senza—the equivalent of throwing a one-hit shut-out against the 2016 Cubs.

"I wanted to do the best version I could," said Sandoval. "I read a lot, bought different pans; it was good, but it wasn't right."

Since Sandoval knew I had eaten a lot of Sicilians (based on my personal and professional Instagram feeds), out of the blue in June 2020 he sent me a picture of one of his early efforts. I recognized the pizza may have been baked in a perforated pan or on a screen, because the skirt of the slice was riddled with evenly spaced, uniform indentations. Without hesitation, I connected him to John Arena in Las Vegas, a majordomo and a father figure to dozens of pizza makers across the country. They quickly began long talks about flour and fermentation.

"I'd send him a side view, and he'd say, 'looks good,'" Sandoval said.

The back-and-forth led to a complete abandonment of Sandoval's original plan for the pizza. Whereas Sandoval was planning on a 70 percent dough hydration, they settled on 62 percent. The fermentation was initially just twenty-four hours, but after talking to Arena, who suggested three to five days, Sandoval is resting it for five days, then baking on the sixth. Even the flour had to be completely changed to Caputo Americana, because it has barley malt in it.

To achieve his crispy, craveable undercarriage, Sandoval uses a thin layer of Crisco (although he learned traditional bakers used lard, he wanted to be able to offer slices to vegetarians). He leaves his five-day fermented dough in the pan for about twelve hours, then bakes the pizzas for just ten minutes at 525 degrees. They'll rest an hour, then get a final bake with toppings for twelve minutes at 500 degrees.

The plan at Pizza Friendly Pizza (the name is intended as a nod to "Music Friendly Dancing" on the awning next door at the Bottle; not to be confused with Friendly Pizza in Uncasville, Connecticut) is to have guests enter through the alley, then serve them slices, a few sandwiches, and salads out through the back window. If you wanted a whole pie, you could certainly order ahead of time. Eventually, once the restaurant figures out the kitchen flow, they'll offer frozen pizzas for sale, which reheat extremely well on a preheated stone.

There are socially distanced tables in the renovated patio space—allowing for about fourteen seats—and they've added a few tables on Cortez along the side of the Empty Bottle for overflow. The inside of the former Bite space is stacked with dough in various stages, a pair of proofing boxes, and a ton of tomato sauce.

Right now there are four options: a cup-and-char pepperoni (again, Ezzo, which is ironic, since Sandoval's inspiration—Prince Street in NYC—uses the Rosa Grande brand) with aged Parmesan and fresh basil; a vegetarian with rapini and chèvre, lemon and garlic (vegan on request); an earthy mushroom with creamy burrata and spicy Calabrian chiles; and then one special pie designed by their chef de cuisine, Ruben Villalobos. Previous iterations of Ruben's special pies have included fennel sausage with his homemade giardiniera and fennel pollen.

I've tasted both the pepperoni and the mushroom, and as delicious as they both are, the experience of eating them is as much textural as anything else. The squares look hefty, but when you lift them, they are as light as an iPhone 4. Biting into them—revealing that tight crumb—you experience not only the top-notch ingredients Sandoval has sourced, but the interplay between sweet and heat, crunch and chew, crisp and soft. The undercarriage is textbook: as golden as a McDonald's french fry, riddled with craters as if you're looking at the moon through a telescope. It's the best Sicilian slice in Chicago, full stop.

The new format completely does away with the old café model of people sitting around inside and, at least through the fall of 2021, service will be strictly on the patio(s) and to go. But I could easily see picking up a whole pie—fresh or frozen—and reheating it at home.

"Our audience is based on the community and the [Empty] Bottle," said Finkelman of his patrons. "We want them to have an experience. We're a slice shop. We're not opening the dining room anytime soon."

PLEASE WAIT HERE FOR CARRY OUT ORDERS
HOT TEAS AVAILABLE
Try Our Grandma Frances Pizza
We Thank You For
Eggplant Parmigiana
Chicken Parmigiana
Sausage, Peppers and Potatoes
Neck Bones and Pasta

POMPEI

1531 W. Taylor Street
312-421-5179
www.pompeiusa.com
@pompei_restaurants

THE DAVINO FAMILY is one of the last remaining vestiges of a Little Italy that doesn't really exist anymore. Despite three generations of baking at Pompei, the surrounding neighborhood has changed drastically. The bakery—which occupies two enormous contiguous spaces at the western edge of Taylor Street's commercial district—still manages to churn out bread and pizza by the boatload, as well as an entire menu of Italian comfort classics.

In the early twentieth century, Taylor Street was the Italian port of immigration. Al's Beef started there in the 1920s, making juicy Italian beef sandwiches; Rosebud, Davanti Enoteca, and Mia Francesca all established restaurants there. Old-school delis like Conte di Savoia still manage to hang on, selling deli items and sandwiches to neighbors and college students. But over the last decade or so, the neighborhood—now referred to as University Village—has changed. The demise of the Italian community was jump-started in the 1960s, as the city took over much of the area to build the University of Illinois–Chicago campus and expand the Eisenhower Expressway, displacing many residents and their family businesses a few miles west to Harlem Avenue and Elmwood Park. Over the last few years alone, Francesca's became an Indian restaurant, 3 Aces turned into a Mexican one, and the number of Asian options on Taylor Street has exploded, with new tea shops, a spicy Szechuan takeout place, and a quirky Asian-themed soft serve and ice cream shop.

All of which is to say that an old timer like Ralph Davino is sensing a sea change in what the neighborhood wants. His grandfather, Luigi Davino, immigrated from Naples in 1924 and promptly established a bakery at 818 S. Loomis, the same address where he and his extended family lived in a six-flat, with a tavern on the other side. Some relatives ended up starting the Gonnella Bread Company, but Davino and his kids spent all of their time baking loaves of bread in an oven that required an 18″ × 23″ peel, where he could bake 250 pounds of bread at a time. Originally designed for burning wood, it was converted to coal and then, after WWII, to gas.

Luigi's sons were truck drivers, making wholesale deliveries in the 1930s, but when the war broke out, they all enlisted, and the

wholesale business dried up, forcing them to commit to retail. After the war, the boys wanted to add pizza to their menu, so they began doing what they knew from their childhood: bakery slices, formed in large sheet pans, topped only with cheese and sauce.

"I never wanted to be a baker and never wanted to be a bar owner and I got both," said Davino. He'd seen the looks on his relatives' faces at the end of each day, tired and worn, and knew he wanted to do something else with his life. But like so many family businesses, the lure was too much. He and his wife took over in 1984.

Davino still uses the same giant Champion mixer from 1946 that his grandfather and dad used; and they still offer bakery slices made from the same dough they use for their bread, it just doesn't proof as long. Cheese is popular, though provolone has been added to the mozzarella, and now they also offer more than a dozen flavors, including eggplant, broccoli, and the Chicago favorite of fennel-flecked sausage (formerly sourced from Scala, now from Greco). Everything is displayed deli-style, so you point to your pizza, they heat it up, and you either eat in or take it to go. The nearby medical district offers an endless supply of lunchtime fans. The slices don't have a lot of complexity in the crumb since they take only a few hours to make from dough mixing to baking, but if you can get them to reheat the slices long enough, you'll get a crispy enough bottom to provide some contrast against the softer middle.

More recently, Davino added a "Grandma Frances" to his menu, a twenty-four-hour fermented dough that is simultaneously thick and light but also appropriately crispy and oily; one of the few grandma-style pizzas in town (the other significant example is by Professor Pizza). It's mostly slices here, but also some jumbos and whole pies. Another variant is the pizza strudel, which is stuffed and rolled, making an excellent to-go option if you're eating on your lap in your car. Another adaptive measure taken recently is the addition of a gluten-free pizza. Davino says he'd love to partner with a national brand to help him fill up the cavernous space, but with COVID wreaking havoc on his private party business, he's hopeful the neighborhood will continue to support his family business, which is steadily approaching the hundred-year mark.

PROFESSOR PIZZA

Fridays and Saturdays only, at the Full Shilling Public House
3724 N. Clark Street
www.exploretock.com/professorpizza
@professorpizza

Nine-inch NYC slices for dine-in
Grandma pies for pickup or delivery

GRANDMA IS A square style of pizza more commonly seen in New York City than the Midwest. Widely acknowledged to have been popularized by Umberto's and later King Umberto's on Long Island in the 1980s, it's usually made in a shallow, rectangular aluminum pan. But unlike the Sicilian, with its overnight (or two or three nights) rest and time to rise in the pan, the grandma is mixed and baked usually the same day, resulting in a shorter slice that's a tad crispier. The tradition stems from Italian grandmothers who would make dough early in the morning, leave it out at room temperature to proof and rise, then top it and bake it in time for dinner. At places like Sofia Pizza Shoppe in Manhattan or Good Pie in Las Vegas, they'll offer an "upside down," which has cheese as a bottom layer, protecting the dough from getting soggy, topped with sauce (ironically, the same order of assembly as a deep-dish). This method results in the sauce becoming slightly reduced from the baking process, concentrating its flavor and thickness. As far as I know, there have never really been any pizzerias in Chicago making East Coast legit grandmas on a regular basis, until I heard about a weekly pop-up in the summer of 2020.

Anthony Scardino, who goes by the moniker "Professor Pizza," worked in the kitchens at Publican Quality Meats and Au Cheval before settling in for nearly two years as the general manager at Dough Bros. (400 N. State Street) in River North, where he came up with several different varieties, including large NYC-style pies with slices meant for reheating. A pizza journeyman, he's logged time in Tony Gemignani's legendary pizza kitchen in San Francisco, then Coalfire here and Paulie Gee's Logan Square, where he was part of Tung's opening team and helped him create his "Logan Squares." He's also spent time working with Rosso Pomodoro, the company overseeing the Neapolitan pizza training for Eataly.

"When the pandemic hit, I started making focaccia, keeping it super simple," said Scardino. At first, he had been taking a break during the pandemic, only to find himself, after streaming a few seasons of *The Sopranos*, itching to bake again. He started off with a focaccia-style pizza. "I put up a Facebook post and the next week, sold sixteen out of my apartment," he said. The following week he sold forty. Then he switched to the grandma-style, selling about eighty pizzas a week.

Scardino says the owner of the Full Shilling—an Irish bar next to Metro, just a block north of Wrigley Field—had been remodeling the space. Scardino had helped him formulate the bar's thin-and-crispy tavern-style pie, and the owner wanted him to come back to teach the staff a refresher course.

Since the grandmas were selling well from Scardino's apartment, he asked if it would be OK to start using the bar's kitchen as a central pickup spot for online orders.

"It might be six months here, or it might be six weeks," said Scardino. He's now in the process of looking for a brick-and-mortar location, and by the time you read this, there's a good chance he'll have moved on from Wrigleyville, so be sure to check his Instagram for the latest information.

Scardino's all-natural starter is used for an initial rest of two days, utilizing Caputo Americana flour. He'll use just a fraction of active dry yeast, but a lot of hydration—about 70 percent of the volume is water. Bakers like higher hydration doughs because they create steam when baked, and, combined with longer fermentation times—giving the yeast more time to eat the sugars in the dough and create carbon dioxide—the interior "crumb" of the dough opens up, resulting in small air pockets. This adds complexity to the chew; the opposite of pizza crust tasting like cardboard, and more like the experience of biting into a tender ciabatta or a firm baguette. Scardino balls up the dough the same day he makes it, letting it rest at room temperature for an hour. Then it goes into a cooler for two days of fermentation. After that resting period, he lines a black steel pan with olive oil, pressing the dough out into the pan and letting it proof for about an hour and a half. A quick four-minute par-bake sets the dough, which is then placed in cooling racks and held until he's ready to bake.

Three flavors of the grandma are available each week, plus one "Extra Credit" pie that will rotate (a recent one featured a spinach-artichoke inspired by NYC's Artichoke Basille). His Margherita features Wisconsin's Grande (a brand used frequently in the industry) *fior di latte*, or fresh mozzarella, but also a fifty-fifty low-moisture shred, Calabrian oregano, slivered garlic, and a special blend of Stanislaus tomatoes. Dotted with a verdant green *pistou* (a sort of pesto without pine nuts), it's remarkable not only for its appearance, but its crunch—a toothsome affair, requiring more jaw work than your standard Chicago thin. His pepperoni with fresh ricotta and Mike's Hot Honey was hard to stop eating after just one slice (four giant slices can be cut from one pie). The undercarriage is riddled with tiny craters, like a view of the moon from ten miles up, quite crispy on the whole, while the interior is definitely thinner than a standard Sicilian.

"I think it's less of a hurdle to explain a non-indigenous style of pizza than it is to explain slice culture [to Chicagoans]," said Scardino of the inherent challenges in communicating something as foreign to Midwesterners as Roman *al taglio* or grandma. "Here they want you to bag up utensils and put everything in a clamshell and it's a whole production. In New York they finish half the slice by the time they pay for it."

Scardino offers his grandma-style pies for pickup every Friday and Saturday, 11 a.m. until 8 p.m. from the Full Shilling, but they're limited, so you need to order ahead. Delivery is also available. Every Monday morning the order form goes up on his Tock page.

TABLE, DONKEY & STICK

2728 W. Armitage Avenue
773-486-8525
tabledonkeystick.com
@tabledonkeystick

DAVID KIRMSE INSISTS his pizza is Roman. Or maybe Northern Italian. It's definitely not Sicilian. Or is it?

"For six months I trained in southeast France, near the Alps," Kirmse, the chef at Logan Square's Table, Donkey & Stick told me. "I made trips to Italy; in Turino I had a pizza like this. It's like Roman," he said.

I respectfully disagree. But I'm happy to explain my reasoning here.

By chance, when Kirmse started working at the restaurant, there was a cook who was making pizzas for a family meal. Once the pandemic hit, they needed an outlet to start a delivery program and it seemed like pizza would be a perfect fit. But they took what they already knew—charcuterie production, dough fermentation, sourcing local produce—and poured all of that knowledge into their new pizza style.

"It's a style that I liked growing up. Typically, you go to a slice joint to get a regular slice, but there were a few places in my town [in New York] that did a really good Sicilian slice that I was always kind of intrigued to have here," said Matthew Sussman, the restaurant's owner. Sussman had to pivot during the pandemic, since his tiny restaurant could no longer host guests. So he and Kirmse began experimenting with pizzas baked in large, rectangular sheet pans, mainly for pickup. Their crusts are thick and somewhat bulky, with golden undercarriages as crispy as chicharrones.

"We always check the bottom to make sure it's dark golden brown," said Kirmse. "When the pizzas are served here [on the patio], we take it a step further, lift the pizza up, put a wire rack under it, then bake it in a convection oven to seal in the oil and make sure it's extra crispy."

Kirmse admits his version is Americanized, in that it leans heavier on the toppings. The dough is a blend of two King Arthur lines: the high-gluten and Sir Galahad, plus a local whole wheat flour. They portion dough into smaller containers, ferment it overnight at room temperature, then the next day will turn it out into the pans, which are lightly coated in oil and Crisco. The entire process takes sixteen to eighteen hours, which would indicate to me, at least, that these lean more Sicilian/grandma than Roman, as I learned from the other Roman bakers in town. (Fermentation times range from thirty-six to seventy-two hours at Bonci, up to ninety-six hours at Bar Cargo.) Classifying this Midwest artisan, Italian American, East Coast–influenced is more about semantics than any kind of scientific category classification, and I don't want to insult anyone here. The pizzas are baked in shallow, rectangular pans, and they're delicious. End of story.

They offer four options: one with a homemade 'nduja—basically pork lardo with fermented peppers (and it's noteworthy that unlike

most local pizzerias who buy 'nduja from the well-respected Tempesta Artisan Salumi, they go to the trouble of making their own); they also make a sausage with fennel and lavender, a basic cheese finished with Parmigiano-Reggiano, and a veggie with a Mediterranean accent, employing olives, artichokes, and local honey, with a note of fermented garlic.

The hefty pies are only available whole (13″ × 18″) or half (13″ × 9″), but they reheat wonderfully on a sheet tray at 350 degrees. Pizzas are available every day (except Mondays, when they're closed) on the patio and for delivery or pickup.

Should you care if this is a Roman or a Sicilian? Do you need to specify which style you're ordering? Of course not. This is a square (technically a rectangle) worth celebrating.

RECIPE

STEVIE'S SQUARES

STEVE DOLINSKY

YIELD: ONE TWELVE-INCH-SQUARE PAN PIZZA, WHICH CAN BE CUT INTO FOUR SLICES

This is a pizza I made that was inspired by the spongy focaccias I love, but also informed by the crunchy bottom on the Sicilians and grandmas I've had over the past few years. The only four tools that are essential are: a digital scale (a worthwhile investment that shouldn't cost more than $30), a pizza stone, a plastic or metal dough scraper, and a twelve-inch-square pizza pan (preferably made by Lloyd). You can find all of them quite easily online.

Toppings are where you can get creative. If you don't want to make my sauce, by all means just open a can of crushed tomatoes, add salt and fresh basil, and you're done. If you prefer a white pie, skip the sauce altogether and add a sautéed vegetable on top of your cheese layer (mushrooms or peppers and onions are favorites); just remember to season well. If you have access to a jar of giardiniera—Chicago's beloved Italian beef (and pizza) garnish—go for it. I love how the crunchy, briny, and sometimes spicy Italian condiment complements the sauce and cheese. The crust is merely your canvas; what you choose to top it with reflects your personality. I've provided a basic red pie here, so if you wanted to add cup-and-char pepperoni on top or maybe some pinched-and-pressed raw sausage, laced with fennel seeds, both would be fine in my book. If you really want to impress your jaded pizza-loving friends and family, tuck a small thimble of 'nduja into a ball of raw sausage and press it onto the pie for what I refer to as "'ndujage" for a sausage accent that is beguilingly spicy and satisfying.

I made this pizza for a pop-up I did at Pizza Lobo in Logan Square the week before Thanksgiving, when the city was facing a surge in coronavirus cases. We managed to sell out in thirty minutes, mostly from the walkup window. I have a feeling I'll do another pop-up in 2021 based on the early excitement—this is a pizza that really isn't being done in Chicago, at least not as of this writing.

INGREDIENTS

DOUGH

400 grams all-purpose, unbleached flour
167 grams fine corn flour
5 grams instant dry yeast
14 grams kosher salt
5 grams sugar
454 grams water
15 grams olive oil
15 grams corn oil
Also: coarse cornmeal and oil or shortening for baking pan

SAUCE

Large can (6 lbs) of whole, peeled Alta Cucina tomatoes from Stanislaus (this will yield two pizzas)
Fresh basil leaves (about 10 to 12 leaves)
1 tablespoon kosher salt
Optional: 1 tablespoon anchovy paste
Also: dried oregano for garnish just before baking
Optional: Mike's Hot Honey for post-bake drizzling

CHEESE

10 to 12 slices of whole milk mozzarella (part-skim will work as well), about 1 ounce per slice
grated Pecorino Romano
Optional: fresh mozzarella or fior di latte

TO MAKE THE DOUGH

Add all dry ingredients (flours, yeast, salt, and sugar) to the bowl of a stand mixer (or just combine in a bowl) and set to low for twenty seconds. (If not using a mixer, just mix with a spatula.)

Add water and both oils, then set on low in mixer, and run for just about ten seconds, until the dry is incorporated with the wet; let sit five minutes to hydrate. Then set mixer to medium setting for about twenty seconds, until you start to smell the corn aroma coming off the bowl, and you see the ends of the dough begin sticking to the sides, pulling away like spiderwebs as the mixer paddle moves around. If you're mixing by hand here, just keep working the dough in the bowl for about a minute. Your arm may get a little tired, but it won't affect the outcome of the dough.

Lightly oil a work surface and remove your dough from the bowl onto it. Using your dough scraper, gather each edge and fold onto the center, one at a time. Cover with a large, upside down bowl for twenty minutes. After the first twenty minutes, remove bowl. This time, oil your hands well, and, one side at a time, pull away the dough and then fold it across to the other side, repeating on all four sides. This helps build gluten structure. The dough will seem really floppy and soggy (and sticky) the first two times you do this, but it will get stronger. Cover the dough again with the upside-down bowl and wait another twenty minutes. You'll do the stretch-and-folds a total of four times over the course of one hour. By the last time, it should be stronger and have some heft to it.

After an hour of covering, waiting, and stretching, lightly oil the inside of the bowl and place the dough—now properly stronger—into it, cover with plastic wrap, and place in fridge for at least two days.

On the day of baking, remove the dough and let it come to room temperature. Lightly oil or grease your pan with shortening. Sprinkle on a few teaspoons of coarse cornmeal. This will help serve as a lubricant, but it will also embed itself into the undercarriage, providing some texture and flavor that will come as a pleasant surprise in each bite.

Recipe continues

Transfer the dough with your scraper directly into the middle of the pan. Wait about thirty minutes. With lightly oiled fingertips, gently press on the dough and start to push it to the edges of the pan. You will need several intervals of pressing, waiting, and stretching to get the dough all the way to the edges and corners of the pan. I typically take my time, doing this over the course of an afternoon; I take around three to four hours to do this. You want to preserve as much air as possible in the crust, without completely destroying all of the carbon dioxide that's built up over the last two days, but you also need the dough to get to room temperature and continue stretching to the edges.

At this point, turn your oven on as high as it goes, ideally to 525 degrees Fahrenheit, but if not, 500 degrees is fine. Be sure to place your pizza stone in the center of the oven when you do this. Once the oven says it's preheated, wait another hour to really get your stone hot. But now—some five to six hours after you initially took your dough out of the fridge, your dough should be rising along the sides of the pan, looking slightly raised in the middle. Place the dough and pan onto the pizza stone and bake for twelve minutes at 525; maybe fourteen to fifteen minutes at 500, until the top is slightly browned.

Remove the crust from the pan (it's now crossed over from raw dough to baked crust) and place it on top of a cooling rack. After an hour or so, I use a serrated knife to cut off the very top layer of crust, slicing parallel to the bottom, so that I have a very even crust that is about an inch high all the way around. You can use the discarded top as sandwich bread or toast it for breakfast the next day.

At this point, you could wrap the crust in plastic wrap and freeze it, as I did for my pop-up, and hold it as long as you want. I think this process may also help with the internal moisture content of the finished crust, but I can't prove it—it's just based on conversations I've had with professionals. If you want to move on to make your pizza though, let's continue.

Recipe continues

MADELINE DOLINSKY

TO MAKE THE SAUCE

Pour half the can of tomatoes (approximately three pounds) into a strainer over the sink. If you are going to use the anchovy paste, then place a small bowl beneath the strainer to collect some of the thin tomato sauce that drains out, and reserve it. Using your hands or a kitchen shears, crush, cut, and mash the tomatoes as small as you can, until you have pieces about the size of a cherry tomato. Let the mixture drain at least an hour or two. You want a very thick tomato sauce. Cut or tear the fresh basil leaves directly into the sauce and mix with your hands to fully incorporate them.

If you are using anchovy paste, blend it with some of the reserved liquid you've captured in the bowl beneath the strainer, then pour this mixture back onto the top of the tomatoes that are draining.

TO ASSEMBLE THE PIZZA

Oil your pan again. (I use strained giardiniera oil, but olive oil is just fine.) Sprinkle on another dose of coarse cornmeal, about a tablespoon, all over the bottom of the pan. Place crust into pan. Cover the dough with slices of cheese, being careful not to overlap them. Try to maintain an even layer of cheese while completely covering up the holes on the surface of the crust. Now add spoonfuls of sauce, being careful to spread just to the edge, leaving about a quarter inch of cheese and crust exposed on the perimeter. You don't want the sauce going over the edge.

At this point, you could add discs of pepperoni or your raw sausage. If you're adding vegetables, I prefer cooking them ahead of time to remove excess water, then scattering them over the sauce. You could also drain a jar of giardiniera, chop it finely and sprinkle over the pizza. This condiment, coupled with raw, fennel-laced sausage, is my go-to. If you had some fresh mozzarella, you could tear it into small pieces and now apply them to the pie as well; you don't need a lot since the base layer is completely covered with those slices of mozzarella, remember?

Grate on an equal layer of Pecorino Romano—about a tablespoon's worth—then sprinkle over about a teaspoon of dried oregano. Place pan onto preheated pizza stone, with oven at 500 degrees Fahrenheit, for about twelve minutes, until cheese is bubbling or slightly browned on the edges.

MADELINE DOLINSKY

You're almost done! Remove the cooked pizza to your cutting board. Don't eat it yet. Cut the square into four equal slices. I have a mezzaluna, a sort of guillotine/rocking knife that allows me to make two easy perpendicular cuts; you'll want to use your largest knife, or, if you have a large pizza cutter, that should work. But ideally, you're cutting from above rather than rolling the cutter through the pizza from the side. You could hold a bunch of slices at this point until your guests ask for them specifically. They can be kept at room temperature for a couple of hours, just like the pizza joints in NYC do.

With your oven still on, and your stone now recovering the heat after you removed the pan from it, place a slice directly onto the hot stone. You'll only need about three to four minutes per slice. Using your peel or spatula, lift up a corner of the slice to see if it's starting to darken. A deep, burnished brown is what I'm going for, but if you're approaching black, it's definitely time to remove it. The slice's undercarriage will now be crispy, and it's ready to serve. If you had some Mike's Hot Honey handy, I would drizzle over a few lines, as the condiment's sweet-heat plays nicely against the sharp acidity from those strained tomatoes.

9 DETROIT-STYLE

DETROIT-STYLE PIZZA HAS DEFINITELY BECOME THE "COOL KID" over the last year or so, and it must put a perplexing smile on the faces of natives who've grown up with it. A pizza that's been around for seventy-five years is suddenly in fashion? What the hell took everyone so long? Emmy Squared started with one shop in Brooklyn; now they're in Nashville, Louisville, Manhattan, and probably coming soon to a town near you.

In 1946, three years after Ike Sewell and Ric Riccardo started selling their deep-dish pizza from the kitchen that would eventually be called Uno's, the Sicilian cooks in the kitchen at Buddy's in Detroit began experimenting. They placed dough in the ubiquitous ten-by-fourteen-inch rectangular blue steel pans left over from the local auto industry, which were more readily available than the larger, shallower rectangular pans they were used to seeing in home kitchens. Today's pans tend to be made of anodized aluminum with nonstick coatings.

Flour is one of several factors. Most Detroit-style pies use bread flour, which has more gluten than all-purpose flour, allowing for more elasticity and a characteristic chew. The crust develops a signature browning from frying in the fat produced by the cheese that gets pushed along the sides. Not just any cheese, but a higher-fat Wisconsin brick cheese, which derives its name from the process of being placed between bricks during the aging process to expel excess whey. The cheese darkens

Detroit-style pizza at Fat Chris's Pizza and Such

as it bakes along the sides, and while it may look like burnt crust, it's simply a crispy, somewhat charred cheesy edge (what's known as a *frico* in pizza parlance). It tastes like the best part of a grilled cheese; you'll definitely fight over the corner pieces.

Detroit-style sauce maintains a lovely balance of brightness, acidity, and a hint of sweetness from sugar. It can be applied at room temperature, once the pizza has been removed from the oven, or placed on just before baking, carefully, in parallel racing stripes (it's the Motor City, remember?), so as not to overwhelm any one slice.

Unlike Chicago, which prizes raw, fennel-laced sausage as the topping most frequently used on pizza, in Detroit, pepperoni is iconic. Traditionally it comes in a natural casing, which results in "cup-and-char" circles of pepperoni that curl up during the baking process. Each porky, charred coin holds tiny flavor bombs of fat while maintaining blackened, somewhat blistered edges. Resting on a cheesy cushion topped by a couple of stripes of room-temperature tomato sauce, the best part is the contrast between the soft, chewy focaccia-like interior, as soft as a down pillow, and the crispy, fried undercarriage—the underbelly of the pizza, also known as the skirt—riddled with tiny craters, usually the result of a thin layer of oil (or in some cases, Crisco, or both) spread on the bottom of the pan before baking commingling with the fat from the melted brick cheese.

I have zero proof of this, but my guess is Burt Katz was influenced by this

Tiny frico *from B Square*

style as he developed his caramelized deep pan pizza at Gulliver's, then Pequod's, refining the process at Burt's Place in the late '80s. Their outer edges sure look a lot alike, with the exception of the shape of the pizza.

A few places closed after my last book came out (Longacre, Union Full Board) but a few more came on the scene, including a surprise in an Edgebrook bar and a Lettuce Entertain You concept with both a city and Wheeling ghost kitchen that deliver within a five-mile radius. On the opposite end of that spectrum, there's tiny, two-person Five Squared, which started life as a food truck and morphed into the little pizza operation that could, making some wacky (but tasty) slices out of a commercial kitchen space in East Garfield Park.

B SQUARE PIZZA

620 N. State Street (delivery only, five-mile radius)
www.bsquarepizzadelivery.com
@bsquarepizza

During the pandemic, a lot of restaurant groups pivoted to pizza. Why not? It's convenient, familiar, and mostly affordable. Chicago's Lettuce Entertain You Enterprises already runs Stella Barra in Lincoln Park and Pizzeria Portofino on the river. But over the course of a few months, the king of local restaurant groups (creators of Ramen-San, Everest, Shaw's Crab House, Big Bowl, and dozens of other local favorites) also launched a pair of ghost kitchen pizza concepts, available only for pickup or delivery. One of them—Bill's Original Tavern Pizza—operates out of the same kitchen as Portofino. The other one—B Square Pizza—is a Detroit-style concept operating out of Saranello's restaurant inside the Westin Hotel in Wheeling (see chapter 15, "Suburban Stars"), as well as from the kitchen at Pizzeria Via Stato in River North. In both cases, they'll deliver within a five-mile radius.

Even though chef Mychael Bonner grew up on thin, hand-tossed pizzas from the East Coast, one of his cooks—Mike Brownell—hails from the suburbs of Detroit. They decided that in addition to the thin, airier style of pizza they were making at Saranello's, they'd take a stab at the beloved pizza of Brownell's childhood. Bonner says the plan was hatched well before Detroit pizza became a trend. After a few successful months of operation on the North Shore, they expanded to the city in December 2020.

Using a pre-ferment or poolish, they add flour and water on Day 1, turn it into a dough on Day 2, then cold ferment it another day. On Day 3 it's portioned and then fermented one more day.

"I didn't want it to be really doughy," said Bonner, who insists on baking the dough on the fourth day, in oiled Lloyd steel baking pans on a stone deck at around 550 degrees for sixteen minutes. The pies come either as twelve-inch or sixteen-inch squares cut into smaller square slices.

Based on height alone, it's more akin to a grandma-style than one from Detroit, but Bonner says that's the plan. It does have that telltale focaccia crumb, a crispy-cheesy edge—though quite a bit narrower than what would be considered textbook—and a sort-of crispy undercarriage that I thought could use some more attention. (Bonner admitted after I posted a picture that the blond undercarriage was an execution error, and it should be more caramelized.)

B Square includes small containers of marinara, ranch, and extra Parmesan on the side, which I guess will come in handy for some. I thought the pepperoni discs (from Greco) were a tad on the stubby side; they don't curl up into cup-and-char territory like those found on the better versions at Paulie Gee's Logan Square. Their cheese blend contains the traditional Wisconsin brick as well as mozzarella and Parmesan. A simple tomato sauce is pleasantly mild and vaguely sweet, which I wasn't complaining about. The challenge here will be consistency. Unless Bonner or Brownell are on the premises, making sure each pie looks as it should, there's a chance there could be execution problems (as I experienced in Wheeling during my one visit). On the other hand, with few Detroit-style competitors downtown, they may not need to worry.

CHEF BILL KIM'S PIZZA & PARM SHOP

1542 N. Damen Avenue (inside Urban Belly)
773-904-8606
www.cbkpizzaparm.com
@cbkpizzaparm

HAVING SERVED two separate terms in the kitchen at Charlie Trotter's, Bill Kim knows his sous vide from his sauté. But the Korean American chef, who grew up in a Chicago neighborhood with a colorful quilt of immigrants, including a lot of Italians, didn't know the first thing about pizza. The pandemic forced him to take a deep dive, and he emerged in late 2020 with a pop-up focused on Detroit-style pizza and chicken Parmesan sandwiches, located inside Michael Jordan's Restaurant in west suburban Oak Brook (see chapter 15, "Suburban Stars"). Due to the popularity there, he installed a similar shop inside Urban Belly in Wicker Park in early 2021.

Kim consulted Peter Reinhart's excellent *Perfect Pan Pizza* and began making doughs in earnest. He lets the doughs rest overnight before panning them out for an hour or so the next day. The relatively short proofing time at room temperature results in a pie that has a little less height than its relatives around town. Topped with brick cheese and some Pecorino, plus his homemade marinara, there are just a few options to choose from: sausage, pepperoni, and cheese. The pepperoni is thin and curls up nicely when baked, revealing slightly charred edges.

The pizzas are pickup or delivery only, and if you are picking yours up from the store in Wicker Park, you might as well get the excellent soft serve as well. The flavors rotate, but the PB&J and the Vietnamese Caramel are both outstanding. They're the best soft serves in all of Chicago.

CITY'S EDGE BAR & GRILL

5310 W. Devon Avenue
773-930-4711
www.citysedgechicago.com
@citysedgechi

THE PANDEMIC CERTAINLY forced restaurants to pivot, but altering course has been a familiar refrain for the family behind City's Edge Bar & Grill. In 2016 they bought a well-liked Irish pub in the Edgebrook neighborhood that had been serving burgers and Guinness for fifteen years. "We were criticized by the neighbors for changing the theme," said Blake Baum, the general manager.

Baum's mom is the owner of the new bar, and while they added barbecue and salads to the menu, once COVID hit, they had to once again make adjustments. "People can only eat so much barbecue," he said.

Baum had been a fan of the Detroit-style pizzas popping up around town, especially Fat Chris's in Andersonville and Union Squared in Evanston. He searched for recipes, tried out a few with the kitchen staff, using their small KitchenAid stand mixer, finally settling on a recipe in the fall of 2020.

He bought Lloyd steel pans ("expensive but worth it") and decided they would offer the pizzas on weekends only, since they had just twelve pans and were baking in their little oven. But Baum tells me if the neighborhood embraces the pizza, they'll figure out a way to offer it during the week. To simulate a stone deck oven, he went to Home Depot to buy quarry tiles that the steel pans bake on. Give the guy credit—he's Macgyvered his kitchen to accommodate his passion.

The dough (consisting of bread flour and a little garlic) proofs for a couple of hours before going into the pan, where it's stretched to the edges and rests for a few hours more. They opt for traditional slices of brick cheese as well as a fifty-fifty blend of mozzarella and provolone, finished with a grating of Parmesan before baking. The only pie that gets red sauce is their pepperoni and banana pepper, and it's a pretty

straightforward marinara—crushed tomatoes, some garlic, basil, and dried oregano. Other pizza flavors include pulled pork with red onion and a smoked chicken with buffalo sauce—flavors you'll rarely see at a pizza place, since few, if any, have smokers. The pizza has that telltale crispy-cheesy edge, or *frico*, while the bottom has a buttery-crunchy crust. It's a great alternative to the tavern and deep pizzas you'll find in the neighborhood, and a twelve-inch-square pie can easily feed a family.

"I'm not the best with dough or with rolling it out and making a circle," said Baum. "But to me, if you have a good dough and get it into one of these pans, you can make a tasty product."

FAT CHRIS'S PIZZA AND SUCH

1706 W. Foster Avenue
773-944-5444
www.fatchrispizza.com
@fatchrispizza

THE THREE MILAZZO brothers grew up about twenty minutes north of Lansing, Michigan. And while Buddy's is certainly a part of their childhood pizza experience, they really wanted to offer a Detroit-style at Fat Chris's that didn't taste exactly the same as the other players' in town. Their no-frills Andersonville restaurant has the requisite Chicago interior design elements: TV, Cubs shirt, W flag, and Blues Brothers painting.

Michael Milazzo opened the restaurant along with his two brothers, but now it's just him and his fiancée, Violeta Bjukic, running the place. He says a lot of their R & D was based on eating trips to Detroit stalwarts such as Buddy's and Shield's.

Their focaccia-like dough is made with oil, and instead of all-purpose flour, he uses regular baking flour, which allows the dough to take on an airier texture. Unlike other Detroit-style pizza doughs, Milazzo said, they add garlic to the dough for a little extra flavor in the chew. The last time I visited—for the *Pizza City, USA* book—they were par-baking their crusts in a pair of conveyor belt ovens. This led to crusts that were just too dough-forward, overwhelming the toppings. The addition of a convection oven has fixed that problem.

In order to achieve their crispy, caramelized edges, Milazzo adds Wisconsin brick cheese they shred in-house directly onto the raw dough. The cheese and dough rest and proof together before entering the oven (this is similar to the process at D'Amato's, interestingly enough). After the pizzas bake at 560 degrees for eight minutes in their convection oven, they carefully ladle on their thick, bright red tomato sauce which is pre-cooked—that allows them to shorten the overall baking time. After a total of sixteen minutes, the pizza is done.

The pies emerge with a gorgeous mahogany perimeter and undercarriage, as burnished as a Coach bag. The upper perimeter is practically jet black, with a crunch you could hear at the next table. Pies are served on an elevated baking rack to promote airflow and keep the undercarriage crispy. Pepperoni discs are thin and slightly crisp along the edges. I actually did not try sausage this time around. But the convection oven has been the game-changer for Milazzo—an upgrade I'm sure he'd equate with Magic Johnson's addition to the Spartan basketball team in '79.

FIVE SQUARED

135 N. Kedzie Avenue,
pickup on Fridays
224-595-5782
www.fivesquared.com/five-squared-friday
@fivesquaredfoodtruck

I first met the owners of Five Squared in the summer of 2019, when they were operating out of a food truck, at a quaint Ravenswood farmers' market. It was a lazy, summer weeknight, so we struck up a conversation. Eager to get some feedback on their new venture, they seemed ready and willing to do whatever they had to in order to improve upon their recipe for Detroit-style squares. I think I recall the bottom not being crispy enough, and gave them some honest feedback. Fast forward a year, and they've ditched the truck for a permanent space on the West Side, baking out of a commercial kitchen inside The Hatchery, a small business incubator in East Garfield Park.

As they continued moving toward that telltale crispy, cheesy square edge with the soft, focaccia-like interior, I'd get occasional updates on Instagram, showing me pictures of the crumb and the undercarriage. The move into a permanent space helped them focus on the product, rather than an ever-changing, nomadic food truck existence.

"Previously we were a food truck, but we have converted to a pickup and delivery service directly out of our commercial kitchen," said owner Steve Kaplan, who runs the business with his wife, Jenn.

They're now open just one day each week—Friday—offering delivery or pickup. Best to get your orders in ahead of time. You can score one of their five-inch-square slices (or whole pies) by sending them a direct message on Instagram or via their website up until Thursday night.

They get creative with flavors like "Chicago Italian Beef," "Chicago Hot Dog," even "Buffalo Chicken" and "Cuban Sandwich," but also stick to the Detroit basics, like cup-and-char Ezzo pepperoni and homemade Italian sausage. All of the pies have that signature soft interior with a crispy, charred cheese *frico* around the perimeter. The buttery crust is enhanced with thoughtful (often locally sourced) toppings, such as organic chicken and Monterey Jack cheese or Gotham Greens basil.

"We've got a lot of fun toppings, like our PB&J—pepperoni, bacon, and jalapeño—which is a favorite. We do spinach and artichoke on our pizza, we obviously do all the standards as well. But every single week we're coming up with new, fun flavors," said Kaplan.

@BESTFOODALEX

JET'S PIZZA

Nineteen locations in Chicagoland—
ten in suburbs, nine in city
www.jetspizza.com
@jetspizza

COURTESY JET'S PIZZA

ALL RIGHT, HANG ON! Before you jump down my throat and send the Twitter trolls on me for recommending a chain, allow me this: not everyone lives near Logan Square and has access to fantastic, independently owned pizzerias making Detroit-style from scratch.

I've driven by a Jet's Pizza so many times that the chain is almost invisible to me—like a Little Caesar's or Domino's (two other Detroit-based chains). The franchise has been around since 1978, and a few friends from the Detroit area told me that Jet's pizza was worth a try (thanks, Jason) after I had posted a picture of the stellar Detroit-style pizza from Union Squared, located in Evanston.

Why am I devoting precious ink to an out-of-town chain? Because even if you don't live in the city, and you can't manage to get over to Logan Square to try Derrick Tung's fantastic Detroit-style squares, I say treat yourself to a reasonable facsimile.

At its core, it's that same focaccia-type dough, riddled with tiny air pockets and heated until it rises at least an inch or two, and with an almost caramelized, crispy exterior. At Union Squared, they add some cheese to the outer perimeter, giving it a wonderful, flavorful chew and texture (kind of like Pequod's). But at Jet's, they omit the outer cheese layer and call their pizzas "deep-dish" (ha, funny). They also allow you to "flavorize" your crust. If you choose the more traditional, circular shape, think poppy seed, sesame seed, Parmesan, or "turbo" (butter, garlic, Romano).

Most of the locations are pretty spartan (couldn't resist) in terms of decor—just a counter and a long red bench like you'd see in a public park. The perfectly square, small "deep-dish" arrives half covered in an addictively delicious pepperoni and half with a generous topping of quite small, misshapen pieces of ground, fennel-flecked sausage. The cheese application is generous, but not stupefying. The sauce has some nice flavor to it, hidden as it is between the high dough and caramelized cheese. The dough is denser than focaccia, and certainly just as high, but it doesn't take away from or overwhelm the ingredients on top of the dough.

If you like deep-dish, and don't feel like using a knife and fork to get it into your mouth, this dough-forward pizza is for you.

PAULIE GEE'S LOGAN SQUARE

2451 N. Milwaukee Avenue
773-360-1072
www.pauliegee.com
@pauliegeelogansquare

WHAT STARTED IN Greenpoint, Brooklyn, in 2010, and spread to several other locations, including Columbus and Baltimore, now has a location in the heart of hipster paradise, aka Chicago's Logan Square. Goofy names aside ("Mo Cheeks," "Ricotta Be Kiddin' Me," "Brian DeParma," etc.), Paulie Gee's intense wood-burning ovens churn out seriously blistered pies with nice leopard spotting throughout the *cornicione* and more than a dozen options for fancy-pants pizzas. The key is the three-day cold fermentation that results in dough with incredible chew and complexity.

Owner Derrick Tung—a former med student turned healthcare administrator—chucked his safe career after earning an MBA and fell hard for pizza. After running some weekend pop-ups from a trailer, he reached out to Paulie Gee in Brooklyn as a potential mentor and partner. They found a soaring space on North Milwaukee Avenue, gentrifying as we speak, and initially launched just doing the wood-fired pies.

But Tung and his wife had driven to Detroit while they were waiting for their business to open, and really went for the thicker, crispy cheese-crusted pies at Buddy's. With help from his devoted staff, he and his crew reverse-engineered a Detroit-style pizza they referred to on the menu as "Logan Squares." One of the quirks allowed Tung to take creative liberties. Since his contract with Paulie Gee mandated no pepperoni—ever—on his wood-fired pizzas, there was nothing in the agreement that referred to other styles of pizza. Thus the

"Paulie's Prohibited Pepperoni" was born, as it's one of the classic toppings on these thicker, focaccia-based doughs.

Tung started offering them as a weekly special, but the neighbors noticed, spread the word, and forced him to put them on the menu permanently. This also meant a demand for a different oven—the wood-fired ones were only good for the wood-fired, neo-Neapolitan-style. So he invested in several new PizzaMaster electric ovens to meet demand. They'll typically offer a carnivore and a cheesavore version, plus his remarkable "U.S. Pizza Cup": a base of sharp white cheddar (rather than traditional Wisconsin brick), mozzarella, Ezzo pepperoni, and a beguiling homemade bacon jam, topped with stripes of red sauce and dollops of fresh ricotta, a chiffonade of basil, and a drizzle of Mike's Hot Honey. It's one of the best square slices in the city of Chicago. You can also sub vegan cheese or gluten-free dough for any of the square pies, which, combined with the fact they have a stellar craft beer list, make it an ideal spot to meet those friends of yours with the dietary restrictions.

10 ARTISAN GAS, COAL, AND WOOD-FIRED

CHICAGO'S PIZZA MAKERS, or if you want to get technical, *pizzaiolos*, usually come in one of two breeds. There are the teenage cooks who are trained to add ladles of sauce to a dough that's been run through a sheeter and then apply handfuls of shredded mozzarella and toppings. The only skills required when it comes to baking are placing the pizza into the oven, setting a timer, and removing it when it's done.

The other type of pizza maker is the salty, old, I've-been-here-for-years cook who dons a company T-shirt, and maybe a sauce-splotched paper hat, and who has the burns and scars from a decade or more of honest service. It's almost always a guy; he keeps his head down, in silence, as he either rolls out or hand-tosses the dough, then works like a surgeon to add the sauce and toppings before getting everything into the oven. He has not only memorized where the hot spots are in the oven, he has an internal timer that knows the status of each of his pizzas and is able to keep track of them without the aid of pen or paper.

The thing these two cooks have in common? Their lack of passion as it relates to the dough-making process. It's usually an afterthought, something that was made a few hours ago, or maybe the night before, and must be rolled out as quickly as possible to get it topped, baked, and sent out to the customer. These kinds of cooks are clock-punchers, just doing their job.

Enter the pizza artisan.

Artisan pie from Stella Barra

Guys like Chris Bianco (Pizzeria Bianco, in Phoenix of all places) started making every pie themselves using local ingredients and handmade sausage. Then master bread bakers like Los Angeles's Nancy Silverton (La Brea Bread) proved you could spend a lot of time mastering a pizza dough, adding the best cheeses and vegetables before baking it off in a wood-fired oven, as Silverton does at her Pizzeria Mozza. These chefs realized people would pay a premium for pies of a higher caliber, and thus ambitious cooks began treating pizza like any other artisan bread. The dough is, after all, the most important component, so why not devote extra time to its care and assembly? In New York City, Scarr Pimentel mills his flour at Scarr's; in Jersey City, Dan Richer keeps a table of times and ambient temperatures, noting the "friction factor" or heat generated by his mixer, so he can add that to his temperature calculations. The result of these obsessive cooks? Next-level pizzas with beguiling chew and char that haunt your dreams and make the pizzas of your youth seem, well, quaint.

Customers have responded, and in Chicago, at least, there has been a nascent movement toward an actual artisan pizza category. Years ago, the lucky few will remember the quirky, iconic Great Lake. Owners Nick Lessins and Lydia Esparza had their Byzantine rules and Soup Nazi rigidity (*No parties over four! Sorry, Beyoncé and Jay-Z, wait outside!*). And there was their minimalist menu, but oh, what Nick could do with dough. I remember seeing a restaurant guest inexplicably break into applause after eating a few pieces.

After Alan Richman deemed Great Lake the best pizza in the country for *GQ*, the lines became impossible and as Yogi Berra famously said, "It's so popular no one goes there anymore." A lease dispute forced them to close, and they never reopened, but they're back in town, taking their time, and will likely have something working by the time this book is out. I got a little preview at the end of 2020 and the beginning of 2021, when Nick was baking out of his home oven.

There are several committed artisan chefs working in Chicago today, giving their ultra-wet doughs up to three days of rest to properly ferment and develop plenty of air pockets inside, which results in extra flavor, character, and a more pleasant chew. Bread bakers refer to this as "open crumb structure." They don't over-handle the dough, treating each sphere as gently and tenderly as they would

Exquisite slices emerge from the PizzaMaster oven at Bungalow by Middle Brow

give a newborn a bath. They meticulously source (or more likely, make) their sausage, and they know most of the farmers who grow the produce for their toppings. Some even have impressive wine lists.

In short, I'm talking about restaurants with very talented cooks in the back who use only the finest ingredients they can get and also happen to make pizzas. To this book, I've added a lot more restaurants that offer fantastic pizzas. Some have opened recently; others, like Avec, have always been there, but I was just so tunnel-visioned looking for pizzerias that I completely overlooked their one pizza option (besides their famous focaccia).

This section has a lot of newcomers, including Bob's in Pilsen (and a few other locations), Roebuck, next to a microbrewery in Lakeview, and one of my favorites, Bungalow by Middle Brow—which opened shortly after my last book came out; it just killed me not to have them in that collection. So welcome to all of our new artisans and welcome back to some of our classics, like Coalfire and Craft. You all make Chicago the premier pizza city it is.

AVEC WEST LOOP

615 W. Randolph Street
312-377-2002

AVEC RIVER NORTH

141 W. Erie Street
312-736-1778

www.avecrestaurant.com
@avecchicago

One of my all-time favorite restaurants in Chicago—where I typically take visitors from out-of-town—Avec is the younger sibling to Blackbird (which sadly closed during the pandemic). It's the brash, free-wheeling upstart with a focus on Midwestern-meets-Mediterranean rusticity.

In early 2021, the ownership group—One Off Hospitality—bought out their former partners at Pacific Standard Time, converting that soaring space into a River North branch of the popular West Loop original. Despite the fact the menus and the management team are similar, each location has a very different oven, so I'll start with the West Loop.

Perry Hendrix was promoted from chef de cuisine to creative culinary director for the entire One Off Hospitality group in 2020, and even though he inherited a menu from the likes of Erling Wu-Bower (and his predecessor, Koren Grieveson), he still wanted to put his own stamp on things.

The restaurant is as narrow as a NOLA shotgun shack, looking like a Swedish sauna. In back sits the hulking Australian-made dual fuel oven. Rather than a beehive shape, it's simply a large, rectangular box. On the gas side, the temperature is set to 712 degrees, but on the wood side, where the famous bacon-wrapped dates fight for space alongside pork shoulders, the oak and hickory wood add another 50 to 100 degrees. Pizzas take about three minutes to bake.

"I think Koren never wanted to serve pizza here, so she called it flatbread," said Hendrix. Not to be confused with the focaccia, which has never left the menu (I can still remember the first time I tried that combination of creamy taleggio and scented truffle oil tucked between the thin, delicate layers of dough).

The focaccia may outsell the pizza, but to be honest, the pizzas have a lot more going for them. For one thing, there's only one flavor per night, often dictated by the season and hidden behind the more popular chorizo-stuffed dates, like Sylvan Esso on the Lollapalooza undercard. But it offers a bigger bang for your buck. With its natural starter, plus a combo of Caputo "00" and King Arthur Sir Galahad flour and a little olive oil, the dough is fermented at minimum one night, although Hendrix prefers two. His tomato sauce is a simple blend of Bianco di Napoli tomatoes passed through a food mill, enhanced with a clove of

garlic, some oil, and a pinch of salt. Simplicity, remember?

About a third of the time, the pizzas will have a red sauce. That means most of the time it's something like pesto or better yet, garlic cream, topped with smoked whitefish and marinated kale, and served with a charred lemon on top—a Midwestern nod to the New Haven clam pie. The same dough might arrive draped over a cast-iron pot of mussels, ready to be torn up and sopped in their juices, or served as a pita with head-on prawns and merguez butter, but do give the pizza du jour a shot. It may not be as popular as the focaccia or the dates, but like Bryan Ferry leaving Roxy Music, sometimes the solo acts deserve your attention as much as the hitmakers do.

Meanwhile, in early 2021, Hendrix was faced with the task of wiping away all evidence of the previous tenants of the space where Avec River North was set to open. Pacific Standard Time had been opened by former Avec chef Erling Wu-Bower and his partner, but the

business relationship deteriorated during COVID, and the One Off partners eventually took it over, rebranding it Avec River North. Hendrix had been overseeing the PST menu for several months leading up to the name change, having inherited a pair of mammoth wood-burning ovens. "I'm a big fan of the charred leopard spotting," he said. "That's what I look for in a pizza crust."

Both ovens look like they came from the Neolithic era, or at the very least, some rustic Healdsburg cook's fantasy of brick, stone, and mortar. Both were built on-site, by hand, courtesy of the Stovemaster company from Canada. One of them, in the middle of the open kitchen, features a trough down the middle that looks like they might do some gold smelting, but it's used for building up charcoals while roasting whole fish or meat along the sides. The other beehive-shaped oven has a smooth, stone hearth, perfect for launching high hydration doughs. Reaching temps around 800 degrees and more, pizzas bake in less than two minutes.

While there are some similarities between recipes at both locations, the dough in River North has an even higher hydration level. Proportionally, there's more natural starter and the dough balls are slightly larger as well. They rest and proof at ambient temperature for two hours, then go into the cooler overnight, although Hendrix prefers if they can last two days before baking.

They typically offer four pizzas (as opposed to the solo option in the West Loop). Hendrix is partial to a tomato base—calling for those Bianco di Napoli tomatoes kissed with oil, salt, and garlic—which will offer a zesty base to a mushroom pizza with burrata cheese and chili crisp, the über condiment of 2020, in addition to the smoked lake fish and 'nduja offered at the West Loop location.

You could get these pizzas to go, I guess, but that would be a shame, like watching a Cubs game from a brownstone across Waveland Avenue. These are pizzas that demand you eat them shortly after they emerge from the kitchen.

BOB'S PIZZA

1659 W. Twenty-First Street
312-600-6155

1512 N. LaSalle Drive
312-869-8006

616 Davis Street, Evanston
847-485-1973

838 W. Kinzie (inside Recess Bar)
slices only behind the bar,
on Peoria Street

www.famousbobspizza.com
@eatbobspizza

Bob's pizza isn't New York–style, or Chicago-style, or any definitive style, for that matter. The owner decided to go in a completely different direction when he launched his pizza joint in 2019. Despite the pitchers of beer you might see back in the kitchen, there isn't a kegger going on. It's the dough room at Bob's in the Pilsen neighborhood, where they're taking a different approach to making pizza from scratch.

"We didn't want to be classified as New York. We didn't want to be classified as Neapolitan or Chicago or New Haven. We wanted to do our own thing," said Matthew Wilde, the owner. That means subbing beer for water in what he casually calls his "Pilsen style" pizza.

After the beer is added to the bowl of a giant stand mixer, they whisk in dry active yeast and sugar, and let it stand for five minutes. Then all of the flour is added—in this case, "00" flour—and they turn the mixer on to its lowest setting. Garlic powder, salt, and oil are added at the end of the mixing process.

Once the mixture is fully incorporated, it rests, for at least two days. Then the dough is pretty supple and easy to stretch. It only takes Wilde about two minutes to stretch it out to fit his wooden pizza peel.

"What is unique about it is how the beer plays with the yeast, or how the yeast is affected by the beer, and vice versa," Wilde said. "Because it's got all that carbonation, so it does almost the same thing as the yeast does."

He can do standard stuff, like use rich tomato sauce, crumbled sausage, and cheese—although his cheese is more than just mozzarella.

"I love Swiss cheese, so I added Swiss cheese to my blend, which is really unique. In the end, we do cut it with a little bit of Parmesan as well, just to add some sharpness," he said.

After it's baked, he adds fresh herbs, cracked pepper, and sea salt, and some pickled onions. Speaking of pickles, he's got a pizza dedicated to them.

"It's one of those pizzas that you read on the menu and you think about it, and you're like, 'Do I really want to eat that?' " he said.

Yes, you do. A garlic cream base is barely covered by slices of mortadella. On goes his three-cheese blend, then a large handful of thinly sliced pickles, plus fresh dill sprigs. Then into the oven for about seven minutes. When it emerges, he finishes it with a generous grind of black pepper and sea salt.

"I always tell everybody, if you're one of those people that dip your pizza in ranch or something like that—which I don't necessarily agree with, each to their own—that's your pizza," Wilde said.

Slices are only available from the back window at Recess Bar in the West Loop, on the Peoria Street side of the building (the window is cut into a storage container).

BUNGALOW BY MIDDLE BROW

2840 W. Armitage Avenue
773-687-9076
www.middlebrowbeer.com
@bungalow_by_middle_brow

GRAINS, HOPS, AND FLOUR are the recurring themes at Bungalow by Middle Brow, located along West Armitage Avenue in Logan Square. The brewpub really started out as a passion project for a former attorney turned gypsy microbrewer.

"We focused in the early days on Belgian styles, yeast-forward styles. But we've matured into a brewery. We like to think we've matured into a brewery that offers something for everyone," said Pete Ternes, the owner, along with his wife, Polly.

Not just IPAs and pilsners, but tart Berliner Weiss styles, like a berry-infused German wheat beer. With so much yeast here, it was only a matter of time before bread and pizza became priorities. Enter Jess Galli.

Galli (an alum of the beloved bakery The Mill in San Francisco) oversees anything coming out of the oven, including the high-moisture loaves that are formed by hand each day, proofed, scored, and baked-off in heavy cast iron, resulting in sturdy crusts and soft, porous interiors, or "open crumb" to use bakers' lingo. Get a rustic slice with whipped mortadella or just the simplest butter, seasoned with French sea salt. If there was an entry for "bread porn" in *Webster's*, they'd set up the photo shoot here.

Pizzas are also majestic, their crusts soft yet crisp, revealing ample open crumb on the heels. There are baseline Margheritas ranging up to more creative options, like one seasonal version I had with a pureed butternut squash base, hearty greens, and a few pieces of roasted kuri squash on top. Fired in an electric oven for about seven minutes, it's garnished with fresh sage, pickled shallots, bracing Calabrian chiles, and briny capers. You need some hipster, artisan bread cred? A pizza this thoughtful pairs nicely with a Kerouac novel, a Third Wave coffee (French press), and some Jungle in your AirPods. All of their pizzas arrive uncut to preserve the bottom crust as long as possible. Since the pandemic, they've also been offering build-it-yourself take-home pizza kits.

"It's kind of a bread-based food program, where we've got pizza at night, and toast and sandwiches and tartines and terrines and such during the day," Ternes said.

There are plenty of pizzas in Chicagoland, though few are making artisan pies as good as the ones at Middle Brow. But a serious bread program to go along with those pizzas? Good luck finding that anywhere in town.

COALFIRE

1321 W. Grand Avenue
312-226-2625

3707 N. Southport Avenue
773-477-2625

www.coalfirechicago.com
@coalfirechicago

Taking pride in their 800-plus degree oven, fed by coal, this West Town favorite also has a second location in Lakeview on Southport Avenue. Several years ago, they upgraded their toppings by using some sausages (specifically the Calabrian 'nduja) from Publican Quality Meats, and things improved dramatically. It's also interesting to note that this coal-fed oven—one of only a handful in the city—is just two blocks west of the city's original coal-fired oven at D'Amato's. Word has it the owners figured they'd have a lot easier time getting the alderman to approve their permits if there was already a history of a coal truck making deliveries nearby.

The pizzas have a nicely charred lip, containing all sorts of odd-shaped nooks and crannies, and there's a good one-inch border of nothing but crust. Sometimes the dough on their pizzas can be a little too thin, but they still offer the opportunity to fold from the heel like an East Coast pro. When done right, these pies have the potential to be complex, with a great chew. The meaty pie was quite good, offering sausage with a nice bite and the slightest amount of heat—I couldn't stop eating it. The pepperoni with whipped ricotta, featuring Berkshire pork 'nduja and smoked mozzarella with fresh basil, is a particular standout for its balance of crunchy and creamy richness, balancing the assertive heat of the 'nduja (referred to often as "pork butter" for its spreadable quality).

The Margherita is extra wide and evenly thin across the entire diameter. Five giant basil leaves, each the size of a playing card, are carefully placed over the large blobs of stark white, fresh mozzarella spreading across the glorious pie as it heats. They're mostly decorative leaves, but they do add a pleasant aroma.

ETTA

1840 W. North Avenue
312-757-4444

700 N. Clark Street
312-766-4444

www.ettarestaurant.com
@ettarestaurant

A LOT OF CHEFS made the pivot from tasting menus to pizza in 2020, but for chef Danny Grant, pizzas have always been in the background during a career that has been spent mostly in fine-dining kitchens. He grew up on Long Island pizzas and the iconic slices at Joe's in the West Village, with fond memories of the granulated garlic, chili flakes, and oregano that permeated his childhood, while his culinary career brought him through some of Chicago's best restaurants: North Pond, NoMI, and Ria, where he was the opening executive chef at the former Elysian (now Waldorf-Astoria) hotel.

Grant left the hotel to become executive chef and partner at Maple & Ash, where cooking *over* fire, rather than next to it, became a

priority for his dry-aged steaks and succulent lamb dishes. When the same restaurant group opened Etta in Bucktown (now with a second location in River North), pizza and pasta became the focus.

Traveling through Italy as an adult, experiencing the wood-fired pizzas of Naples and the crispier ones from Rome, helped inform his opinion, despite having strong memories of those New York slices. Living in Chicago the past fifteen years, his desire for a more sturdy, stable crust took precedence over the typical Neapolitan version cooked at blazing heat for just ninety seconds.

With his shiny new Marra Forni oven, Grant says he wanted to embrace the fun parts of wood-fired cooking without strict adherence to AVPN rules. He runs the oven at around 750 Fahrenheit, resulting in a bake time of about four and a half minutes. The artisan pies—made from a combo of natural starter and commercial yeast—rely on a combination of all-purpose, barley, and high-gluten flours. Dough is fermented for three days, resulting in a thin and delicate but sturdy crust that stands up to a panoply of toppings.

"The outside crust has to be airy and delicate," he said. "But I also want to check the box of a great sausage and pepper pizza in Chicago."

There are typically five pies on his menu, but one that never changes is the Fire Pie—a nod to a pizza he and his staff from Ria would get almost weekly at a nearby Pizano's. Dressed with hot giardiniera, fresh sausage, and garlic, Grant's version uses chile de arbol over a base layer of his house cheese blend: mozzarella, provolone, and a kiss of raclette. But other seasonal and local farm-influenced pies (think ramps in spring, butternut squash or the leaves of brussels sprouts in fall) might be topped with thick, creamy slices of fresh mozz or even runny burrata, spooned directly onto a pie after it emerges from the oven. The emphasis on using high-quality olive oils and imported cheeses is clearly a mentality he maintains from his days in fine dining.

"The more I play, less is more," said Grant. "I want to let just a few ingredients shine."

GREAT LAKE

Google "Great Lake Pizza"

WHY AM I INCLUDING a pizza place with no address and no phone number or social media presence? Because Great Lake is back, and I, for one, would tell you it's worth the trouble to go online now to see where they decided to sign their lease or buy their building. In March 2020, Nick Lessins and Lydia Esparza moved back to Chicago from their native Detroit, where they had recently thrown in the towel on plans to open a pizza place. Even though they were from the Motor City, it didn't feel like home.

"Chicago is where we became adults, and it became home to us," said Esparza. "The Corktown I grew up in lost all of the schools; the cleaners were gone. It wasn't the city I remember. It became a very suburban city," she said.

The couple missed the farmers and friends they'd met in Chicago during their brief but successful run in a tiny Andersonville storefront with all of four tables. Back then, pre-Recession, Nick was making every pie himself, as quiet and focused as a monk, while Lydia would handle customers, talking about the provenance of the day's salad option or pointing out some of the quirky design books on display. Her experience at Herman Miller revealed itself in minute details either on the menu or in the physical space that seated all of fourteen.

In 2009, an era when magazines had budgets to send writers all over the country, Alan Richman declared Great Lake to have the best pizza in America for a story in *GQ* (ahead of Lucali, Delfina, and Bianco!). You can imagine the overwhelming response. "No man is slower. He makes each as though it is his first, manipulating the dough until it appears flawless, putting on toppings one small bit after another. In the time he takes to create a pie, civilizations could rise and fall, not just crusts," Richman wrote. But then this: "His cheese pie, prepared with fresh mozzarella made in-house, grated Wisconsin sheep's-and-cow's-milk cheese, and aromatic fresh marjoram instead of basil, was slightly shy of unbelievable. The next day I returned to try the same pie topped with fresh garlic and mortadella . . . this pie—creative, original, and somewhat local—represents everything irresistible about the new American style of pizza making." After a few years in business in Andersonville, they couldn't see eye to eye with their landlord on a lease, so the couple moved back to Detroit to try to start anew.

They returned for a one-night pop-up at Cellar Door Provisions' five-year anniversary in 2019 (I attended), and the line stretched down the block like a bunch of teenage girls waiting for BTS tickets. The pizza that night was quite a bit different from what he'd made before in Andersonville. It wasn't as swoonworthy. But now Nick and Lydia are back. They bought a condo on Lake Shore Drive and were in the process of negotiating a lease as the calendar shifted to 2021.

"We keep seeing a pattern with landlords," Lydia told me on New Year's Day. "We may want to just own a building."

In late 2020 and early 2021, they were doing "UP" (Underground Pizza) Nights for friends and family. Because they'd run into old friends or former customers, it gave Nick a chance to workshop his

LYDIA ESPARZA

ideas. Here's what I ordered then: "Tomato, Fresh Mozz, Aged Mozz, Parmigiano-Reggiano, Greek EVOO, French Sea Salt (Breton)—$20." A natural starter kicks off the twenty-four-hour ferment with 50 percent freshly milled whole-grain wheat and rye from Illinois. The pizza was delicious, if quite a bit nuttier than anything I'd ever had. A rye Manhattan would have paired nicely.

"I don't want to change what we did," said Lessins. "I'm still gonna make them with the same taste and texture, but I want to use more local grains we have a connection to. They're better tasting and better for your health."

These "nutritionally responsible" grains—like rye or Turkey Red Wheat from Janie's Mill in Ashkum, Illinois—are what gets Lessins excited about baking these days. He still wants the light airiness and open crumb he was known for in Andersonville. He just wants the pizzas to reflect more of the terroir of our region.

His R & D took place in his condo, from a tiny, twenty-four-inch-wide Blue Star custom range. I know once he gets into a permanent space with a proper stone deck firing at a consistent temperature, this pizza will shoot to the top of my radar once again.

Note: Lessins is not a fan of social media, but there is a chance Lydia may have convinced him by now. Try @granlago or @greatlakepizza on Instagram. If nothing is there, just Google "great lake pizza" and I'm sure you'll find them.

PAULIE GEE'S LOGAN SQUARE

2451 N. Milwaukee Avenue
773-360-1072
www.pauliegee.com
@pauliegeelogansquare

PAULIE GEE'S INTENSE wood-burning ovens in hipster Logan Square churn out seriously blistered pies with nice leopard spotting throughout the *cornicione* and more than a dozen options for fancy-pants pizzas. The key is the three-day cold fermentation that results in dough with incredible chew and complexity.

Owner Derrick Tung chucked his safe career after earning an MBA and fell hard for pizza. After running some weekend pop-ups from a trailer, he reached out to Paulie Gee in Brooklyn as a potential mentor and partner. They found a soaring space on North Milwaukee Avenue, gentrifying as we speak, and initially launched just doing the wood-fired pies.

But, while they were waiting for their business to open, Tung and his wife drove to Detroit and were smitten with the thicker, crispy cheese-crusted pies at Buddy's. To read more about what happened afterward, and how Tung integrated those "Logan Squares" into his menu, see chapter 9 ("Detroit-Style").

From the wood-fired lineup, the sweet Italian fennel sausage is a favorite, but so is anything with pickled cherry peppers, fresh mozzarella, or Berkshire *guanciale* (cured pork cheek). The beer list is vast, matching the pizza quality in terms of variety and depth.

Once COVID and shutdowns are over, I have no doubt Tung's spacious dining room will be back to normal, humming with the sounds of metal peels scraping the hearth stones, turning and baking the delicate, blistered pies, and brimming with the delighted squeals from fans after they devour his neo-Neapolitan pies just minutes out of the oven.

PIZZERIA BEBU

1521 N. Fremont Street
312-280-6000
www.bebu.pizza
@pizzeriabebu

HUGE GALDONES

Pizzerias are typically the kinds of places you expect to have a beer or a glass of wine with dinner—although you probably don't expect to see a '78 Mt. Eden Cabernet, for $200 a bottle, on the wine list. But Zach Smith is trying to change your idea of what a pizza joint can be.

A veteran of the Gold Coast's Nico Osteria and Lettuce Entertain You's corporate ecosystem, he and his business partner, Jeff Lutzow, created a hidden gem among the caverns of unidentifiable apartment and light industrial buildings just south of North Avenue, near the massive Whole Foods. It seems like an odd neighborhood—after all, Sono Wood Fired didn't last a few blocks away—but there are lots of new high-rises nearby, plus a ton of single-family homes just to the north in Lincoln Park.

The restaurant doesn't look like much from the outside. Tucked into a long, narrow room at the base of a micro-apartment building with floor-to-ceiling windows, it could just as well be a furniture store. But from the looks of it, the neighbors are excited to have some artisan pies in the 'hood. Servers stand sentinel, in "Feed Me Pizza" T-shirts, waiting to take your order and happily guide you through the wine or craft beer list.

The high hydration dough gets a gentle two-day rest before being hand-stretched and launched into a gas-fired, brick-lined Marsal oven, kept right around 700 degrees. The pizzas take six to eight minutes to bake. A trio caddy of dried oregano, chili flakes, and grated Parm arrive at your table just in case you want to doctor up your pie—but it's unnecessary. These are truly transcendent pizzas, achieving what few artisan or Neapolitan pies can: an ultra-thin middle that manages to stay firm, upright, and impossibly crispy.

The Margherita has a generous heel with an even char on the undercarriage. Five large basil leaves top off the pie, along with a half-dozen amorphous blobs of fresh mozzarella. Unlike those of many shops in town, Pizzeria Bebu's tomato sauce is more generous (I guess when you know that your bottom crust can hold its own—and hold things up—you feel more confident adding liquid or sauce on top of the crust). I also loved the "Jalapeño Business," with broccoli rabe, pickled jalapeño, red onion, and ricotta, and an "Ode to Rubirosa" from New York, with vodka sauce and nutless pesto. Next time, I'm getting the "Sausage & Broccoli Rabe," with its generous knobs of fresh ricotta and homemade Italian sausage.

Note: Bebu has remained closed during the pandemic, and they have stopped doing takeout until the situation improves. As I'm turning this book over to the publisher, there are now two vaccines, so by the time this book is published, there's a good chance they will have reopened. Regardless, call ahead or look online just to make sure.

RENO

2607 N. Milwaukee Avenue
773-697-4234
www.renochicago.com
@renochicago

On a rainy, dreary Wednesday night in Logan Square, the hipsters are jammed into booths, music playing loudly. Many are here for Reno's $25-for-two-pizzas-and-PBR night.

The focal point here is the wood-burning oven, which also finishes off Montreal-style bagels for the morning crowd. But at night, nearly every table has a fourteen-inch pizza on it, and I can see why. They offer about a dozen creative pizza options, including "Fancy Nancy" with burrata and fresh basil, and a "Hog" with pork carnitas, salsa verde, and cotija cheese.

I opt to go baseline, with a "Reno" (fresh domestic mozzarella, a chiffonade of basil, and a base of Valorosa tomatoes) and add-ons of sausage and pepperoni.

The homemade fennel sausage is the standout here. It's crumbled onto the pie in generous handfuls and packs a mouthful of fatty-rich flavor with the barest whisper of anise. Even the pepperoni—sourced from elsewhere—is sliced a shade thicker and contains the slightest amount of chili heat, just as a sort of wake-up call. The naked lip, about a half-inch wide, is softer than on most artisan pies, but I like seeing a pair of char domes on one side, indicating some texture, fermentation, and extraordinary heat from the oven, which hovers around 800 degrees. The undercarriage is also suitably charred, but the slices are so thin that they flop beneath the weight of just about any topping. You can fold them if you prefer, since the outer lip is soft and chewy and folds easily, which will come as a relief to displaced NYC ex-pats seeking a three-finger fold.

After ten years in business, the owners have decided to finally upgrade their beehive oven, which has seen the stones begin to separate; it just doesn't hold heat the way it used to. They planned on splurging on a new oven at the beginning of 2021, so chances are pretty good by the time you read this, the newer, more functional oven will be in use.

ROBERT'S PIZZA AND DOUGH COMPANY

465 N. McClurg Court (entrances on Illinois and McClurg)
312-265-1328
www.robertspizzacompany.com
@robertspizzaco

There are plenty of mediocre pizzas within walking distance of Michigan Avenue. So when I tell people about the transcendent deep-dish pies at Labriola, or the next-level artisan pies at Robert's, even locals tend to scoff, since they're already predisposed to turning their noses up at anything located within striking distance of The Bean, the architecture tours, and the Michigan Avenue bridge. Robert Garvey's pizzas are not only worth taking a detour from those tourist attractions, they're worthy of a special trip in from the suburbs. That they happen to be in Streeterville—a quick cab ride from most of the downtown hotels—makes them one of the pizzas most tourists will never experience, since they're singularly focused on stuffing their maws with stuffed pizza.

Consider the fact that Garvey has spent the past twenty years with an obsession. He says he had a slice-a-day habit in New York City. After stints with the Merchant Marine, living on large ships, then getting his MFA in creative writing and working for a time at a theater in Pittsburgh, his wife's family business brought them to Chicago. He realized pretty quickly the kind of slices he had growing up in Queens didn't exist in his new home. That led to five years of almost daily baking experimentation to come up with his ideal pizza. Like any good pie, it's all about the dough. It's a cold rise in a refrigerator for three days, and then he gives it a long time to proof when it comes out of the cooler.

Garvey handles the dough like Lang Lang on a Steinway, careful not to overwork it. He uses his fingers rather than a roller to put a little bit of air in the crust, which gives it a nice, light chew in the finished product. The sauce and sausage are homemade, vegetables and cured meats are carefully sourced, and additional toppings include brussels sprouts with bacon, a seafood version with clams and shrimp, and Peking duck with hoisin. The fennel pie has become a personal favorite, featuring fennel in several forms: pickled and roasted; in sausage as well as using the fennel fronds. After about ten minutes in a gas-fired oven, the pizzas emerge beautifully crisp on the edge. The crust has the characteristics of a really good ciabatta or a fresh baguette. There is ample crunch and chew, with the slightest whiff of a sourdough tang that will make it hard to leave any crust orphans behind. A wire rack beneath elevates the pies, preventing them from getting soggy and maintaining a crisp bottom crust.

It's all part of the plan to create the perfect slice. "The middle is kind of a nice, soft chew; then it moves to a nice crunchy chew, then you finish with that nice big heel, which is a terrific finish to the slice," he explained.

I couldn't agree more. And good news for celiacs: Robert's Pizza and Dough Company has a gluten-free option (which I hear is spectacular).

ROEBUCK PIZZA

3159 N. Broadway Street
773-857-2229
www.roebuckpizza.com
@roebuck.chicago

WOOD-FIRED PIZZAS are nothing new in Chicago, but you don't see a lot of all-natural starters using wild yeast. At Roebuck Pizza in Lakeview, they worked on their recipe for months, even employing a pizza consultant from New York City before opening. He not only helped create the dough, but also worked on launching the pies into their mammoth brick-red Pavesi oven, until they emerged with blistered edges.

"We bring to pizza making a philosophy that brewers bring to beer, which is yeast can have a really big impact on the flavor of the finished meal, so we wanted to do that with pizza," owner Greg Shuff said.

Shuff is also owner of DryHop Brewers, right next door, so beer is definitely a part of the experience. It's mostly of the IPA and lager variety, but certainly appropriate with the thin, charred pies emerging from the oven.

It's sopressatta instead of pepperoni here, added to handfuls of fresh mozzarella; the pies bake directly on the stone hearth, a few inches from the fire. Post-bake, the sopressatta gets some pickled jalapenos and a drizzle of hot honey. Purists might opt for the sausage, pinched and pressed Chicago-style of course, with red onions. And they're not necessarily going for traditional Neapolitan heat levels, which require faster baking, and thus, wetter middles. These beauties are baked a bit lower and a bit longer. The end product is leopard-spotted without the soupiness.

"You get a lot of that softness that you'd expect, but then you get a little bit of crispiness on the bottom that we think people really like," Shuff said.

STELLA BARRA PIZZERIA & WINE BAR

1954 N. Halsted Street
773-634-4101
www.stellabarra.com
@stellabarra

With locations in Hollywood, Santa Monica, and Bethesda, Maryland, this Lincoln Park sibling to Summer House Santa Monica is part of the Lettuce Entertain You empire. Chef Jeff Mahin helped create the original menus at both restaurants, and now chef Ben Goodnick carries on the mission, creating a pretty lovely lineup of pies that takes a farmers' market approach.

Alongside the homemade sausage and fresh mozzarella, you'll also spot fennel pollen, fresh ricotta, and peppery arugula, plus an outstanding mushroom pie with truffle oil, but I digress.

The star here is the crust, and I can't overstate its importance. Too many pizza fans rave with misguided loyalty about places that have crusts so substandard I wouldn't serve them at a

six-year-old's birthday party, and I'm sure those same fans will berate me for touting a pizza joint in Lincoln Park that has leather couches and hand-crafted cocktails. But if you consider yourself a pizza lover, you have to give this crust a try. The kitchen staff are bread bakers. They start with a lot of hydration (about 70 percent water) along with wheat flour grown and milled in California, then ferment the dough for eighteen hours. The result is an artisan bread that eats like a baguette. It's everything I want in a chew: salty, slightly textured (is that cornmeal on the bottom?), and with an enormous *cornicione* revealing air pockets the size of edamame beans.

The middle of the pizza is also impressive, with a sturdiness despite its shallow depth, which is only a millimeter or two, that holds up under the fresh mozzarella and organic California-grown tomatoes. For the record, that sauce has more intensity than most, as if the kitchen first reduced it before adding it to the pie. Goodnick says they marinate the tomatoes in olive oil and salt, plus a few secret ingredients, for forty-eight hours.

"We buy really good stuff and put that on pizza and let that shine," he said. Lettuce founder Richard Melman gave him some advice that stuck: "If you're going to make onion pizza, let the onions sing."

The pizzas bake directly on the stone hearth of an American Baking Systems oven for about twelve minutes. They also offer a second style of pizza—kind of a hybrid between Roman and Chicago tavern-styles (referred to as "thin and crispy" on the menu), but the artisan makes up most of their orders.

One thing they don't want is to be confused with that other pizza company with California origins. It's not California Pizza Kitchen fare, not even close. There are no "stunt" pizzas with over-the-top flavors. "It's a Chicago-California hybrid," said Goodnick. "It very much speaks to who we are as a group." The presence of sausage, fennel, and giardiniera is a reassuring sign to any Midwestern doubters.

That said, even after taste-testing a few other pizzas on the day I visited Stella Barra, I still managed to eat an entire slice—a compliment to the person who did the baking. My recommendation? Get thyself to the corner of Halsted and Armitage and dive into one of Chicago's best artisan pizzas.

11 ROMAN

ONE OF THE GUYS ANTHONY "PROFESSOR PIZZA" SCARDINO refers to, when praising Chicago's willingness to adopt new styles, is Gabriele Bonci. The founder of Pizzarium, with several locations in Italy, has expanded on a style called Roman *al taglio* ("by the cut") that's been around for about fifty years. With the help of people like Rick Tasman, a former P. F. Chang's executive, the brand is now slowly expanding around the United States. Under the LLC of Bonci USA, their first outpost was in the West Loop. A second location in Wicker Park closed, but they have plans to add stores in the suburbs and another in the city; a shop in New Orleans has opened while another is planned for Miami.

The "*al taglio*" refers to a process involving scissors. You tell the employee behind the counter how much of the pizza you'd like—using your fingers or other pantomime—then they'll cut it from the rectangular pan and weigh it. You pay by the pound. The slices are topped with all manner of seasonal and regional specialties. Personal favorites include a thinly shaved zucchini accented with freshly ground black pepper and bright lemon zest, but you'd be just as struck by how good the potato-mozzarella is, or the octopus. They recently started making an "Italian Beef" flavor with the namesake, thinly shaved, plus homemade giardiniera.

Assortment of Roman al taglio *flavors at Bonci*

The pizzas are stretched and baked in large steel rectangular pans, but after they've baked on the stone decks of the Castelli ovens imported from Italy and you've placed your order, the employee will reheat the slice in a different oven, then cut them into tiny, almost tapas-sized squares for easy eating. The focaccia-like interior is a result of three flours, a lot of water in the dough, and a thirty-six- to seventy-two-hour fermentation. The second bake ensures a hallmark of all Roman pies: they *must* be crispy.

Almost twenty years before Bonci opened its first store here, Marco Schiavoni opened Pizza Metro on a long-neglected block of Division Street in Ukrainian Village. Unlike *al taglio*, his slices were not cut to order, and the flavor options stayed more basic but always included a very Roman cheeseless marinara and a potato-rosemary. The restaurant gets its name from the Roman style "*al metro*" or "by the meter" since whole pies are typically about a meter long before being cut. The squares here remain fairly small—again, perfect for a snack or a light meal for one, and the crusts are adequately crispy.

Bar Cargo in River North (part of the Stefani Restaurant Group) is making Roman pizza *al metro*, claiming they do a ninety-six-hour rise and baking in the same Castelli stone ovens as Bonci uses, but the smallest size they offer is about the size of a child's boogie board—made for two or more people—so dining solo is nearly impossible unless you want to take home lots of leftovers (and snob that I am, I rarely eat cold or reheated pizza, unless it's a proper slice on a preheated pizza stone).

Roman pizza al metro *at Bar Cargo*

Even Greg Wade, the James Beard Award–winning baker at the venerable Publican Quality Bread (808 W. Lake Street) is getting into the spirit. On Mondays, he has a Pizza Night (suspended during COVID), crafting a hand-tossed artisan pie as well as a puffy Roman version (each served cut). The open crumb in the Roman is off the charts when compared to the other options in town. Get ready to chew.

In 2019, another great option within the Roman repertoire launched in Chicago: *pinsas*. They're sort of a cross between the light *al metro* interior and the crispy *al taglio* bottom. L'Aventino in Streeterville was the only place making them. The chef there, Adam Weisell, left in late 2020 after a dispute with the owners, who wanted to add New York–style pizzas to the menu. Weisell, who had lived in Rome and wanted to preserve the singular focus, left the business, but is working on finding his own space in Avondale. By the time you're reading this, there's a good chance he'll also be back to making his *pinsas*. A manager at L'Aventino told me in early 2021, as I was turning in the book to the publisher, that they would keep the *pinsas* on the menu, but would add New York–style pies and slices as well.

The scene at Bar Cargo

Other Roman variants include a tavern-style, a lot like the Chicago version, cut into tiny squares (the only local version I've seen of this style is at Pizzeria Via Stato in River North). Danny Meyer tried creating a whole brand with this cracker-thin style, at a restaurant called Martina in New York City's East Village, but couldn't make it work; Martina closed in 2019.

One thing all Roman pizzas have in common is their propensity for crunchiness. Unlike their soft, supple brethren down the coast in Naples, the Roman ideal must always have, at the very least, a crunchy bottom.

BAR CARGO

605 N. Wells Street
312-929-0065
www.barcargo.com
@barcargochi

I FIRST ENCOUNTERED THE Stefani Restaurant Group in the '90s, at their bustling Tuscany on Taylor Street. One of the must-visit Italian restaurants at the end of the twentieth century, it was also a haven for Bulls pre-game dinners back in the Jordan era. But since those heady days, the company has expanded into Mexican (three Broken English Taco Pubs), bro bars, and Viagra Triangle crowd pleasers (Mad Social and Tavern on Rush, respectively), and operates a couple of concepts at Navy Pier, North Avenue Beach, and a few in the suburbs (Tuscany Wheeling, Stefani Prime in Lincolnwood). All of which is to say they are good at feeding the masses, rarely drilling down to focus on something that's truly unique or noteworthy, for fear of scaring off the roasted chicken and pear–stuffed ravioli crowds.

Perhaps it's the next generation that will turn the tide. Anthony Stefani, Phil and Karen Stefani's son, came back to the restaurant business in 2017 after a career with the Blackhawks and Breakthru Beverage (formerly Wirtz Beverage). He created Bar Cargo after having eaten around Rome, falling for the long (and long-fermented) pizzas served on wooden paddles the size of a boogie board. He grew up in the business, starting at the pasta shop at the original Stefani's on Fullerton, so he's no stranger to recipe development and customer service.

The pizzas at Bar Cargo are long (my small could easily feed three people with its twelve generous squares) but also fermented a long time—about four days. The dough is a blend of three flours, imported

from Italy on cargo ships (hence the name). Just like Bonci, they stretch and bake them in Italian Castelli Forni ovens, but unlike Bonci—which first bakes them in rectangular pans—they bake them directly on the stone hearth, resulting in a seriously crispy undercarriage producing a crunch that could wake a sleeping child in the next room. The extra-long fermentation allows for some impressive open crumb in the middle, creating a pizza that is deceptively light, despite its apparent heft upon first glance.

I had the Chicago-style—with crumbles of fennel sausage and thin rings of green and bell pepper, but since giardiniera is available as a $3 extra, adding some briny, spicy chilies and carrots to this excellent Roman ambassador was a no-brainer. Bring a few friends. This is pizza to share, and offers quite a bit more complexity and chew than your standard Chicago-thin bar pie.

BONCI

161 N. Sangamon Street
312-243-4016
www.bonciusa.com
@bonciusa

NOT MANY *PIZZAIOLOS* look like they could wrestle a crocodile. But Gabriele Bonci certainly looks the part. As wide as a linebacker, bald, and tattooed, he sports a short-sleeved chef's coat and speaks in rapid-fire Italian to his young cooks. They all race around the narrow West Loop kitchen, filling orders and answering questions from customers. I witnessed this scene only two days after the highly anticipated pizzeria opened. The Pizzarium, as it's known in Rome, has several locations. But now Bonci and his partners are on a mission to bring Roman *al taglio* to the masses.

Teaming up with a former P. F. Chang's executive, Bonci has been slowly expanding in the United States, but it's notable that they planted their first flag in the US in Chicago. Why Chicago?

"We wanted to get to an area where people were food savvy, where they understood food and were willing to try new things," said Rick Tasman, whose company—Bonci USA—has the rights to open more stores outside Italy. "We weren't trying to redefine what pizza is for Chicagoans, but we wanted people to try it. We liked the urban area and the good foot traffic," he said. "With the [Morgan Street Green Line] train stop and the young people here, it's the perfect location."

A second location in Wicker Park closed in 2020, but they have plans to add stores in the suburbs and another in the city; a shop in New Orleans has opened, while another is planned for Miami. The Roman style of pizza is something Chicagoans have only seen elsewhere. Maybe they were on vacation in Europe and tried it; perhaps they saw Anthony Bourdain feature Mr. Bonci on his TV show. There really is nothing even close to what Bonci does in Chicago, even if you count Pizza Metro in Wicker Park or Bar Cargo in River North. Bonci makes pizza *al taglio* (literally, "by the cut"), always baked and presented in sturdy rectangular trays, which also help evenly distribute heat.

Besides the shape, the other important point of difference is the crust's texture. It somehow maintains an impossibly crispy, light bottom crust—showcasing browned spots and uneven surfaces on the outside. That delicate undercarriage supports a fluffy, pockmarked interior, as light and airy as an artisan bread that's been left to ferment for days.

Calling it simply focaccia or Sicilian doesn't do it justice. Those pizzas have a density and sponginess that Bonci's pizzas manage to avoid. Tasman says the secret is Bonci's dough, which contains a blend of Italian "00" flour as well as whole-grain and minimally processed organic flour (as well as spelt). There are two separate fermentations of at least twenty-four hours each, which build structure and complexity. Baked in imported Italian handmade Castelli ovens with terra-cotta decks, the pizzas bake at 575 degrees. But due to the ovens' special construction, the heat is controlled on both the deck *and* the ceiling. Dough this delicate doesn't need a blast furnace; it needs to be coaxed to life.

Bonci really gets creative with his toppings. Using as many local sources as he can (for example, 'nduja from Tempesta Salumi, and cheese, olive oil, and cured meats from local suppliers), he thinks seasonally about what goes on top. If it's summer, you'll see thinly sliced zucchini with tiny blobs of fresh ricotta and black pepper; fall means pureed pumpkin; spring offers ramps and young garlic. They recently started making an "Italian Beef" flavor with the namesake, thinly shaved, plus homemade giardiniera.

You'll never see pepperoni, since that's an American invention. "Ask for pepperoni in Italy and you'll get green peppers," said Tasman. They're more likely to pair up fresh, peppery arugula or seasonal mushrooms with 'nduja—my favorite spreadable, spicy Calabrian sausage—often referred to as "pork butter."

The other aspect of the *al taglio* style of pizza is how it's ordered. You're paying by the pound, so simply tell your friendly counter worker how much you'd like by making a sign with your thumb and forefinger. They'll position their kitchen shears along the rectangular pizza, ask if that's sufficient, cut across the width of the tray, and then weigh it for you. This allows you to try several styles without committing to enormous slices. The slices are then reheated, cut into smaller, tapas-like squares, and served on paper-covered boards. The second bake ensures a hallmark of all Roman pies: they *must* be crispy. I was able to try four different flavors on my first visit, including the strangely addictive mozzarella and potato, and got out of there for $15. Bonci has more than a thousand flavors in his portfolio but will most likely rotate about fifty of them on the Chicago menu. I, for one, hope to try them all.

L'AVENTINO

355 E. Ohio Street
312-964-5112
www.laventino.com
@laventinochicago

THE INTERESTING THING about Roman-style pizzas is they come in several forms. There's *al metro*, by the yard; *al taglio*, which is cut with scissors to-order; a cracker-thin Roman tavern; and something called a *pinsa*, which is now available at exactly one place in the city, where they spend an inordinate amount of time on their dough, which is unlike anything in town.

Most of the menu at L'Aventino Forno Romano, located in a tiny corner of a Streeterville high-rise, revolves around this subcategory of Roman-style pizza.

"When you eat *pinsa*, you look at the crumb structure, it's really recognizable as a Roman thing—it's got big air pockets, lots of fermentation going on, it's light, airy and crispy," said Adam Weisell, the opening chef who lived in Rome, but who ended up parting ways with one of the most difficult landlords in the city (in less than five years, the space has been Flour & Stone, Robert's, Urban Crosta, Streeterville Pizzeria, and L'Aventino). By the time you're reading this, they may have given up on *pinsas*, but a manager there told me in early 2021 they were going to stick with them, while adding New York–style slices as well.

The dough has an all-natural starter, lots of moisture, and rests for at least two to three days. It's pliable to the point of creating finger-width craters when pressed with hands.

"This is a next-generation one, and what I mean by that is it also incorporates some non-GMO soy flour, as well as some rice flour. This lowers the gluten content and just aids in the digestibility," said Weisell.

They drizzle on olive oil, then par-bake the crusts for a few minutes and hold them on a wire cooling rack until orders come in. A basic Margherita begins with fresh tomato sauce, some shards of basil, and a generous handful of *fior di latte*, or fresh mozzarella. Just a little drizzle of oil and then into the oven for about three minutes, until the outside has formed a sturdy crust, while the interior portion of the heel has that nice, complex, open crumb structure.

The white pies are just as impressive. Cooked prosciutto is set over a bechamel-covered dough, which gets a shower of mozzarella and then grated potato. To finish, some fontina cheese, Parmigiano, and rosemary. The *pinsa* is light, with a soft interior and crisp edge.

"It's definitely for a certain type of person, someone who is looking for something beyond the red sauce," said Weisell, who was, at press time, working on opening his own place in Avondale.

PIZZA METRO

1707 W. Division Street
773-278-1753
www.pizzametro.com
@pizzametro70

Marco Schiavoni finishes every pie himself

GROWING UP IN ROME, Marco Schiavoni had a cousin who was a master baker there, and as a kid, he always helped him out any way he could. He also, coincidentally, had an uncle who owned a restaurant, so when he was sixteen, he was already working in the business. For Schiavoni, the only pizza he really knew growing up was Roman *al taglio* (by the cut—a style perfected by Bonci).

When Schiavoni opened his tiny shop in Chicago in 2001, he asked his cousin to come over and stay here for two months, just until he felt comfortable working with the dough and making his small pizzas. The idea at that point was to offer the cut-to-order pizza slices, just like back home, but he realized the neighborhood was quite different then (as in sort of rundown and shabby). Chicago was still more than fifteen years away from getting its first Bonci, and customers had a problem with the rectangular shape of the pies.

"People weren't open-minded," said Schiavoni. "Here they only saw one type of pizza, the giant wedge."

They decided that rather than cutting the large rectangles into smaller slices to order, they would simply bake a rectangular pie and pre-cut it into six equal-sized squares. Dough gets an overnight cold ferment and it's baked in sturdy blue steel pans in a convection gas oven.

Since the shop specializes in pies with toppings such as potato and rosemary, or simply anchovy, they certainly look and taste more like Roman pizzas than ones born in Chicago. Marco's favorite slice is actually the Marinara, a cheeseless pizza that's very Roman. (I've seen this flavor also available at Finestra, the Tuesday–Wednesday pop-up inside Superkhana International.)

There are a few seats at the counter and a few tables outside on the sidewalk. It took all of thirteen minutes to get my small, which was really the perfect size for one relatively hungry person. The crust is seriously thin, almost creeping into tavern-style territory, and the crumbled sausage, buried beneath a snowdrift of cheese, certainly had me coming back for extra slices. The pepperoni is standard stuff, but I liked how simple yet tasty this pizza was, especially how good the OBR of toppings-to-cheese-to-crust was. Metro is a great option if you're nearby at one of the bars or just shopping along Division Street and craving a snack. Pro tip: save room for one of Marco's incomparable hazelnut cookies. That cousin—the master baker—didn't just teach him how to make pizza.

PIZZERIA VIA STATO

620 N. State Street
312-642-8450
www.osteriaviastato.com/pizzeria
@osteriaviastato

Pizzeria via stato, next door to its sibling, Osteria Via Stato, is easy to miss as you walk down State Street on your way to a River North bar or club. But this little pizza joint that's been around since 2004 does quite a bit with a simple gas-fired oven. They bill their pizzas as "cracker-thin, Roman-style," which has to be one of the only Roman tavern-thins in town, considering most of the Roman appearances here are in the *al taglio* or *al metro* camps. But instead of cutting them into wedges, they make them a little bit more Chicago-style by employing a square cut. These tavern pizzas, as they're listed on the menu, have a serious chef behind them, who also creates the menu at the Osteria. Consider the stellar options with mushroom, sausage, and vegetables, as well as a couple of white pizzas and a pizza of the month. (The special pizza when I was there included cruciferous green rapini, goat cheese, homemade sausage, and caramelized onions. Sounds pretty good to me.)

Their pie size is a bit smaller, about ten inches, which is perfect for one hungry person or a great snack to share. Even though I had taste-tested a few slices from other places before arriving at Pizzeria Via Stato's, I almost polished off their entire Margherita. It was that good, with its juicy, naturally sweet San Marzano tomatoes, an ultra-thin, cracker-like, crispy crust that prevents you from getting too full, plus a generous garnish of torn basil and a drizzle of olive oil.

The edges have a wonderfully rough, misshapen border to them, with all kinds of air pockets scattered throughout. I even appreciated the ventilated tray that the pizza was served on, preventing the middle and undercarriage from getting soggy.

PR ITALIAN BISTRO

3908 N. Sheridan Road
773-404-8955
www.pritalianbistro.com
@pritalianbistro

Finding a hot dog joint, taqueria, or Thai restaurant near the intersection of Irving Park Road and Sheridan is surprisingly a lot easier than tracking down decent pizza. There's a hospital down the street and a bunch of single-family homes in the neighborhood, not to mention the Sheridan stop on the CTA Red Line, so I'm kind of surprised there aren't more pizzerias catering to the employees and residents nearby.

Pizza isn't even the main thing at PR Italian Bistro. They're listed way down on the menu, below soups, antipasti, salads, pasta (*primi*), and entrées (*secondi*). They offer just four reds and three whites, in either quarter-sheet size (for one), half-sheet (for two), or a full-sheet tray for a group.

Served on a wooden pizza peel, the pizza presents a beautifully crisp edge that continues underneath, resulting in extremely delicious small bites. The fennel-laced sausage is a pleasure to eat, roughly crumbled and buried beneath a perfectly respectable layer of mozzarella, which is nicely browned in splotches. On my second visit, the topping was a simple combination of fresh, peppery arugula and chopped tomatoes.

Not that I'm a sucker for sauce, but I think a few ounces would have improved this pie. Each bite is basically crispy dough (light, somewhat airy), melted cheese, and your topping, contributing to an OBR that every pizza joint should aspire to. I also like how pepperoni slices are placed on top of the pie, so the discs render some of their fat in the oven and remain crisp on top.

THE PIZZA PUFF

A CHICAGO ORIGINAL

The convenient snack known as the Pizza Puff may be known to millions of hungry football fans, convenience store shoppers, and itinerant snackers throughout the United States, but few people know this self-contained, personal-sized panzerotti was created in Chicago in the 1970s.

Having grown up in Minnesota, I'm familiar with Totino's Pizza Rolls, based on a Minneapolis pizzeria. Totino's actually owes its origins to Jeno's Pizza Rolls, created in 1951. These Matchbox car–sized frozen snacks changed their name to Totino's after the company was bought by Pillsbury in the 1980s. In 1993, Jeno's Pizza Rolls were rebranded Totino's.

But the Pizza Puff is an altogether different creation, invented by a Chicago family with roots in the Middle East. After arriving in America in 1898 at the age of fourteen, an Iranian Assyrian named Elisha Shabaz ended up settling in Chicago. He began working with a tamale guy, rolling them each morning and then selling them from a pushcart for a penny each. He went on to eventually buy the pushcarts, creating the Illinois Tamale Company in 1927. Ten years later, his only real local competitor, Tom Tom Tamale Company, opened for business on the South Side, selling a similar coarse cornmeal-based tamale stuffed with ground beef, rather than the shredded beef traditional in Mexico.

In 1964, Elisha's grandson, Warren, took over the management of the company, incorporating the business and condensing the name to Iltaco Foods Company (IL-Ta-Co). He helped move the headquarters to its current location in West Town in 1973. It's important to note that in the early 1970s, a number of important pizzerias were launching in the Chicago area—Lou Malnati's, Pequod's, My Pi, Nancy's, and Giordano's among them. Some were making deep-dish, others stuffed. It was the dawn of Chicago's second major pizza wave.

"They were delivering tamales to all of these hot dog stands. But pizza places were becoming more prominent," said Andrew Shabaz, Warren's son and the executive vice president of sales and marketing at Iltaco Foods. "The hot dog stands wanted to compete, so they asked my dad if they could make something similar." Warren had grown up in an Italian neighborhood in Chicago and loved calzones. All of their customers had deep fryers, so Iltaco could stuff an outer wrapping similar to a tortilla dough with local sausage, mozzarella, and tomato sauce, then let the restaurants fry them to order, resulting in a phyllo dough–like consistency. The Pizza Puff was born in 1976.

First there was sausage, then a "Deluxe" with peppers. Eventually a beef flavor, because "not everyone eats pork," said Shabaz. "Although as we've expanded to forty-two states, it's amazing how popular pepperoni is outside of Chicago. It's catching up to the original sausage in sales," he said.

Shabaz says when they developed the Pizza Puff, they wanted to make sure it could be baked as well as fried. But he admits the wrapping does get a little flakier when deep-fried. His employees are split down the middle on how they prefer cooking them.

Sold primarily to hot dog joints, snack shops, and grocery stores, at six ounces they're quite a bit larger than the typical one-ounce pizza roll. They're also assembled by hand rather than machine.

"All of them are hand-folded," said Shabaz. "Machines will never take that part over. There's a whole level of quality that goes into it. The filling is made from scratch in our kitchen every day."

While baking is acceptable, microwaving will render the outer layer—a flour tortilla-like wrapping—just too flaccid and lacking in textural contrast to the filling. Better yet, fry them in some vegetable oil at around 360 degrees in a cast-iron skillet. "Sales in convenience stores and restaurants are good," said Shabaz. "But I think the pandemic has increased awareness."

Over the years, they've expanded well beyond the original sausage and pepperoni, adding flavors like Four Cheese, Spinach & Cheese, Gyro, and Breakfast Sausage. More recently, Buffalo Chicken and Reuben have been added to the lineup to broaden their appeal, no doubt because in a category with brands like Hot Pockets, competition is fierce. A pepperoni Pizza Puff has 450 calories and twenty-four grams of fat, so while it's great stoner food or maybe an occasional after-school snack, the nutritional content is something to consider before making them a regular meal replacement.

Shabaz is the fourth generation now involved in running the business, and he says the fifth generation is already on deck. As iconic pizzerias like My Pi and Lou Malnati's gear up for their fiftieth anniversaries this year, remember there's a little tamale company that's still making Pizza Puffs, heading full-steam into its ninety-fourth year in business.

12 THIN

It took me all of twelve chapters to get here, and yet, the thin scene is as exciting as ever! Typically, in Chicago, "thin" means tavern-style, as we've already established. But the thins I'm talking about in this chapter walk a fine line between long-fermented artisan, sturdy, foldable NYC-style slices, and crispy, light Chicago-thin. They are typically fermented for a day, maybe two. They bake in gas, wood, and electric ovens. East Coast ex-pats can relate to their tight heels, easy to pick up and do a three-finger fold. Demerits for tip sag; bonus points for the stability to withstand a fold, hold their shape, and maintain an interior height of just a few millimeters.

I've got a full dozen entries here in this chapter, with new additions including Le Pizza, which is hidden away inside the Whiner Beer Company at The Plant on the South Side. If you miss the chewy, delicious Brooklyn-style pizzas at Roxy's in Bucktown (now Small Cheval on Milwaukee Avenue), then you'll dig Le Pizza, since it's the same guy in the kitchen. And I do mean one guy, as it's a solo job.

Crushed was a pleasant surprise near Lincoln Square. Former employees of the ORD space on Montrose Avenue (which I wasn't a fan of) took it over and ramped up their game. The pizzas are worth a detour.

I've also added a surprising addition, by way of Istanbul. Turkitch Turkish Kitchen is a next-generation fast-food concept, featuring Turkish street food presented in modern surroundings. The owner has modified the shape of his *pide*—a

Thin at Crushed

My off-season weekend tradition was watching NFL and college football games with some professional players and my Chicago friends. We would put two tables together at Yakzies on Clark. Our typical order: two large THIN CRUST pepperoni, mushrooms, and garlic, and one with just cheese. I also would walk across the street and bring a few home during the season. We probably finished about nine every Saturday and Sunday.

—**MARK GRACE**, former first baseman for the Chicago Cubs

traditional flatbread filled and topped with cheese and other toppings—and now offers both the narrow rectangles as well as the more familiar circular pies Americans will recognize. But it's his homemade dough, sheeted, stretched, and topped to order, then baked in a fancy Turkish convection oven in about seven minutes, that is truly impressive.

I also included a little place—Stunod's—in a neighborhood (Clearing) literally no one ever recommended for restaurants. Hidden in the shadow of Midway Airport, about a mile west of the southwesternmost runway, it sits near the border with Bedford Park and Summit. But right next door is a fantastic *pupuseria* I did a story on for ABC7, and there's another little Mexican joint next to that. Farther east along Sixty-Third Street, there are Polish delis and old man bars, but it's this sort of Land That Time Forgot, restaurant-wise, and the family running Stunod's has a long history of food service in the city. I wish them well.

Most of these places are going to be new to pizza fans, and I hope you get a chance to go give them a try. Get out of your usual pizza rut and go explore the city.

CRUSHED PIZZERIA

1607 W. Montrose Avenue
773-327-9200
www.crushedpizzeria.com
@crushedpizzeria

ONE OF THE BEST parts of researching (ahem, eating) my way around town for this second volume was encountering new places. In some cases, I had the chance to revisit establishments I had tried early on, but where, for whatever reason, I didn't have a good experience the first time (for example, the StopAlong)—and was happy to be proved wrong by their legion of fans. In other cases, as was the experience at Crushed, I was hesitant to visit, only because I thought the address—formerly held by the so-so ORD Pizzeria—would lead to more disappointment. I'm happy to report those demons have been exorcised.

Ronnie Khoshaba and Foruzan Namdari took over the old ORD after working there briefly, renaming it Crushed in the spring of 2019. They tweaked the former owner's recipe by subbing in Bacio cheese (supplemented by a kiss of buffalo milk), Stanislaus Alta Cucina tomatoes (my favorite), and a dough featuring unbleached organic King Arthur flour. The key is their fermentation time: a full four days in the cooler before baking. All of the pies are baked on a beautiful old Faulds rotating deck oven that's as old as Steve Stone, but the oven has steel decks rather than stone ones. I was surprised by the relative crispness on the undercarriage, considering they're not baked on stone, which, due to its porosity and ability to pull moisture, usually results in crispy bottoms. Perhaps in this case, it's a result of the longer fermentation? Regardless, it's still certainly a well-made pie you'll have no problem, er, crushing.

It's a thin crust (available in twelve- or sixteen-inch) with some heft—the sides are a good inch higher than most thin pies around town, but maintain a beautiful, golden-colored crust. The interiors remain thin, albeit cheesy, and slices will still allow for proper folding when removed from the pie. Big bonus points for serving their pizzas on metal screens, allowing for airflow and the proper maintenance of a crispy undercarriage while you eat and imbibe one of their craft or classic soda flavors.

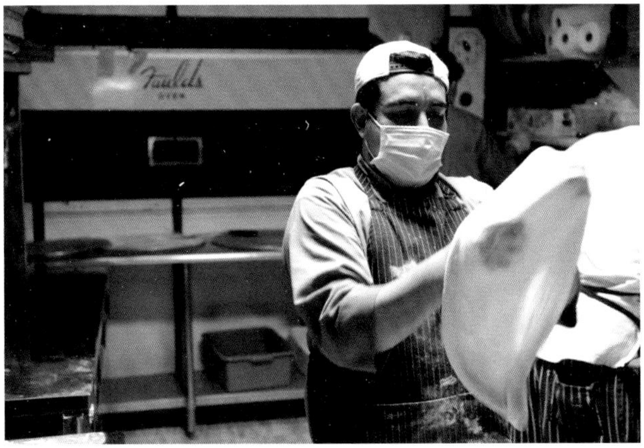

LE PIZZA AT WHINER BEER CO.

1400 W. Forty-Sixth Street
www.whinerbeer.com/book-experience
@lepizzagram

Thursdays through Sundays (recommended to make reservations via Tock)

FANS OF THE LATE, lamented Roxy's—which occupied a sliver of a space in Bucktown, before eventually being converted to the first Small Cheval—remember Chad Anderson's oversized, Brooklyn-inspired pies with lots of char and chew. Anderson disappeared for a time, but thankfully, the team at the Whiner Beer Co. asked him to come on board to help inject some new life into their moribund pizza program.

Located in The Plant, a gigantic food company incubator in the Back of the Yards neighborhood on the South Side, Anderson works under the "Le Pizza" moniker inside Whiner's tasting room.

"I'm doing kind of a classic take on a New York–style slice but using sourdough. It's nice and crunchy," Anderson said.

His "Bee Sting" has lovely pepperoni with thick handfuls of fresh mozzarella, baked for just five minutes on a stone deck, then post-baked with a drizzle of hot honey. It's a cheesy, crunchy, chewy pleasure, all the way through the slice. As you lift a slice, folding it on the heel, there is very little tip sag—indicating a dough with remarkable structure, even though it's as thin as a CD sleeve.

"The goal is, I always see people throwing away their crust at the end and I wanted to make a pizza that you actually ate the crust," said Anderson.

Anderson also makes cast-iron pan pizzas, but only offers them on Friday and Saturday, and even then, only two are available each night, since he only has two pans, so if you're interested, be sure to call ahead or send him a note on Insta.

PICCOLO SOGNO

464 N. Halsted Street
312-421-0077
www.piccolosognorestaurant.com
@piccolosognorestaurant

TONY PRIOLO's Piccolo Sogno (Italian for "little dream") has always been one of my favorites for Italian in the city, since everything—including the breadsticks—is made in-house. At lunchtime, expect to see plenty of suits and shiny cuff links while Loop office workers travel a few blocks west for handmade pastas. (There's also a convenient parking lot.) The crystal chandeliers and white tablecloths, along with exposed brick and deep-blue walls, make this a slightly more elegant option for pizza eating, but no less comfortable. The expansive, lush patio provides a perfect respite on a warm, breezy day (and COVID compliant!).

TODD ROSENBERG

With the house olive oil bottle standing sentinel, my pizza arrives, and it is majestic, hiding a few well-placed basil leaves and lots of *fior di latte* mozzarella, which is combined with a buffalo milk starter. Priolo uses a little bit of the previous day's dough to add complexity and lift to the finished crust. Once the dough is made, it rests overnight.

The ultra-thin center and relatively even heel indicates this is not a traditional Neapolitan pie. Also, the middle isn't as wet as a Neapolitan. That's just fine with me. As I pick up a slice, it holds its shape, despite the generous application of San Marzano–based sauce. Clearly, the dough gets a little oven spring as it bakes, revealed in the tiny air pockets spread throughout the heel.

I thought the undercarriage could have used some more charring, but that's a minor quibble. This is an "Italian-style" pizza, as Priolo calls it, and it does its country of origin proud.

PISOLINO ITALIAN MARKET

2755 W. Belmont Street
773-293-6025
www.pisolinochicago.com
@pisolinoitalianmarket

Located in a former barbecue joint, Pisolino sits, almost hidden, near the busy intersection of Elston, California, and Belmont, and the free parking on the side of the building is a big plus. James and Rachel De Marte had to do something once the pandemic hit, as they realized they wouldn't be able to accommodate dine-in guests anymore. Switching to a full-time market, they still offer Italian subs for lunch, catering, and made-to-order pizzas (either hot from the oven or take and bake later). But now, thanks to Rachel's eye for design, they've turned the entire dining room into a showcase for imported Italian ingredients and a staging area for assembling elaborate gift boxes.

They avoid the cliché-driven Italian American entrées and stick to the basics: antipasto, pasta, pizza, and panini. The cozy bar still holds a massive Simonelli espresso machine, but now the bar is filled with to-go orders ready to be picked up. You'll find everything you need for a make-at-home dinner here, from steaks and sausages to pasta and prepared meals like lasagna and chicken vesuvio. Desserts are homemade, and their small batch wine collection (thanks to James's industry connections to niche importers) is impressive.

There are a dozen pizzas on the menu, including some really creative ones, such as a homemade fennel sausage with castelvetrano olives, black truffle puree, and stracciatella cheese. I may have to go back to try the whipped ricotta with roasted garlic, mozzarella, and pepperoncino. Either way, I'm definitely going back. Here's why.

The dough gets an overnight rest and two separate periods to rise, or proof. That's part of the reason the crust has so much integrity—but the dough recipe itself is

another reason. Even after the pies bake, they maintain their wonderful structure, despite the relatively heavy toppings of San Marzano tomato sauce and cheese.

On the Margherita, enormous pools of *fior di latte* rest among the gargantuan basil leaves, and when you remove a wedge from the pie it doesn't budge. There are extremely small air pockets lining the lip, along with some mild charring, but the use of a dough docker helps to punch out air pockets in the middle, keeping the center über-thin. Underneath, the bottom has a few interesting craters with random charring and brown spots. They brush the perimeter of each pizza with a little bit of herb oil just before baking, which results in a barely greenish hue at the farthest edges (no, it's not pesto). Just before serving, they sprinkle a bit of Parmigiano-Reggiano over the top—as they do on all their pizzas—adding a subtle note of umami.

This pizza doesn't need chili flakes or oregano or anything shaken from a cheese container to enhance it. The kitchen does all the heavy lifting. Why would you mess with it?

PIZZA ART CAFÉ

4658 N. Rockwell Street
773-539-0645
www.pizzaartcafe.com
@pizzaartcafe

THIS QUAINT NEIGHBORHOOD café, on the border of Ravenswood and Lincoln Square, sits directly next to the Rockwell CTA Brown Line stop, at a point in the city where the train rides along at street level so that, during rush hour, the security gates are constantly rising and falling.

Once you step inside Pizza Art Café, take notice of the handmade pizza oven just to your left and behind the bar. It's wood-fired, of course, and the insulated bricks bring the internal temperature up to around 800 degrees. This would, at first glance then, indicate they are making Neapolitan pizzas, but that's not so much the mantra as it is an inspiration. The pizza menu lists thirteen vegetarian options, seventeen with meat (they're particularly proud of their house-smoked meat), and another five with seafood.

The Margherita, which takes about four minutes to reach your table, arrives with a slightly puffy edge and a respectable amount of leopard spotting. It has a nice, easy chew and a fair number of tiny air pockets within, indicating some fermentation. The top of the pie is dominated by fresh mozzarella—not a bad thing, but also not very Neapolitan. Rather than the balanced splotches I was expecting, this pie has a little too much cheese for my taste, but cheese lovers will appreciate the kitchen's generous hand. You can always ask them to back off, I guess. You know me, all about the Optimal Bite Ratio. Oregano flecks and a half-dozen or so enormous basil leaves cover the pizza, making it a pleasure to eat—even though the tomato sauce might be a tad too thick for some.

Since the owner and pizza maker is from Serbia, he also offers smoked meat as a possible topping (just no cevapcici). If you live in the neighborhood, it's a fantastic option, although like all wood-fired pies, it does not travel well, so try to eat it within minutes after it emerges from the oven.

PIZZA LOBO

3000 W. Fullerton Avenue
312-265-1745
www.pizzalobo.com
@pizzalobo_

ONE OF THE prouder byproducts of a pandemic, with its forced shutdowns and chef shuffles around the city, is pizza. Oriole's Noah Sandoval shifted to make Sicilian slices at Pizza Friendly Pizza; Dean Zanella (Tripoli Tap) and Kevin Hickey (The Duck Inn) are launching thin doughs into their wood-fired ovens on the back patio. For Dan Snowden—a veteran of One Off Hospitality and the executive chef of the short-lived (and dearly missed) Bad Hunter—his response has been to make glorious thin pizzas with artisan-inspired toppings at Pizza Lobo, on the corner of Fullerton and Sacramento.

"I would definitely call it a New York–style, New York-inspired," said Snowden. "It's a three-day ferment on a 70 percent hydration dough."

There are three sauce options for the sixteen-inch pies, including one with a pinkish vodka sauce that reminded me of Rubirosa in New York City. This pie, however, is then topped with slices of provolone and dollops of Tempesta Salumi's 'nduja, the spicy, spreadable Calabrian sausage that has the entire city's pizza corps in rapture. After only six or seven minutes, Snowden applies dollops of fresh ricotta and parsley leaves. The pizzas here are baked directly on the stone deck of the seemingly ubiquitous Pizza-Master electric oven, which allows cooks to control the heat intensity on both the deck and the ceiling. They emerge properly blistered but firm; easily foldable. Snowden's experience in the kitchen is apparent with his judicious use of ingredients—every slice has that Optimal Bite Ratio (OBR).

They also have a pickup window on the Sacramento side of the building which would be perfect for picking up a slice, but, as of this writing, they're still only selling whole pies. Imagine, if this were NYC, they'd be firing off slices all day (and night) long. Paulie Gee's around the corner is allegedly going to offer their NYC-style slices late night on weekends only.

"I love the super-thin but super-crispy crust; but also a nice, big, bubbly, chewy crust with nice char on it as well," said Snowden. Couldn't agree with him more.

PIZZERIA PORTOFINO

317 N. Clark Street
312-900-9018
www.pizzeriaportofino.com
@pizzeria.portofino

DEERFIELD NATIVE Sam Dickstein grew up on the thin, crispy, crimped-edge pies at Barnaby's on the North Shore. Little did he realize he'd be elbow-deep in thin pizzas all day, every day in the summertime, running the kitchen at Pizzeria Portofino on the Chicago River downtown.

"We'll go twelve hours straight, making six hundred pizzas on a busy day," he said.

The thin pies are inspired, perhaps, by the postcard views of Portofino. Looking at their website made me want to book a flight on Alitalia or at least watch a Marcello Mastroianni film. Dickstein is just trying to keep his thin pies simple, while sourcing top-notch ingredients like Ezzo cup-and-char pepperoni, Grande cheese, and Mama Lil's sweet hot pickled peppers.

His dough is a blend of King Arthur Sir Galahad and rye flour, bulk fermented overnight, then balled and shaped. It works really well with a sauce containing not just the expected fresh garlic, bright Italian tomatoes, and sugar (to balance the acidity), but also fresh Calabrian oregano and chili flakes. Baked in his electric Pizza-Master oven at 600 degrees for about three to four and a half minutes, the pies emerge evenly charred, slightly crisp, and not too filling, in case you're going to be doing some power shopping (or power drinking) in River North later in the day.

You can see why they get slammed in warm weather: the patio has a commanding view of the glass-and-steel skyscrapers across the river along Wacker Drive, as well as the busy boat traffic in the foreground. Sipping a Negroni with the sun on your face, eating a thin Pugliese-inspired pie with sharp broccoli rabe, fennel-flecked ground sausage, and chili flakes, while listening to Wilco a block from Marina City, you're in the midst of your own Chicago film. It may not be Fellini, but it's worth the wait.

QUARTINO

626 N. State Street
312-698-5000
www.quartinochicago.com
@quartinochicago

WITH A VETERAN like John Coletta manning the kitchen, you know that this Italian restaurant in River North isn't just going to serve average pizza. He's going to take it to the ultimate level, using as many homemade ingredients as he can. The author of *Risotto & Beyond* takes the provenance of his ingredients as seriously as Mayor Lightfoot does producing her "stay at home" memes.

The restaurant is lively at night, with purposefully dim lighting and TVs showing old black-and-white Italian films. Subway tiles and wooden floors lend an air of urban rusticity, as if you're dining in a curated West Village bistro that had the budget for an interior designer.

Surprisingly, there isn't a wood-burning oven here. It's a gas-fired, man-made, stone hearth from Italy that gets up to 700 degrees. That said, the guy still manages to churn out some impressive pies. There's an entire side of the menu dedicated to Neapolitan pizza (though it doesn't adhere to the strict AVPN bylaws regarding oven or baking temp), ranging in price from $10 for a simple bianca with no tomato sauce, or marinara with no cheese, all the way up to $16 for elaborate pizzas featuring homemade duck prosciutto and wild arugula or smoked provolone with spinach, speck, and Grana Padano cheese.

My Margherita arrived with the largest basil leaves I'd ever seen (no small feat in the middle of winter). Beneath the leaves, homemade *fior di latte* is almost completely incorporated into the San Marzano tomato sauce, and there is cheese complexity, thanks to a shower of Parmesan, I'm sure. A very small *cornicione* indicates a shorter resting time for the dough, yet there are ample air pockets and a very good chew. The edge stays crispy, and each slice is a pleasure.

I visited after a long day of trying other pizzas, but somehow managed to fit in a taste of the smoked provolone pizza as well as a unique version with homemade

ricotta, roasted cherry tomatoes, and a rich, melted-cheese fonduta instead of tomato sauce. Too full from the antipasti? Who do you think I am? Now go get me a Negroni and don't let your pizza get cold.

STIX 'N BRIX WOOD FIRED PIZZA

220 W. Thirty-Third Street
312-265-0219
www.stixnbrix33.com
@stixnbrixwoodfired

IN THE SHADOW OF Guaranteed Rate Field, the Scalise family is now into pizza. Known in Bridgeport as the original family behind the well-loved Italian deli Gio's, they converted one of their buildings directly across the street from Armour Square Park into two businesses: one serving as an all-day café, the other, a wood-fired pizza operation that is not trying to be just another Neapolitan joint.

The dough is made each day in bulk, cut into portions and weighed, then formed into balls and left to proof overnight before baking. The process is familiar to most any Neapolitan pizza maker, but at Stix 'n Brix Wood Fired Pizza, Neapolitan-style was only an inspiration, not a requirement.

"On the South Side, it's pretty bare, not many options; there's obviously several on the North Side, some in the West Loop. We had this empty building, it's been in the family for many years, we're just kind of brainstorming, what could be there?" said Mario Scalise, the owner. "Our goal wasn't

necessarily to come up with the best Neapolitan pizza, it was to come up with the best wood-fired pizza."

So while they use "00" flour, they don't use San Marzano tomatoes, and rather than some other name brand *fior di latte*, they prefer Galbani mozzarella. A Margherita is the baseline, but you can get more creative from there—add thin slices of prosciutto or maybe make the base from pesto, adding shards of Parmesan and then topping with roasted tomatoes before taking it to the oven. And here's the biggest point of difference: rather than bake the pies in ninety seconds with a 900-degree oven, they take a bit longer, since the oven temp is intentionally kept a little lower. That results in a crust with more even baking, like bread, but still results in some slight open crumb on the heel and—most important for folks who aren't fans of sloppy, wet Neapolitan pies—an undercarriage that's charred and evenly browned, with a middle retaining some integrity and little, if any, tip sag.

"A nice, crunchy outside, not burnt, just slightly nicely cooked outside, and then a chewy middle. Then the middle won't flop, it'll be a nice, steady pizza," Scalise said.

STUNOD'S PIZZERIA & BUDDY'S ITALIAN ICE

6535 W. Sixty-Third Street
773-586-7373
stunodspizza.com
@stunodspizzeria

Growing up on the South Side, the Battaglia brothers were always surrounded by homemade Italian food. "Every Friday, we had a competition between the men and the ladies," said Frank. "Austin and I would use our great grandmother's recipe from Sicily [for a sheet pan pizza]; our mom and sisters would try to beat us to see who could make the best pizza. Mom eventually started rolling hers out into circles."

The brothers—just two years apart—had always wanted to be entrepreneurs. In 2017, they started making Italian ice and selling it at summer festivals. The next year, at the ages of twenty and twenty-two, they fell in love with the food industry after taking restaurant management classes, but were too impatient to wait for graduation, so they dropped out of college.

"We wanted to keep our Chicago roots," said Frank. "We grew up on Phil's in Bridgeport and Oak Lawn, but we liked the crust our mom made, hand-rolling to keep some air inside."

For Battaglia, that meant ditching a traditional dough sheeter, which would compress the dough too much and knock all of the air out of it.

As they searched the city for a space—looking in Wrigleyville, Lakeview, and Pilsen—the old D'anardo's space suddenly became available. Knowing they'd have to renovate the entire '80s-era kitchen, the location—just a mile or so west of Midway Airport in the Clearing neighborhood—allowed them to save a bundle on rent. "It just fell into our lap," said Battaglia.

The name of the business is Sicilian slang for "knucklehead," as in "don't bruise the fresh basil, you stunod!" Once they decided on Sixty-Third Street, in a block tucked among tidy brick bungalows, next to a fantastic El Salvadorean *pupuseria*, they realized they needed to differentiate themselves.

"We didn't want cracker-thin like everyone else," Frank said.

"But they have high standards around here."

The easy part would be relying on their cousins at Battaglia Foods for things like ground sausage with fennel, ground, peeled tomatoes, and low-moisture mozzarella. But it's the dough that sets them apart from the neighborhood's other stalwarts. They let it rise at least two days. It contains a little olive oil and sugar, and the hand-rolling keeps some air intact, resulting in a slightly raised middle and some tiny pockets of air in the crumb, after baking directly on the stone deck of their Bakers Pride oven. For this reason, even though they cut their pizzas into squares, I'm classifying them as a thin pizza, rather than a crackery "Chicago-style thin."

Battaglia says there is truth to the rumor that South Siders like their sauce sweeter. "Lou's [Malnati's] has a harder time down here. They [locals] like a thin, sweeter sauce like Obbie's or Palermo's," he said. While they don't add any sugar themselves, he attributes the brighter flavor of their sauce to fresh, ripe tomatoes with a natural sweetness.

"We were nervous the neighborhood wouldn't like it, but they've really welcomed us," he said.

TRIPOLI TAP

1147 W. Armitage Avenue
773-477-4400
www.tripolitap.com
@tripolitap

FOR SPORTS FANS from other cities, Chicago can be a lonely place. It takes research and some digging to find a Packers- or Vikings-friendly tavern where they always have the games on; a place where you can proudly wear that Favre jersey without getting heckled. I've even found the one lonely pub in the entire city dedicated to my son's (and now mine) favorite Premier League football club, Tottenham Hotspur (the Atlantic, on North Lincoln Avenue, by the way). But for Pats, Celtics, and #redsoxnation fans, the city has generally been a non-starter. Until the Tripoli Tap came along.

My friend Vince—a guy who knows the final score to every playoff and championship game ever played by a New England sports team, and probably memorized *Good Will Hunting*—spends as much time at Tripoli as a stoner in a dispensary. But you can't just drink Sam Adams all day long. Yelling at the TV, dropping your *r*'s, also makes you hungry. That's where Dean Zanella comes in. A veteran of Chicago Cut, Rhapsody, and 312 Chicago restaurants, he oversees the minuscule kitchen, which contains a pair of electric, stone-deck ovens.

Over the summer, he borrowed a wood-burning oven from his friend at Pizzeria Deville in Libertyville and was firing pizzas on the back patio. But with winter approaching, that wasn't feasible any longer. The 700-degree decks do just as good a job, in fact, sometimes a little better than the wood-burning ovens, since they have a faster recovery time. When you launch a pizza onto a stone hearth in a wood-burning oven, it drops the temperature of the hearth's surface, but in an electric oven, the temperature recovers more quickly, allowing you to cook more pizzas in less time. Zanella's pies take about six minutes. They emerge thin and crispy, although they are not cut into Midwestern squares. This is a pie with an East Coast accent.

Zanella still picks up his dough from Deville a few times each week, letting it ferment a full three days before baking, adding a little extra flavor to his blistered pies.

"We're using Italian tomatoes because I think they have a better bite," said Zanella. "California tomatoes tend to be a little sweeter." He adds fresh marjoram to his sauce as well. From his lineup of a half-dozen pies, the most popular is the soppressata, which gets a final drizzle of Mike's Hot Honey just before serving. They also make their own sausage in-house, for the occasional Pats fan who wants to actually eat like a local.

TURKITCH TURKISH KITCHEN

565 W. Diversey Parkway
773-453-3323
www.turkitch.us
@turkitch

Breakfast is one of the most important meals in Turkish culture, and you can certainly find it at Turkitch Turkish Kitchen. But this is not your usual mom-and-pop DIY storefront with a few rugs hung on the walls and a stash of hookahs near the front door. It's Turkish 2.0, with a strong nod to the idea of scalability. The clean lines, digital signage, and pristine interior give it the feel of a Chipotle, albeit one with roots in Istanbul, not Colorado. You can imagine seeing branches all over the US someday. Be sure to peruse the refrigerated and frozen case back near the coffee station to pick up some *gözleme*, *borek*, or *manti* for dinner later.

"We're trying to serve authentic Turkish street foods in the United States," said owner Ozkan Yilmaz.

And dough plays a significant role here. *Simit*—the ubiquitous, circular, sesame-covered bread—is eaten throughout Turkey, and here, they get the dough shipped in and then bake them off. But they also get creative, using them for sandwiches, housing cheese and *sujuk*—a Turkish dried beef sausage. Those traditional Turkish flavors—kebabs, sumac, ground beef skewers—also show up on the surfboard-shaped *pides*. Yilmaz wisely markets them on his LCD screens as flatbread pizzas. They're finished with a shower of fresh flat-leaf parsley, chopped tomatoes, and some lemon wedges (similar to that other famous Turkish flatbread, *lahmacun*). He also makes some traditional round pizzas, called *trabzon*, cut into squares either for easy eating or perhaps as an homage to his adopted city.

Since Turkey is a Muslim country, pork is forbidden. But you won't miss it, as their turkey sausage, chicken, and *sujuk* fit the bill nicely. In fact, *sujuk* bears a strong resemblance to pepperoni, albeit a few shades darker.

Yilmaz sheets his dough to order, topping the pizzas, then crimping the edges like a *pide* maker might in Ankara, baking them for just a few minutes in an imported Rokon rotary convection oven. The crust is delicate and airy, barely crisp, and just sturdy enough to hold the mozzarella and other toppings. Turkitch is one of the few places where they encourage having an egg baked on top of your pie, and it's definitely the only place in town where you can have a bracing Turkish coffee after your meal.

"We brought the Turkish coffee machine and Turkish tea machine from Turkey. All of our teas come from Turkey too," said Yilmaz.

13 NYC AND BY-THE-SLICE

LET'S FACE IT: CHICAGO IS NOT A SLICE KINDA TOWN. Over the course of a day, we never really have the opportunity to walk by a window on the street, point to a slice, have it reheated in a gas or electric oven for two to three minutes, and be on our way. Pizza eating in Chicago is about making an appointment. Pizza eating in New York City is about a spur-of-the-moment decision to abate hunger before making your way to the train. In Chicago, we soak up alcohol with tacos, tamales, and sub-par slices. In New York City, the possibility of a transcendent slice is almost always right around the corner.

What is a "New York slice"?

According to my friend and colleague Arthur Bovino (@nycbestpizza and www.thepizzacowboy.com), New York–style pizza is

> *a style of pizza that originated from Italian-American immigrants in New York City. New York–style pizza is thought to have first been born in coal-fired brick ovens with fresh mozzarella. Subcategories of New York pizza like Neapolitan-American, $1 slice, VPN Neapolitan and Neo-Neapolitan can feature extreme differences in style, but generally, the characteristics of New York–style pizza include a pie about a foot-and-a-half wide divided into eight slices with a thin, pliant crust that bends or cracks when folded but never breaks and that*

NYC-style slices at Jimmy's

is layered with a thin layer of shredded, low-moisture mozzarella and thin, mildly seasoned tomato sauce that completely covers each slice out to the crust, a raised, slightly browned, crunchy end about a half-inch thick.

Arthur eats more pizza in a given year than I do giardiniera. That's saying a lot. The guy sweats San Marzanos and dreams of *bufala* mozz. Would I have a hard time showing him around Chicago? I'd say it's getting easier to find NYC-worthy slices every year. The pandemic absolutely kick-started the movement. A new Paulie Gee's Wicker Park opened in 2021 in the old Bonci space. They'll be NYC-style slice HQ after bar time. A few blocks south, Craft is offering slices during the week, for commuters. All of the new Sicilian joints offer their rectangles and squares as slices to go, so take that, Williamsburg. We even have the previously unseen deep-dish slice, served in a circular personal pan, so you can eat lunch and get back to work without needing a nap.

Several of the slice options here are second mentions (Pizza Fried Chicken Ice Cream, Foxhole, etc.). That is, the pizza places are listed elsewhere in the book, but because they specifically offer noteworthy slices in addition to full pies, I felt they deserved to be included in this one-stop shop for slice hounds. Other mentions in this chapter might include a place like the StopAlong, which isn't necessarily a slice joint, but if you're longing for the New York–style pizza you had in college, or foraged from that place in the West Village, their pizza will bring back memories for sure.

We're never going to have the density and demand here to support an army of slice shops. That's just a fact. But if you're walking near a CTA train stop, or heading back after a show at the Green Mill or Thalia Hall, you've got some dynamite, dare I say legit slices to practice your three-finger fold on.

Slice options await at Dough Bros.

One of our Pizza City USA tour participants demonstrates how to fold a slice at Dante's

BEATRIX MARKET

23 E. Jackson Blvd.
312-583-0598
www.beatrixrestaurants.com
/beatrix-market/depaul-loop/
@beatrixmarket
Style: Deep-dish

WITH THREE restaurant locations in Chicago and one in Oak Brook, Beatrix is becoming its own brand, despite being a part of the Lettuce Entertain You Enterprises family. Executive partner and divisional president Marc Jacobs has worked with Lettuce for many years, launching several brands in the city and suburbs. While Aba might be their most popular (they've already opened a branch in Austin, Texas), Beatrix also has its devotees—they plan to open a location in Disney Springs.

There are four Beatrix Markets as well. These are extensions of a sort, from when Jacobs ran Foodease inside Water Tower Place. They're bright, clean, grab-and-go markets with extensive salad bars and tempting sweet stations usually tucked into high foot traffic areas with a mix of office workers, students, and tourists. But within that portfolio, only the Loop

COURTESY BEATRIX MARKET

location within DePaul's downtown campus offers individual deep-dish pizzas served in Lilliputian seven-inch pans. It's not large enough to share, but it's certainly the equivalent of an XL slice, which is why I decided to include it in this slice chapter as opposed to the deep-dish one.

"We wanted to create a deep-dish, but with a lighter touch to it," said chef-partner John Chiakulas. "A little lighter crust with less olive oil—flakier and less dense."

Indeed, the thought of tearing into a whole pie at lunchtime is a non-starter for solo diners (unless your job involves taking naps in the afternoon), and no one in town offers deep slices for quick consumption. But Chiakulas's creation solves for both problems. All of the hallmark flavors are still there: the whole milk mozzarella slices on the base; the chunky, reduced Stanislaus Alta Cucina tomatoes, with a whiff of garlic, salt, and sugar; the final sprinkle of grated Parmesan, chili flakes, and oregano just before baking. Only in this scenario, you're experiencing a full circumference of crispy-edged pizza, rather than a single slice with a limited heel, which may or may not have held its shape after being reheated.

The positively adorable pans (I could see them used for a children's make-believe deep-dish pizzeria sold by Fisher-Price) bake twice on a conveyor belt oven. The first time is for seven minutes, forty seconds, and then held until orders come in. The second bake takes just two and a half minutes—ideal for a busy lunch rush pickup. A knife and fork are acceptable, but since the entire perimeter of this personal pizza is crisp and firm, there's no shame in using your hands. A circular slice, you say? Only in Chicago.

BOB'S PIZZA

838 W. Kinzie (inside Recess Bar)
www.famousbobspizza.com
@eatbobspizza

There are Bob's locations in Pilsen, Old Town, and Evanston, but the only location selling slices is the sprawling Recess Bar space, tucked into a warren of stacked shipping containers in the West Loop. This makes for a great late-night impulse buy if you're walking back from one of the dozens of bars in the neighborhood.

Bob's Pizza isn't New York–style, or Chicago-style, or any definitive style, for that matter (as discussed in chapter 10). The owner decided to go in a completely different direction when he launched his pizza joint in 2019. That means subbing beer for water in what he casually calls his "Pilsen style" pizza.

Besides beer, they also use "00" flour plus some garlic powder, salt, and oil. It's not a standard thin-crust dough by the usual standards.

"What is unique about it is how the beer plays with the yeast, or how the yeast is affected by the beer, and vice versa," Wilde said. "Because it's got all that carbonation, so it does almost the same thing as the yeast does."

Wilde also gets creative with his cheese blend. It's more than just mozzarella.

"I love Swiss cheese, so I added Swiss cheese to my blend, which is really unique. In the end, we do cut it with a little bit of Parmesan as well, just to add some sharpness," he said.

After it's baked, he adds fresh herbs, cracked pepper, and sea salt, and some pickled onions.

Slices are only available from the back window at Recess Bar in the West Loop, on the Peoria Street side of the building (the window is cut into a storage container).

BOILER ROOM

2210 N. California Avenue
773-276-5625
boilerroomlogansquare.com
@boilerroomchicago

FROM THE FINE FOLKS who brought you Simone's in Pilsen, the Boiler Room—nearly hidden beneath the California Avenue Blue Line CTA stop—delivers a recycled DIY aesthetic, complete with old *Twilight Zone* episodes on a screen behind the bar. But their pizza puts this program front and center. Take a quick look to your left as you enter. You'll see the pizza guys hand-tossing their dough, then launching the enormous discs into a rarely seen multi-deck oven that spins like a turntable. They also stockpile several pies at a time, all of which will eventually be sold by the slice to a late-night crowd wandering over from one of the several bars along nearby Milwaukee Avenue.

I visited the Boiler Room with a friend, so we weren't interested in slices and opted for my usual order when assessing a Chicago pizza: a half-sausage, half-pepperoni whole pie. There are plenty of other wacka-doodle options here, including Thai cream-cheese sauce, curry, serranos, and beet bruschetta. They offer a vegan slice every day and also have a Thursday vegetarian special . . . but for this stop, we stuck to the half-and-half rule.

My friend and I let out an audible gasp when our server placed a comically large, twenty-inch pizza in front of us. Even if we hadn't been planning to try other pizzas on this day, there would have been plenty to bring home. Aside from its scene-stealing size, the pizza is a beauty. On the pepperoni side, wide circles cover every possible bit of real estate, looking like a map from Dubai's urban planning department. On the other side, crumbled, beautifully seasoned sausage complements the melted cheese. Beneath it all, a delicate, cornmeal-flecked dough maintains a crispy edge. This is OBR at its finest among the thin-crust cool kids. If you close your eyes while listening to the traffic outside, as you raise the giant slice to your mouth, folding it with three fingers along the crusty heel, you'll be transported—ever so briefly—to the Lower East Side (minus the endless garbage bags out front on the sidewalk).

Fun fact: PB & J Special is offered all day, every day: a slice of thin crust, a PBR tall boy, and a shot of Jameson for $10.

They've also added a personal, ten-inch pan pizza that I haven't tried, but it sure looked good coming out of the kitchen.

BONCI

161 N. Sangamon Street
312-243-4016
www.bonciusa.com
@bonciusa

When stopping into a traditional slice shop, you expect to see squares and rectangles or triangles sitting behind a sneeze guard, assembled on large baking sheets. You point to one, the cook pops it into an oven (usually gas or electric, with a stone deck) and two to three minutes later you're eating a hot slice. Bonci is anything but traditional.

First, there's its shape. Baked in large, rectangular trays, the customer must decide how much of the flavor in question they'd like. A helpful cook will guide their scissors up along the sides of the pan, indicating the thickness. Sometimes they'll just hold up their fingers and make a guestimate, based on the customer's interest level. Then they'll cut a strip of pizza and weigh it, which determines the price. At this point, any cold toppings are removed and the base of the pizza is baked a second time in a smaller oven to ensure the bottom gets crispy. The cold toppings are replaced and the strip of pizza is then cut into small squares, about three inches wide. Think of it as pizza tapas, a perfect snack to have with a beer while standing against the glass window or sitting outside on their porch.

Toppings go well beyond pepperoni or sausage. 'Nduja from Tempesta Salumi is a highlight, as are cheese, olive oil, and cured meats from local suppliers. Personally, I'm a big fan of the thinly sliced zucchini with tiny blobs of fresh ricotta and black pepper.

One of the hallmarks of Roman pizza is the crispy undercarriage. Roman pizzas, unlike their Neapolitan cousins, must be crispy. The pockmarked bottoms, with their light, focaccia-like interiors, offer a delicious contrast in textures.

Bonci has more than a thousand flavors in their portfolio but will most likely rotate about fifty of them on the Chicago menu.

CRAFT PIZZA

1252 N. Damen Avenue
773-442-7238
www.craftpizzachicago.com
@craftpizzachicago

Everything at Craft Pizza screams "farm-to-table," and they attempt to highlight the quality of their ingredients—that their sausage is made by Anichini Brothers or that they bring in Mama Lil's hot pickled peppers from Portland and Ezzo cup-and-char pepperoni from Columbus, Ohio. John Ortega, a longtime employee, has taken over the shop as a partner now, and he's usually working the ovens, so it's reassuring knowing one of the owners is always on hand, keeping an eye on every pie that comes out of the gas-fired oven. The dining room is cozy; facing the open kitchen, you can see every pie being made. Floor-to-ceiling windows offer glimpses of busy Damen Avenue, with all of the pizzas featured on a massive blackboard on a back wall.

They may want to tweak their name to Craft Dough, since the dough is the real star. It gets a three-day proof, which helps it develop incredible texture and a nice, even chew. No need for a wood-burning oven here. The pizzas emerge from a standard, gas-fired deck oven, much like some of the best pizzas in town now—Bebu, Robert's, Pizza Friendly Pizza—and they only take a few minutes to bake.

Internally, they call their pies "Neapolitan American East Coast," which implies there is a wide lip, some puffy blistering, and a thin interior. The East Coast thing either refers to coal-fired ovens (which they do not have) or the fact that you can fold the slices in half lengthwise (sure).

One of the house specials—and a pie we typically order on our Sunday Pizza City USA tour through Bucktown and Wicker Park—is the "Devil in the White City": whole milk and fresh mozzarella, Pecorino Romano, hot capicollo, Mama Lil's spicy peppers, peperoncinis, red onions, lots of fresh garlic, herbs, black pepper, and extra virgin olive oil. The creaminess from the cheeses keeps the chilies in check, but you'll still get a burst of heat in each bite.

The Margherita is excellent—they combine canned tomatoes and a bit of tomato paste to intensify the sauce—and the fresh mozzarella is top-notch, like a glorious, shapeless amoeba spreading itself across the surface, ensuring a small taste in every bite. I love the generous handfuls of whole milk

mozzarella. The top is also dressed with a bit of Pecorino Romano and Grana Padano cheeses, quite a few fresh basil leaves, and a healthy drizzle of olive oil.

Each slice is a thing of beauty, holding its shape and integrity without drooping. Does it need the whole milk mozzarella? Probably not, but since they prefer crafting their own style, it goes with the territory. I doubt you'll see anyone complaining, as they'll be too busy crushing these pies.

On Tuesdays, they offer fourteen-inch pizzas for just $10 and eighteen-inch pies for $15. Slices are available every day from 5 to 6:30 p.m., first-come, first-served. Options typically include sausage, pepperoni, or cheese.

D'AMATO'S BAKERY

1124 W. Grand Avenue
312-733-5456
www.damatosbakerychicago.com
@damatosbakery1

ONE OF THE FEW Sicilian-style bakeries left in Chicago making memorable slices to go. Clearly a throwback to a bygone era. The part of West Town the legendary bakery sits in is a sort of hollowed-out Little Italy, with a few trattorias and markets nearby. The glorious Tempesta is just a few blocks west; the busy-but-tired Bari deli is right next door. D'Amato's celebrated seventy years in business in 2020, an awful year to be celebrating anything, so they just sort of went about their business, not drawing a lot of attention to their milestone.

Sausage slices are clearly the most popular. By Chicago standards, the sausage balls are mini, and D'Amato's takes a different approach to their assembly, following the Sicilian tradition of adding toppings and cheese before the dough is fully proofed. While still raw, the dough is embedded with both cheese and sauce, and then left to rise a second time. Finally, it goes into the oven, where the cheese-sauce-topping mixture literally bakes into the soft, supple dough.

And that dough is what you come for. The undercarriage is riddled with tiny craters and ridges providing extra crunch and a caramelized texture (when heated up properly), while the top is pillow-soft, as light as cotton candy but with a sturdy density that holds up the cheese and sauce so well. The edges are also what you need to try, with their blackened and charred exterior. It's a perfect crispy counterbalance to the softer interior. For that reason, make sure you ask for a corner or an edge piece, and if you're going to eat it right away, ask them to heat it up. The other option is to take it home, preheat your pizza stone, and then finish it directly on the stone for about five minutes. I much prefer a crispier undercarriage.

DANTE'S PIZZERIA

3028 W. Armitage Avenue
773-342-0002
www.danteschicago.com
@dantespizzachicago

THE DEATH METAL–THEMED Avondale location closed in early 2021, but the Palmer Square joint on Armitage Avenue is just as gritty. Still, it has its charms. With an in-your-face attitude and lots of ink on the staff, the BYOB café offers both enormous, twenty-inch specialty pies and gigantic, Fred Flintstone–sized slices. As much as I was curious about the Charon option, with its shrimp, prosciutto, pineapple, and jalapeños, and the Minotaur, with Italian beef, giardiniera, provolone, mozzarella, and garlic sauce, I opted instead for a humbler slice with sausage.

These mammoth pieces dwarf anything from the East Coast, and in some cases, are superior to them. Let's begin with the heel, which is at least an inch wide and brushed with garlic butter, Parmesan, and herbs, packing a lot more flavor than you'll find at 97 percent of the by-the-slice joints in Chicago. Then there's the dough itself, slightly crispy with a number of air pockets. My slice offered two pockets that looked like the United Center from 35,000 feet above—the result of at least a twenty-four-hour rest before baking in one of Dante's numerous Blodgett ovens on a stone deck.

Dante's Pizzeria uses a homemade tomato sauce that is applied cold and raw, and then cooks in the oven. The owner emphasizes that there is no sugar in the sauce; any sweetness comes from the quality of the tomatoes they're using. The knobs of sausage are pretty generous and somewhat mild. (The sausage comes from the same supplier who handles the orders for South Side icon Aurelio's.)

A well-charred undercarriage and an excellent dough-to-topping ratio make this chewy, blistered mega-slice great any time of the day—although I can see why it would taste even better to late-night by-the-slicers. A three-finger fold is not only recommended, but required. Ex-pat New Yorkers, rejoice!

Note: At the beginning of 2021, Dante's was also having a pop-up at 1938 W. Chicago Avenue, and the owner, Tim, told me it will eventually become a permanent space, pending their remodeling plans. So, as always, consult their Instagram to see the latest updates.

DIMO'S PIZZA

1615 N. Damen Avenue
773-525-4580

3463 N. Clark Street
773-525-4580

Dr. Murphy's Food Hall
1811 W. Harrison Street

www.dimospizza.com
@dimospizza

DIMO'S ISN'T AFRAID to push the boundaries of what's considered "traditional" on a pizza. With both locations in bar-dense areas (Wicker Park and Wrigleyville) and signs out front advertising their PBR Tall Boy nights along with delivery until 2 or 3 a.m. on weekends, their typical demographic is definitely a little younger than I am.

The dining room in Wicker Park feels like an industrial loft, and the assortment of enormous pies gives you a sense of "choice paralysis." Buffalo chicken? Macaroni and cheese? Sriracha-marinated tofu tucked into a creamy peanut sauce? How about fried chicken, mozzarella, and mini-waffles on a crème fraiche base with honey?

"The piece of dough for us is our blank canvas on which we create our art, and nothing is off limits for us," said Jay Wescott, the chief operating officer.

Despite all of these options, however, the most popular whole pie is still a traditional pepperoni pizza, featuring cup-and-char discs that curl up nicely in the oven.

Their dough is made with unbleached, unbromated flour, which undergoes a twenty-four-hour cold ferment to achieve the desired crumb structure, texture, and flavor.

Two surprising ingredients are found in their red sauce: coffee and red wine vinegar. Wescott says they add them to elevate the flavor, balance the acidity of the tomatoes, and add a note of umami.

Since they are one of the few pizzerias in Chicago that goes to the trouble of hand-stretching their mozzarella, the cheese arrives at the pizzeria in curds. From there, Dimo's salts them, then soaks them in boiling water before hand-stretching.

Four flavors, one pie, ready for reheating

This allows them to control the salt content and achieve the desired texture before adding it to the pizza.

During COVID, pizza wasn't the only thing baking in their stone deck ovens. As of March 2020, Dimo's began making and donating acrylic face shields as personal protective equipment. The face shields are still being donated and can be purchased on their website.

Sticking to my baseline plan of either sausage or pepperoni—so I can better assess the crust and chew—my slice of pepperoni wasn't all that bad. Incidentally, they get their pepperoni from the well-regarded Ezzo Sausage Company in Columbus, Ohio. I also tried one with spinach and cherry tomatoes, just to cover my vegetarian bases as well.

Heated up in a Bakers Pride oven for just a few minutes, the slices emerge slightly crispy. The middle of the slice is super thin, just sturdy enough to hold up the generous sauce and cheese, while the lip is a bit more substantial. I love how the undercarriage is evenly charred and the pepperoni on top maintains a nice kick. I think Dimo's is also a bit more generous with the sauce than most. It's a slice my twenty-year-old son adores, and no judgment if he decides to get the mac and cheese; I understand late-night cravings tend to be irrational.

DOUGH BROS. PIZZERIA & SUB SHOP

400 N. State Street
312-600-9078
www.doughbrospizza.com
@doughbrospizza

THIS QUICK-SERVICE joint, nestled among a slew of bars in River North, knows its audience. Sure, a few office workers stop in when the sun is out, picking up a sub or a slice to go, but with a closing time of 4 a.m., Dough Bros. isn't focused on sober diners after dark. With just five tables and a half-dozen gargantuan pies up front behind the glass case, this is alcohol-soaking food. That said, the recipes here were coaxed to life by none other than Anthony Scardino ("Professor Pizza"), who worked here for a time before stints at some other notable shops and then opening his own grandma-style project (see his story in chapter 8).

My large slice of sausage pizza arrives, heated up nicely after a few minutes in their deck oven, and it's served cafeteria-style, atop black-and-white checkered paper sitting on a paper plate. It has an appealing aroma and a significantly thick lip.

The top is slightly greasy, which is odd since there was no pepperoni, but the homemade sausage pieces have a very pleasant aroma and chew. It must be the fat that's rendered from the raw sausage. The crust is ultra thin in the middle and tapers off from the lip, where it's just a lot of dough that needs seasoning. There is an audible crunch when biting into the slice, even though much of it is buried beneath cheese.

The sauce is pleasant (though there isn't much to speak of), and I like how some of the spots on top

of the pizza slice have a little bit of browning from hot spots in the oven. Since some of that cheese is from the well-regarded Grande Cheese Company, it tastes that much better.

Even better, and *highly* recommended, is the grandma-style slice. Maybe an inch high, showing some impressive crumb with an undercarriage as black as my newly tarred alley, it's as crunchy as a tortilla chip with all kinds of riddled holes underneath. The tomatoes on top are bursting with juiciness. There's a hint of salt and a row of cup-and-char pepperoni that looks like a bunch of satellite dishes pointed at my mouth, awaiting instructions for what's next. I say, get in here.

The key to Dough Bros is Scardino's influence. I've been there when his instructions obviously were not being followed. Hopefully you'll manage to score one of their grandma slices that's been lovingly re-created in his image (and to his specifications).

FOXHOLE

3335 N. Southport Avenue
773-687-8568
tinyurl.com/ybsp498v
@cdvolpe_chi
#thefoxholeatcdv

For chef Salvatore Lo Cascio, garnering a VPN Certificate for his Neapolitan pies at Coda di Volpe wasn't enough. The Sicilian native wanted to also share his childhood pizza with his regulars in Lakeview. How do you carve out a separate personality from within an established restaurant on a busy corner? By cutting a window out of the side of the building and calling it Foxhole.

Lo Cascio makes a focaccia-style dough with a spongy-soft interior, crispy bottom, and crunchy sides. Its shallow height makes it appear more grandma than Sicilian, despite a seventy-two-hour dough-making process.

The menu is tight. First choose a size: slice, half pan (serves six) or full pan (serves twelve). Then flavor: Margherita, sausage and red onion, or that spicy pepperoni. Even with a pie as seemingly simple as the Margherita—cheese, sauce, fresh basil—Lo Cascio's Sicilian instincts overrule taking the easy way out. He insists on finishing it with wild oregano.

The other key to the success of these slices is the trio of bakes. First, a five-minute naked bake in the pan—just the crust. Then a second bake with the toppings on for five minutes more; finally, removed from the pan and baked directly on the stone hearth of the oven for five minutes to properly crisp the undercarriage.

GIGIO'S PIZZERIA

4643 N. Broadway Street
773-271-2273
www.gigiospizzachicago.com
@gigios_in_uptown

Unrelated to the Gigio's in suburban Evanston and Des Plaines.

GIGIO'S OPENED FOR business in 1965, and has moved just once, up the street to where it is now. The brightly lit slice joint sits across from the renovated Wilson Avenue CTA station, next to some random businesses that never seem to keep their leases for very long, but notably, right next door to one of my favorite Thai restaurants—In-On—that's also worth seeking out. There are a few tables here, along with a high counter at the window overlooking Broadway. I first visited in 2015, while researching *Pizza City, USA*, and I'm happy to announce they finally invested in new flooring and wood paneling, ditching the garage sale Italian-themed prints, and adding a swanky digital menu.

Decor isn't likely a top priority, since Gigio's is a late-night mainstay for the after-show crowds coming from the Green Mill or the Aragon—so the pizzas probably don't even need to be that good, especially when the guy in front of me in line yells he wants his fried chicken wings "extra hot."

The slices, however, exceed expectations. Gigio's also makes whole pies, but clearly, they do most of their business by heating up slices in their enormous rotating deck oven.

Ruddy knobs of homemade sausage, laced with plenty of fennel, stand sentinel among the even spread of mozzarella and zesty tomato sauce, all of which rest on a cushioned bed of firm crust that's still pliable enough to bend in half, NYC-style. There is a slight char on the lip, supplying additional crunch. The bottom manages to maintain its crispness (it's a hand-tossed dough), and even though it's served on flimsy paper plates à la New York, this is not throw-away pizza meant only to fill your stomach on an alcohol-fueled night out. It's solid, respectable pizza that fits firmly into the canon of quality late-night munchies. Just don't ask for a glass with your can of pop. It's not that kind of joint.

ITALIAN FIESTA PIZZERIA

1919 E. Seventy-First Street
8058 S. Halsted Street
1306 E. Forty-Seventh Street
773-684-2222

Also in suburbs:
Dolton
15425 S. Cottage Grove
708-849-9204

New Lenox
2021 Calistoga Drive
815-462-5555

italianfiestapizzeria.com

Even though the shop is known for its tavern-style pizzas cut into squares (see chapter 3, where I give its history), a few years ago they also started cutting up some of those whole pies into traditional wedges so customers didn't have to wait fifteen minutes to eat, and more importantly, didn't have to commit to a whole pie. There is a fair amount of foot traffic along Seventy-First Street, so it makes sense that people getting off the Metra train across the street might want a quick snack on the way home. It's the only place in the city I've seen cut traditional tavern-thin pizzas into giant triangles, but it works. They may not fold as elegantly as a traditional NYC slice, but if you're walking along Seventy-First, and don't feel like getting barbecue from Slab across the street, a big slice of sausage or pepperoni will certainly do the trick.

The most popular topping is sausage, and since this is Chicago, it's a mass of raw sausage, seasoned with fennel and other undisclosed spices. Pinched and pressed onto a tomato sauce–covered dough, the sausage—or really any topping you choose—is ultimately buried by handfuls of whole milk mozzarella, shredded in-house.

JIMMY'S PIZZA CAFÉ

2434 W. Montrose Avenue
773-293-6992
www.facebook.com/jimmyspizzacafe
@jimmyspizzacafe

THE NYC-INSPIRED SLICE at Jimmy's is one of the best deals in town. They manage to crank out just a few simple items and do them extremely well: New Orleans–style beignets covered in powdered sugar, calzones, chicken wings, garlic knots (essentially dough topped with Parmesan and basil, served with a side of marinara), and by-the-slice pizza options. They hold six large pies in the front glass case. You choose your slice and they pop it into a small Bakers Pride oven that heats your selection up in about two minutes.

Jimmy Kang grew up in suburban Hoffman Estates, where his parents maintained high expectations (they wanted him to become a doctor). After a brief stint acting and modeling in Korea, he returned to the United States in 2009. A trip to New York City as a kid had exposed him to the delicious simplicity of pizza there, and it made such an impact, he dedicated himself to learning how to make that style when he opened his eponymous shop in 2011.

The slices are generous, and somehow maintain their crispiness. The undercarriage is almost universally blackened, and there's an audible crunch when you bite into it. The slices claim to be New York–style (yes, you can fold them), but they seem to have more heft and substance than those I've had in New York. And there is certainly a welcome lack of grease. In fact, the Grande mozzarella from Wisconsin is divine, and with the large crumbles of sausage (his recipe, ground by local manufacturer Greco) embedded within, Jimmy's Pizza Café devises an excellent ratio of dough to toppings. (FYI, they use Black Angus for their meatballs.) They also offer specials. On the day I visited Jimmy's, the menu featured an eggplant pizza and a chicken-and-bacon pizza.

Regardless of flavor, the dough is almost bread-like in appearance and texture, sort of like ciabatta (an Italian white bread), with a slightly raised heel and just enough crumb to provide ample chew. The hole structure indicates they let the dough rest and ferment enough to create those lovely air pockets. The tomato sauce is zesty without being overpowering; it plays a nice supporting role, especially if you get the crumbled sausage.

NONNA'S

925 W. Randolph Street
312-690-7323
www.nonnaschicago.com
@nonnaschicago

As a child of Racine, Wisconsin, David Schwartz has spent most of his life in the Midwest. Growing up on the thin tavern-style pies at Wells Brothers, he moved to Chicago for culinary school, and worked at restaurants like La Madia in River North, where he was responsible for pizzas and pasta. But the pizza of his childhood was strictly tavern-style, and there didn't seem to be any desire for the thin and crispy, square-cut slices at Nonna's, a tidy little sandwich shop around the corner from its more sophisticated sibling, Formento's.

When faced with overhauling and updating the menus at both restaurants, he had to immerse himself in two very different styles that would present a unique challenge. First, he wanted to change up the Sicilian slice he inherited on the menu. The previous version already used King Arthur bread flour (no need to change that), and his dough would continue to be made at night, kept cold, then removed the next morning to proof in the pans for about two hours. Pies are built with sliced mozzarella then sauce, and here is where he diverged from his predecessor's recipe. Instead of just pumping up Formento's marinara with lots of chili flakes, Schwartz decided to start from scratch—sweating garlic, adding crushed tomatoes, oregano, and chili flakes, then cooling it down. He grates on a Parmigiano-Pecorino blend just before baking in his Blodgett deck oven at 400 for about 20 to 25 minutes.

The slices are thick but not too cumbersome. They definitely look heftier than they taste. There's plenty of crumb to chew, and the pepperoni is nicely charred while maintaining its porky characteristics. The sauce on this new-and-improved version is also worth noting. If you had the Sicilian when they first opened, be sure to give this newer version a shot.

Schwartz's next task, in early 2020, was to bring a taste of New York to the West Loop. Specifically, creating a slice anyone from the East Coast could relate to. Schwartz had never been to New York, but went online, diving deep into research. "Everyone said it's the water," he told me. "We probably tested thirty to forty doughs, and it came down to three we liked."

After a few more tweaks, success: they make a *biga* (a pre-ferment), let it rest for sixteen hours, then hydrate it and let it sit in the cooler for another day or so. After they remove it cold from the cooler, they hand-stretch it, launching it onto the stone deck of the Blodgett oven he made his new employer purchase. He uses Caputo "00" flour and likes the crispy texture he gets on the heel. "We wanted something that would travel well, even if a delivery driver had it sitting in his car for thirty minutes," he said. He'll typically bake them at 600 degrees for seven to eight minutes.

The basic Margherita has generous dollops of buffalo mozzarella and fresh basil set over a simple sauce of San Marzanos, garlic, and chili flakes. He also makes a pepperoni with white truffle—a nod to his days at La Madia—as well as a crumbled meatball (instead of the usual sausage) with briny, crunchy giardiniera. Slices range in size. Most whole pies are about eighteen to twenty inches, so the resulting slices may vary, but believe me, they're not only generous enough for one, they're also quite good, and if you close your eyes, a few bites may even transport you to Williamsburg.

PAULA & MONICA'S PIZZERIA

1518 W. Chicago Avenue
312-929-3615
www.paulaandmonicaspizzeria.com
@paulaandmonicas

PRACTICALLY HIDDEN along a busy stretch of Chicago Avenue in Noble Square, where you're more likely to stumble into a mom-and-pop Cuban joint or a dive bar, Paula & Monica's prides itself on its range of slices. The owner, George Dragne, is a Romanian immigrant who opened here in 2007, when the neighborhood was significantly shabbier than it is today. He garnered some good press from *Chicago* magazine a few years later, and I give him and his staff credit for maintaining consistency for the past decade.

Slices come in regular, medium, and jumbo, and are available either thin or deep. They're baked on rotating steel decks inside a hundred-year-old Marshall oven the size of a tank, which he rebuilt himself. They also have a few specialty pizzas, including a Hawaiian (pineapple, ham, and barbecue sauce), a BLT, and a "meat lovers" version with ground beef, bacon, sausage, and pepperoni (BYO Lipitor). I got there right when they opened on a quiet Wednesday, ordering a jumbo sausage slice, which is both comically large and puzzlingly cut into four smaller pieces.

"A lot of customers ask us to slice them in half," said Dragne. Really? Please, George, stand your ground and don't give New Yorkers another reason to make fun of our pizza habits.

The slices here are served on either a no-frills industrial tin plate or a styrofoam one. They have quite a bit of heft, making a fold nearly impossible, but even more so if you ask for them cut into smaller pieces (don't). They must have been paying attention the last time I wrote about them, because they've increased the ratio of sausage to cheese, so almost every other bite includes a knobby piece of the fennel-flecked sausage (made by Greco). There's an undeniable richness—the full-fat cheese blending with the rendered pork fat on a very respectable base layer of evenly baked crust. I'm getting just enough fennel essence in each crumbly bite.

As for the crust, it's very good—even better, I imagine, than last time, and certainly better late at night. There is a nice chew and crunch in the lip, but it's not as impressive in the middle and on toward the point, where the cheese can border on overwhelming.

PAULIE GEE'S WICKER PARK

1566 N. Damen Avenue
www.pauliegee.com
@pauliegeeswickerpark

SOME SPACES IN Chicago just never had the mojo to last very long. 355 E. Ohio is a great example (five pizza concepts in seven years). But I think 1566 N. Damen is finally poised for greatness. The former home to a Bongo Room and, most recently, a Bonci, it's now a NYC-style slice shop, as Derrick Tung expands his Paulie Gee footprint in the city.

After running some weekend pop-ups from a trailer, Tung reached out to Paulie Gee in Brooklyn as a potential mentor and partner. They found a soaring space on North Milwaukee Avenue, and initially launched just doing the wood-fired pies in Logan Square.

After a lot of tinkering, Tung also started making exquisite Detroit-style pizzas too, and during the pandemic, when the dining room was closed, he started selling giant slices on paper plates through the front window. Turning to Paulie for his slice recipe, Tung was doing a brisk business, at first, heating them to order in his portable Breville ovens, then later, in the electric PizzaMasters.

The six corners at Damen, Milwaukee, and North Avenues present a great opportunity, if they're the right fit. I lived in the neighborhood for twenty years and saw plenty of businesses come and go. As much as I loved having Bonci there, the format was almost too smart for the audience. Twenty-somethings don't want to be lectured about "how this works" with the Roman backstory, the measuring of slices, the cutting to order, paying by the pound, and the reheating. They want to point to a slice—choosing from maybe three or four options—and wait two minutes while it's heated up. You know, New York–style. Oddly enough, despite the immediate area offering about nine pizza concepts, it's hard to find a front window promising big, foldable slices. As Bonci decided to leave the Wicker Park space, an opportunity arose. Tung plans to have two of his dedicated employees take it over—William Ravert and chef Tony Dezutter. They'll have the usual suspects of pepperoni, sausage, cheese, and probably one special; maybe even a vegan option. Meanwhile, back in Logan Square, Tung says they'll probably only offer the big slices late on weekends. Here's hoping the Wicker Park spot gains a following and enjoys some longevity.

PAZZA PIZZA

1543 N. Sedgwick Street
312-774-0303
pazzapizza.net
@pazzapizza.chicago

Fisnik "Nik" Halimi and his brother, Adi, moved to Chicago in 1999 from Kosovo, Albania. Their father and uncle ran a pizzeria there for many years, and they'd occasionally work in the kitchen when they went home for visits. In Chicago, Nik worked construction jobs, but the brothers had the idea to do a slice shop for years.

"There's not a whole lot of them here," said Halimi. "We visited New York plenty of times. We really got excited about the idea because of the location."

After a night out seeing a show at The Second City, or stumbling out of one of the bars near North Avenue or Wells Street, Pazza Pizza is an excellent choice for a slice. It has that Old Chicago feel, tucked into the first floor of a prewar brownstone. Its proximity to the Sedgwick stop on the Brown Line CTA also makes it a good option for commuters.

There's not much to the dining room; it's basically a giant case with an assortment of twenty-inch pies, all ready to be divvied up and reheated by the slice in one of two electric Moretti Forni ovens. Halimi says he and Adi demolished the old 5 Boroughs Pizza and Subs and rebuilt it. They do also have a back patio for seating.

My sausage slice has several generous pieces, each flecked with enough fennel, and a base layer of cheese that is melted expertly. Just like a slice from Joe's in the West Village, the surface resembles the sun's reflection on a lake in midsummer—it shimmers, with equal spacing between the fatty white mini blobs of mozzarella. Special flavors include *sujuk*—the beloved fermented beef sausage from back home—as well as a dried beef similar to jerky. They rotate about a half-dozen flavors for slices, but offer another two dozen pies, including some dessert versions.

The crust is sturdy but not leaden, with an appropriate-sized

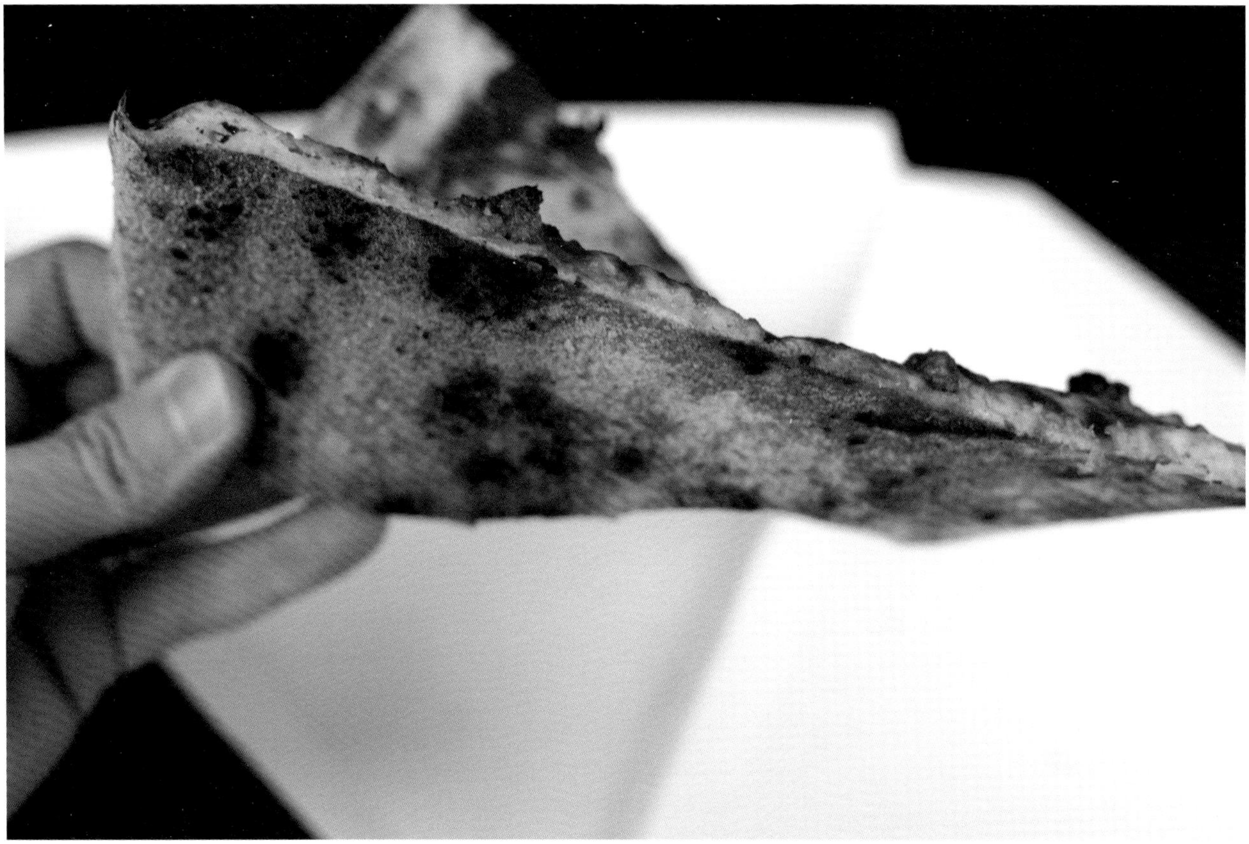

width and height, the result of a forty-eight-hour fermentation. It's blond but freckled, and it folds easily, making a telltale cracking sound as you press your pointer finger into the heel's vortex to get it into a V shape. There is no tip sag once folded. Admire the undercarriage while you're at it, because those blackened spots didn't just happen on the reheat; they likely are a result of the pie's initial firing on the stone deck.

The brothers plan to open more locations once they test the brand in Old Town. With Adi in the kitchen and Nik handling the business side of things, they'd love to eventually franchise.

Each bite yields an optimal bite ratio (OBR) and I couldn't help but think about the kids who are growing up nearby. If Pazza becomes their childhood pizza—the one they'll have on walks home from the train or at birthday parties and for after-school snacks—think how funny it would be that this New York–style pizza will become their PIGUE (Pizza I Grew Up Eating), thus informing their pizza opinion as adults . . . from Chicago!

PIZZA FRIED CHICKEN ICE CREAM

960 W. Thirty-First Street
773-565-4192
www.pfcic.com
@pizzachickenicecream

Childhood friends Bradley Shorten and Billy Federighi (along with Billy's fiancée, Cecily Rodriguez) are really into crispy edges and chewy interiors (the result of high dough hydration and long fermentation) and employing toppings of the highest quality, sourced from as many local artisans and farms as possible. You can read about their tavern-style and artisan pizzas in chapters 1 and 10.

Their Sicilian is inspired by trips to New York City. And they've opted to use brick cheese—favored by Motor City adherents—rather than mozzarella, hand-shredding it themselves. The resulting slices are downright majestic, baked on a stone deck oven—in large rectangular pans using either fresh vegetables or carefully sourced meats—until they emerge crispy-edged but still toothsome, topped with freshly snipped basil, just like they do at DiFara, in Midwood, Brooklyn.

"It's designed to be a square slice to go, kind of like a New York square slice place," said Rodriguez.

They offer to-go slices from the window; if you want a whole pie, you'll need to order ahead of time.

PIZZA FRIENDLY PIZZA

1039 N. Western Avenue (enter through the alley)
773-395-2483
www.pizzafriendlypizza.com
@pizzafriendlypizza

THE ONLY SLICE OF pizza in Chicago currently being produced by a Michelin-starred chef is emerging from a walk-up window adjacent to a twee backyard patio in Ukrainian Village. Forced to make a pivot during the pandemic, Oriole executive chef Noah Sandoval dedicated himself to coming up with a stellar example of a Sicilian slice.

Sandoval, a native of Richmond, Virginia, grew up on large, triangular slices, but fell hard for the thick and airy Sicilian slices he and his wife devoured at Prince Street Pizza in New York City.

The problem with replicating that style was, he didn't have a clue.

"I wanted to do the best version I could," said Sandoval. "I read a lot, bought different pans; it was good, but it wasn't right."

He sent me a few pictures in those early days, asking for my reaction. I could see there was an issue with the undercarriage and the crumb. I connected him to John Arena in Las Vegas, a towering figure in the industry. They quickly began long talks, peppered with Sandoval sending frequent pictures of the side of the pizza for feedback.

Arena's suggestion? Start over.

Sandoval shifted the hydration level of the dough, the fermentation time; even the flour.

To achieve his crispy undercarriage, Sandoval uses a thin layer of Crisco (although he learned traditional bakers used lard, he wanted to be able to offer slices to vegetarians). He leaves his five-day fermented dough in the pan for about twelve hours, then bakes them for just ten minutes at 525 degrees. They'll rest an hour, then get a final bake with toppings for twelve minutes at 500 degrees.

When I visited, there were four options: a cup-and-char pepperoni (again, Ezzo, which is ironic, since Sandoval's inspiration—Prince Street in NYC—uses the Rosa Grande brand) with aged Parmesan and fresh basil; a vegetarian with rapini and chèvre, lemon and garlic (vegan on request); an earthy mushroom with creamy burrata and spicy Calabrian chiles; and then one special pie designed by their chef de cuisine, Ruben Villalobos. Previous iterations of Ruben's special pies have included fennel sausage with his homemade giardiniera and fennel pollen.

The squares look hefty, but when you lift them, they are as light as a pair of AirPods. Biting into them—revealing that tight crumb—you experience not only the top-notch ingredients Sandoval has sourced, but the interplay between sweet and heat, crunch and chew, crisp and soft. The undercarriage is textbook, and it's not really going that far out on a limb to proclaim it's the best Sicilian slice in Chicago.

POMPEI

1531 W. Taylor Street
312-421-5179
www.pompeiusa.com
@pompei_restaurants

FOR OLD TIMERS like Ralph Davino, "Little Italy" as it was known for most of the twentieth century, is no more. Indian, Chinese, and Mexican restaurants have replaced a lot of the Italian favorites near Pompei, the bakery his grandfather, Luigi, started in 1924.

Davino still uses the giant Champion mixer from 1946 his grandfather and dad used; and they still offer bakery slices using the same dough they use for their bread, it just doesn't proof as long. Cheese is still popular, though provolone has been added to the mozzarella, and now they also offer more than a dozen flavors, including eggplant, broccoli, and the Chicago favorite of fennel-flecked sausage (formerly sourced from Scala, now from Greco). Everything is displayed deli-style, so you point to your pizza, they heat it up, and you either eat in or take it to go. The slices don't have a lot of complexity in the crumb since they only take a few hours to make from dough mixing to baking, but if you can get them to reheat the slices long enough, you'll get a crispy enough bottom to provide some contrast against the softer middle.

More recently, Davino added a "Grandma Frances" to his menu, a twenty-four-hour fermented dough that is simultaneously thick and light but also appropriately crispy and oily; it's one of the few grandma-style pizzas in town (the other significant example is by Professor Pizza). It's mostly slices here, but also some jumbos and whole pies. Another variant is the pizza strudel, which is stuffed and rolled, making an excellent to-go option if you're eating on your lap in your car. Another adaptive measure taken recently is the addition of a gluten-free pizza.

THE STOPALONG

1812 N. Milwaukee Avenue
773-394-4694
www.thestopalong.com
@thestopalong

Tucked behind some trees along a random stretch of North Milwaukee Avenue, the StopAlong is one of several businesses to have sprouted up along the 606—the three-mile-long narrow park occupying a former freight train line. The theme is pure '80s, with arcade games like Galaga and Ms. Pac-Man in back, plus lots of comics and movie nostalgia that also find their way onto the pizza menu.

I had visited early in 2017 and for whatever reason was unimpressed. But a return trip in late 2020 proved me wrong (as I had been not-so-casually reminded by several people in the industry). I dodged the prosciutto and the pepperoni on my most recent visit, opting instead for the "Old School"—their Margherita. Homemade sauce and mozzarella—practically unheard of in Chicago—led to giant sun splotches of fresh, white mozz, their color a bright contrast to the even browning around the heel. Slices are generous (large pies are sixteen inches—not quite NYC diameter, but resulting in perfectly manageable slices). I loved the slightly raised heel, its crust still plenty crispy as I took my first bite on the tailgate of my car. The interior crumb offers a pleasant chew with a yeasty, slightly tangy note of fermentation. Bonus points to the cook who goes to the trouble of cutting a chiffonade of fresh basil, resulting in tiny strands of the verdant green herb that find themselves woven into nearly every bite.

This is textbook OBR and I daresay even picky New Yorkers would have a hard time finding fault with any aspect of this delicious pie. How delicious you ask? I visited the week of Thanksgiving, after visiting three other places that same day, and still somehow managed to find room to polish off nearly three slices.

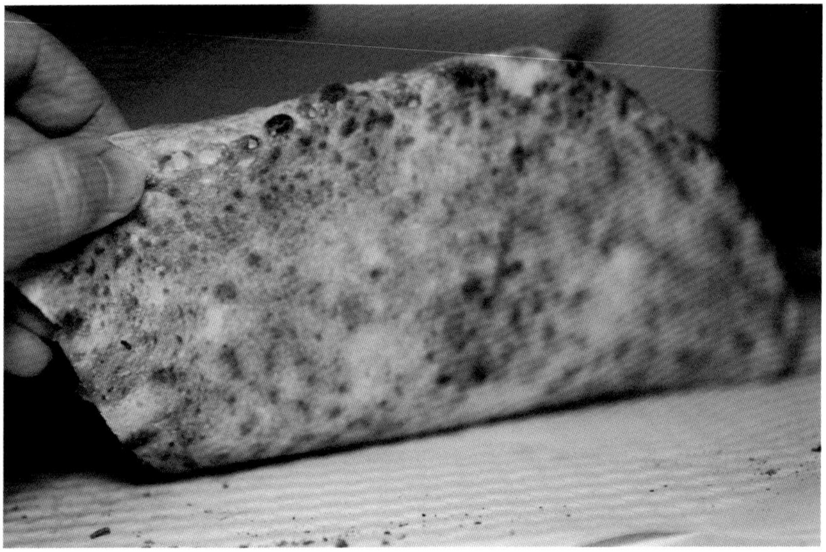

BAM!

14 PIZZA NIGHTS AND POP-UPS

THIS CHAPTER COULDN'T HAVE EXISTED in *Pizza City, USA*. The pandemic forced people's hands. Pizza, it turns out, can be a draw for people who might not otherwise bother visiting a bakery or restaurant in their neighborhood. In some cases, making pizzas in 2020 went from hobby to fledgling business or charitable endeavor.

I'm guessing John Carruthers is perfectly content working in the marketing department at Revolution Brewing, but his love of tavern-style pizza became a mild obsession during lockdowns. His Crust Fund Pizza requires customers to make a donation to a charity of his choice, then send him a DM of the receipt so they can order one of his fabulously thin and crispy pies. Oh, don't forget you have to meet him at his Uptown garage in the alley on a Thursday night to pick up your pizza. (Not kidding!)

On Tuesdays and Wednesdays at Logan Square's Superkhana International, where an Indian-ish menu prevailed in the Before Times, one of the young bakers is hawking thin and crispy (and cheeseless) Roman pies.

Outdoor, wood-burning ovens on a Bridgeport back patio; Sunday-only Sicilian squares from an Edgewater bakery; a young couple's business plan, making Roman-inspired pan pizzas as pizza nomads, moving to a new space every month; a former Soho House cook making killer wood-fired pies in a portable

Sicilian slice at Sauce and Bread

oven from inside a taqueria in Pilsen. All of these pivots happened in 2020, and I'm sure I'm missing a few more. Even Giant, the much-loved Logan Square farm-driven restaurant, shifted to a giant food truck in 2020, selling square slices as high as the Great Wall, designed by one of their cooks.

The nature of these "Pizza Nights" and pop-ups is all about being nimble. They can turn on a dime if need be, and updating information is as easy as editing an Instagram profile. All of which is to say, there is a decent chance some of these options may not exist in late 2021, or whenever you're reading this. While I'm sure the Wednesday Pizza Night at The Duck Inn isn't going anywhere, the monthly pop-ups might be more tenuous. Just check out their Instagram account before making the decision to try them; many of these require prepayment via social media channels anyway. It's definitely not going to be a traditional pizza eating experience, but I can think of worse things than cracking open a beer and eating a pizza on my tailgate in the summertime.

The alley handoff in Uptown, at Crust Fund Pizza

Backyard oven at The Duck Inn in Bridgeport

CHI PIE GUY

1726 S. Racine Avenue (inside La Luna)
www.lalunachicago.com/chipieguy-pizza-pop-up
@chi.pie.guy
Weekend pop-up

THE 1200 BLOCK of West Eighteenth Street has come a long way over the past ten years. Like a lot of the neighborhood, it's been changing. Bars, restaurants, and coffee shops seem to be slowly displacing the bodegas and clothing stores with quinceañera dresses. Some longtime residents are unhappy with the gentrification—higher property values lead to higher tax assessments and, eventually, higher rents—there have been graffiti tags on some newer restaurants. But there's no denying Pilsen's ascendance in terms of food, drink, and entertainment. On that one block alone, there's Thalia Hall, one of the city's great live music venues; next to it, Dusek's Board & Beer (with the Punch House in the basement). Stephen Gillanders' S.K.Y. is across the street; at Racine and Eighteenth, there's Honky Tonk BBQ, and on the opposite corner, La Luna, a tequila-and-tacos joint that, during COVID, started offering a weekly pizza pop-up that suddenly became Pilsen's second-best pizza option (I still give top honors to Bob's over on Twenty-First Street).

Chi Pie Guy operates only Fridays through Sundays, and even then, only after 4 p.m. I'll say upfront there's a good chance owner Samantha Sanchez may have moved the location of the pop-up by the time you're reading this, so best to check the hours and location via their Instagram. Going to a taco joint to get a part-time pizza didn't inspire a lot of confidence. Fortunately, she has a secret weapon in chef Marco Colin—a veteran of the pizza program at The Allis inside the Soho House (one of my favorite pizzas featured in *Pizza City, USA*).

One of the things Colin learned at the Soho House was a near religious devotion to Italian ingredients: imported burrata, prosciutto, *fior di latte*, and San Marzano tomatoes are all featured throughout the compact menu.

"I want the real deal," he said. "My dough is really rustic too. Neapolitan-style with minimal yeast."

The "00" flour proofs for twenty-four hours at room temperature. He'll roll it out, then let it rest another three to four hours before making his pizzas. Using a commercial Gozney wood-burning oven, the small mouth only allows him to bake one twelve-inch pie at a time. But because the oven is so small, burning cherry and oak wood so close to the pizza, the high temperature allows him to bake a pie in about seventy seconds, and yet, he avoids the typical pitfall of an overly soupy middle.

"I don't like watery pizzas. You've gotta be consistent with the weight of the dough, the type of cheese," said Colin, who credits the drier middle to an imported *fior di latte* from Viola Produce with less water.

The pizzas have a glorious, even charring around the *cornicione*, with just enough rise in the heel to offer chewiness. And yet, unlike traditional Neapolitans, they have an earthy rusticity to them; the char makes you feel as if you're eating a pie that was baked in some nonna's

fireplace oven in the hills outside of Naples with the sun setting. The light touch with the tomatoes and the creamy richness from the cheese burst in your mouth with each successive bite. Fresh basil leaves are torn onto the pie immediately before serving. Pies this good would cost $16 to $18 downtown; here, they're $12 to $14.

"We're also making our spicy sausage with fennel in-house and we always include a little side of homemade giardiniera. I'm now working on a chili oil too. We want to have fun and innovate," said Colin. When I saw the gratis container of giardiniera with my Margherita, I literally yelped with joy.

Once COVID ends, and La Luna gets back to serving tacos and tequila, there's a good chance the pizza pop-up will move. No matter where Sanchez decides to locate it, those Gozney ovens are portable, so make an effort to seek out @chi.pie.guy for one of the most surprisingly delicious pizzas in town.

CRUST FUND PIZZA

@nachosandlager
Monthly pop-up

JOHN CARRUTHERS calls himself a "proprietor of a bootleg pizza shop." He started making pizzas in his Uptown kitchen after the Black Lives Matter protests in the summer of 2020. Feeling helpless, he started cooking tavern-style pizzas and giving them away in exchange for a donation to a Chicago-based charity, since he's legally prohibited from selling pizzas made in his home oven with a pair of baking steels.

Carruthers—whose day job is working in the marketing department at Revolution Brewing—takes orders via his Instagram account once a month, always on Monday, for Thursday night pickups. The final result is an ode to the pizza his family had growing up in McHenry County: square cut, tavern-style, light on the cheese, with a pronounced cornmeal base.

Carruthers uses a food processor to form his dough into balls, which he says leads to the best rise. The dough rests for up to one week to cold ferment, which allows it to reach its desired texture and sharp flavor.

His slow-cooked sauce takes about an hour to make, and contains a secret weapon—fish sauce—which Carruthers adds for a jolt of pure umami. It's interesting to see young cooks playing with traditional recipes. Obviously, there's no way the pizzas of his childhood in rural McHenry County ever saw fish sauce, but over the last few years, I've seen guys like Frank Pinello at Best Pizza in Williamsburg, Brooklyn, use anchovy paste in their sauce to achieve the same result: umami. First, Carruthers fries tomato paste for a few minutes, until it becomes dark. Then he adds tomato sauce and fresh garlic cloves that have been fried in butter and oil; finally, the fish sauce, plus sugar and salt, using an immersion blender to combine everything. He finishes it with a splash of sherry vinegar. The addition of vinegar and fish sauce helps the sauce develop a richer flavor, along with aromatics and dried herbs such as marjoram, basil, and oregano.

While most of his ingredients are donated, Carruthers prefers to pay for the full-fat Wisconsin deli block mozzarella, which he likes to grate himself to achieve the proper melt and finish.

All of his pizzas must be picked up at a designated time on a Thursday night from his garage. He sends you specific directions, noting the large bourbon barrel as a marker to look for in the alley as reference. He greets you just outside the garage, usually wearing his "Tavern Style" T-shirt. Get your pizza, then either devour it in the car or just try to hold off not eating too much on the way home. I pulled over across the street from Winnemac Park and tasted a few squares before making the twenty-five-minute drive back home. That weeklong cold ferment makes such a difference. Just like at Pat's and Pizza Fried Chicken Ice Cream, it gives the thin dough time to dry out, losing a lot of its moisture, resulting in a thin, brittle crust that is more cracker than bread.

THE DUCK INN

2701 S. Eleanor Street
312-724-8811
theduckinnchicago.com
@duckinnchicago
Wednesdays

KEVIN HICKEY HAS never forgotten his roots. Despite years of traveling the globe as a chef for the Ritz-Carlton hotels, the Bridgeport native has always been proud of his South Side working-class roots. When he finally resettled in Chicago, opening The Duck Inn in his old neighborhood, he wanted to create some kind of pizza night, no matter how humble.

In the summer of 2015, an opportunity presented itself. The restaurant's original general manager worked out a deal with the Chicago Brick Oven Pizza Company, where Hickey would do some "how to" videos in exchange for a wood-burning oven he could use in the restaurant's massive backyard. Wednesday Pizza Night was born.

Using an instant dry yeast, the dough is made the same day and topped with local favorites like Tempesta Salumi's pepperoni and 'nduja; Hickey makes his own sausage and gets what he calls "bootleg" soppressata from some guys in the neighborhood. They get together every year, make the soppressata, and turn it over to a USDA-certified butcher to hang and age; then, a few months later, Hickey buys about $200 or $300 worth of the product to get him through the season. That "local" cured meat is paired with hot giardiniera, a tomato sauce featuring San Marzanos, fresh garlic, chili flakes, and oregano.

The ten- to twelve-inch pies bake for about two minutes inside the tight applewood-burning oven. Five of the six weekly pies are cut into wedges, but the "South Side" (sausage and giardiniera) is cut into squares as a nod to its origins.

Most of the pies get a cheese blend consisting of mozzarella, fontina, and provolone, which adds an extra dimension of richness. For his Margherita, Hickey uses an imported *fior di latte* from La Mozzarella; the fresh basil comes from his late father's garden down the street. These are pies with a strong Bridgeport accent.

He always manages to offer a Garden Pizza featuring local legends like Klug and Nichols Farm; hyper-seasonal greens and squash blossoms are typical ingredients. If you can call ahead, find out if he's offering a clam pie. Whole littlenecks are placed on the pies—paired with either chorizo or spicy 'nduja. The shells, opening upon contact with the heat of the oven, release their briny juices, which meld with a ton of fresh herbs and parsley. It's a long way from sausage and giardiniera, but just as welcome on a backyard patio on a warm summer night.

MILLED2SPILL

@milled2spill

A pop-up about once a month, usually for two consecutive nights

CARMEN CHAPARRO and Sean Malone met while working in the restaurant business, never realizing they shared a passion for pizza. Chaparro used to work as a server at Parachute, then as a host and floor supervisor at Bad Hunter—the vegetable-forward restaurant in the West Loop that, sadly, closed during the pandemic. Malone would stop by the restaurant frequently, since he worked for a boutique wine importer. A budding romance formed over cooking and "geeking out over food," said Chaparro. "We started baking together, and we found that during the pandemic, we had a lot more time to concentrate on it."

Since they wanted to mill their own spelt and rye grains, someone joked about the band Built to Spill. The funny name stuck.

They begin with an all-natural starter, seeded with spelt, pumpernickel, dark rye, whole wheat, and bread flour—specifically, the Central Milling High Mountain Flour from Utah. The combination of the starter and the additional grains resulted in a dough that was chunkier, at least visually.

In January 2020, about a month before the first lockdowns, they took a European trip and went to Rome. In search of places like Digeribile and Alice, they wanted to learn more about the open crumb, focaccia-inspired squares in the Roman repertoire. Malone had grown up near Detroit and was always fascinated by Jet's sourdough Sicilian, while simultaneously respecting the style at Buddy's, the birthplace of Detroit-style pies. The couple returned to Chicago and began experimenting with doughs, determined to combine the chewy, open crumb styles from Rome with the focaccia-like Sicilian pizzas available in Detroit.

They hand-knead the dough (which contains some olive oil), letting it spend a couple of hours to ferment in the fridge. After two days, they place the dough into their twelve-inch-square Lloyd steel pans, dimpling it with their fingers, then letting it rise a final time before topping and baking at 500 for about twenty minutes (depending on the oven).

They usually offer just two options: one is an homage to Italian American pizza, what they call their "Original." A sauce of stewed San Marzano tomatoes, Parmesan rind, puttanesca (olives and capers), and dried parsley is topped with some freshly torn pieces of fresh mozzarella—it's pure simplicity. Their signature is to season the crust with butter, parsley, black pepper, and freshly grated Pecorino Romano around the perimeter—another nod to Italian American flavor profiles.

The other option is the "Siciliano"—essentially a tomato pie. The base is an even layer of cooked Bianco di Napoli crushed tomatoes with salt, some grated Grana Padano, and that Pecorino-seasoned crust. The pizzas are tasty, if a little chewy. I appreciated their baking them a tad longer the next night, to fully crisp up the undercarriage. You have to respect their spartan approach, using just a few ingredients on top, while letting the complexity of their dough do most of the talking.

One of the big challenges for pizza nomads is always popping up in different locations with different ovens. The first night I tried

their pizzas, they were operating out of the kitchen at Wicker Park's Enoteca Roma. They were clearly having issues with the bake times. But I returned the next night and found the pizzas much improved. Maybe wait to order a pie on their second night in residence, so they have time to work out the kinks. The other challenge involves their lives outside of pizza. Carmen wants to go back to art school. Sean wants to be a restaurateur. In the meantime, they ask customers to send them money electronically, and then after expenses, they make one big donation to an organization of their choosing. They're also making bagels, baguettes, and sandwich bread—you might see their handiwork show up on the lunch menu at Boeufhaus one of these days—but plan on seeing more of their pizza pop-ups as they get more adept at making adjustments with their starter, always adapting to the challenges an unfamiliar space provides.

NUDE DUDE FOOD

3530 N. Clark St.
www.nudedudefood.com
@nudedudefood
Weekend pop-up

WHAT HAPPENS WHEN your catering business for private dinner parties runs face-first into a pandemic? You bake bread, naturally. But Seth Bradley and Ryan Van Voorhis, the tattoo-clad gentlemen behind Nude Dude Food, also make a convincing pizza. They just might be the only bakers in town producing a weekend-only sourdough version that melds the best of Sicily and Detroit.

The name of their business comes from the fact they use the simplest ingredients, stripped down to their essence, but also because they will occasionally show up at events or media appearances in just overalls. Their motto is "Eat well, feel sexy."

Bradley says they started recipe testing in the summer of 2020, then opened up in the former Cemitas Puebla space on Fulton Market in December of that year.

They're making an enriched dough with extra virgin olive oil that includes their own natural starter. The dough gets a nice, long three- to five-day cold ferment, which helps break down the organic whole grains they source from Janie's Mill in Central Illinois (the same mill Great Lake is using). Several hours before service, they remove the dough from the cooler to bring it to room temperature.

"Long fermentation on the grains is something not typically talked about in Chicago," said Bradley. "It's all about the crust and the bread experience. We really want you to taste the grains."

Once the dough is panned out and has rested for four to six hours, they rim the pan with Wisconsin brick cheese, just as a traditional

Detroit-style place would, but they're not trying to make a Detroit-style pizza. They then add a basic San Marzano tomato sauce and shredded mozzarella. The night I visited, we also had a delicata squash and roasted carrot pie (no sauce) topped with pickled red onions and dollops of lemon truffle cream.

Like a slice of Swiss cheese, the crust is riddled with holes, a result of that long fermentation. The grains they're using give the interior a more rustic hue. The bottom is barely crispy; I would have preferred it a bit crunchier. (I learned later, when I interviewed Bradley, that they were having issues with the bottom burner on their French oven. I'm sure by the time you're reading this, they'll have solved that problem.) The top has a gorgeous, evenly browned surface of baked mozzarella, embedded with larger than normal slices of pepperoni from Tempesta Market that have just barely crisped-up around the edges. A few chopped fresh basil leaves are the only post-bake garnish.

Even though the sides have a consistent *frico*—the burnt cheese crisp—around the perimeter like a Detroit pie, there are no stripes of tomato sauce across the top, which makes it resemble a standard Sicilian from above. Even the height of the slice seems to be more in the grandma or Sicilian vein than a Detroit, but I'm splitting hairs here. At the end of the day, it's a solid nine-inch-square pan pizza with an artisan crust and a crispy cheese edge.

The squares are plenty for two people. I recommend you ask for the pizzas uncut, waiting until you get them home to cut yourself.

I'm normally not one to dip my crusts into ranch or other sauces. I find them gimmicky and unnecessary, like piling capers and eggs onto perfectly good caviar. It's usually a method of covering up something that should be able to stand on its own. But the three sauces they threw in with my order were on a different level. Especially the "Umami Thousand Island" with star anise, soy sauce, rice vinegar, and lemon juice. The tomato one, essentially extra sauce from the red pie, had only San Marzanos, fresh basil, salt, and olive oil, while the vibrant, herby "Green Goddess Ranch" proved to be a surprisingly delightful dip. I didn't need to wait until I was at the end of the slice, faced with just the crusty cheesy handle either. I dipped them throughout, and have no regrets.

Note: As of Spring 2021, they were hoping to expand pizza nights to Wednesday–Saturday instead of just Friday and Saturday. Be sure to check their Instagram for the latest information. Will still, however, just be pickup or delivery.

PAPER THIN PIZZA

At Soho House, 113–125 North Green Street
708-546-8462
www.exploretock.com/paperthinpizza
@paperthinpizza
Wednesday through Saturday

Andrew Anthony grew up in Naperville but bounced between Michigan and the East Coast growing up. His family is originally from Ann Arbor, so, not surprisingly, local icon Domino's plays an important role in his early pizza memories. He recalls visiting the Domino's farms just outside of town, as well as a franchise in North Carolina owned by one of his dad's friends, which made an early impression.

But the idea behind Paper Thin Pizza stems from wanting to create a hybrid of two thin pizzas: one, inspired by the über-thin pizzas at Fricano's, in Grand Haven, Michigan (where the pies are cut into wedges using a large scissors); the other, a richer, buttery Chicago crust.

"I wanted to combine an East Coast bar pie with a low-fat dough and a buttery Chicago-style crust" he said.

The low hydration dough is sheeted immediately after it's mixed, then left to dry out in a refrigerator between sheets of parchment paper for nearly a week.

The reason Anthony cuts them into wedges is to see if they pass his structural integrity test, which is not as dramatic and much harder to ascertain when you lift up a tiny square. St. Louis natives will appreciate the off-menu special request: homemade provel, inspired by Imo's, but made by combining mozzarella, provolone, and Wisconsin brick cheeses. He offers four different pies, and in addition to the usual toppings of fennel sausage (homemade), pepperoni, bacon, and vegetables, he always has broccoli on hand. "If it were my choice, every pizza would come with broccoli," said Anthony, an idea he got eating them at Arnie's in Wheaton when he was a kid.

PHLOUR BAKERY & CAFÉ

1138 W. Bryn Mawr Avenue
773-293-6135
www.phlour.com
@phlour_chicago
Sundays

Phlour is certainly the best bakery in Edgewater. Their rustic sourdoughs, flaky croissants, and hearty cinnamon rolls show the kitchen's command of bread and pastry. But like many pop-ups, there is no indication on their website of any pizza (beyond some round, tomato-topped focaccias). Yet stroll into the bakery on a Sunday, usually between 10 a.m. and 3 p.m., and you'll see three or four flavors of rectangular pizza set out in a sheet pan. They market them as Sicilians, but they're closer to a traditional bakery-style slice, with their spongier, focaccia-like interiors and cushioned undercarriages containing mammoth air pockets.

The day I visited, they had cup-and-char pepperoni (from Ezzo), with mozz, asiago, a homemade tomato sauce, fresh basil, balsamic glaze, and Parmigiano; a veggie-friendly option with black kale pesto, shaved fennel, and lemon zest; and an ode to Chicago with double fennel sausage and hot peppers. That's what I gravitated toward, and I just loved the toothsome boulders of sausage, with their punch of black pepper and fennel seeds. The chew is impressive, and easy sauce application provides an acidic balance, while whole milk mozz brings the richness. Had I not been impatient, I would have gone home, preheated my stone, then baked it for about four minutes, just to crisp the bottom and provide some additional texture.

I rarely say this, but the size of the slice is too large to be able to pick up and eat without using utensils. It could easily feed two. The only sizes available are the half sheet for $36, quarter sheet for $18, and eighth sheet for $9. Hey guys, how about a sixteenth sheet for $4.50? That would be the optimal size for grabbing and noshing on the go.

PIZZA FINESTRA

3059 W. Diversey (inside Superkhana International)
Tuesdays and Wednesdays, 10:30 a.m. to 2 p.m.
www.toasttab.com/superkhana-international/v3
@pizzafinestra
Tuesdays and Wednesdays

DURING THE PANDEMIC of 2020, the kitchen at Superkhana International in Logan Square began tapping into the secret desires of its staff, friends, and family. Not only could you order ahead and pick up a *tikka masala* calzone from the side window, but the kitchen also became a testing ground for former Lula Café pastry chef Kelly Helgesen, who started running Takeaway Bagel from the same spot.

With their double-stacked Blodgett ovens routinely cranking out blistered naans and now bagels, it was only a matter of time before pizza became an option. Simplicity is the key to the trio of Roman-style pizzas made each Sunday. The Bianca is made with white and whole wheat flours, brushed with olive oil and dusted with flaky salt. There is no cheese, so I'd recommend using it for dipping, toasting, or even forming the base of a sandwich. The Rossa, meanwhile, is their über-simple assembly of baked dough and reduced tomato sauce, with a drizzle of olive oil. I loved how crispy and thoroughly Roman it chewed but would have liked a bit more salt and a sauce that wasn't quite so thick. I could see myself taking home a Rossa, tearing a few pieces of fresh mozz on it, then finishing in the oven for five minutes.

Important note when ordering: in order to see the pizza options, you have to go to their order tab from the Superkhana website, then request a pickup. You can also link directly from their Instagram page.

SAUCE AND BREAD KITCHEN

6338–40 N. Clark Street
773-942-6384
www.sauceandbread.com
@sauceandbread
Fridays

FINDING A BILLIARD HALL, car repair, Ethiopian restaurant, or taqueria along the 6300 block of North Clark Street in Edgewater is easy. Artisan pizza? Not so much. But the Sauce and Bread collaboration proved in 2020 that having a weekly "Pizza Night" could mean many things.

The charming shop offers exquisite baked goods, hearty, two-fisted sandwiches, meal kits, and an assortment of fresh pantry items. Anne Kostroski previously had a baking business called Crumb; her friend Mike Bancroft had worked at a fundraiser for a youth art camp, where he and the campers started growing peppers. That led to making and selling hot sauces as another form of fundraising, under the Co-op Sauce brand, which would usually find its way into local farmers' markets. The two decided to join forces to share expenses like city licensing and permits, opening Sauce and Bread Kitchen in a former Venezuelan restaurant next door to an Irish pub.

Pre-COVID, they started a Friday "Pizza Night" served buffet style, with all of the proceeds donated to a different nonprofit each week. Back then, sales could generate up to $3,000 in one night. Now, however, whole pies are sold for pickup only, and proceeds go toward providing free meals to those in need due to the pandemic.

In an effort to end the week with zero waste, the pair have come up with some creative pizza toppings, including some with fried rice or bacon and fennel. Their most outrageous pie is likely "The Kraken"—a white pie with squid ink, umeboshi plum sauce, and fried yakisoba noodles, topped with caviar.

On a typical Friday, they'll have cheese pizza, homemade sausage, and three to four different oddball pies. Customers can also call in and request custom toppings.

They use high-gluten all-purpose flour and oil for a wet, focaccia-like dough. It's mixed two days before

baking, so the dough can cold ferment in the cooler. The shallow pan pizza resembles a cross between grandma- and Detroit-style, with a crispy, firm crust but a somewhat chewier interior featuring some impressive open crumb. "I just call it pizza," said Kostroski.

While her specialty is the bread, Bancroft takes over when it comes to the sauce. Sourcing most of his ingredients from the Midwest, the simple sauce includes tomatoes, onions, fresh garlic, and dried spices. They also make occasional white pies with chili crisp for some of their non-tomato-based pies.

PAIRING PIZZA WITH (LOCAL) BEER

JOSH NOEL

Whiner Beer with Le Pizza

There's no more elemental pairing than beer and pizza. Yet for years, Chicago's pizza production far outstripped its brewing output.

The craft beer revolution helped balance that equation. With about two hundred breweries in the Chicagoland area at the beginning of 2021—up from just a handful in the late '80s—rare is the pizza place that doesn't have at least a couple of Chicago-made beers on draft or in the cooler.

But dig deeper and there's a wonderful truth about the modern intersection of Chicago pizza and Chicago beer: there's a locally made beer for every locally made pizza, no matter the style, the toppings, or the occasion.

The pairing of beer and pizza in this city can be a carefully considered fete or a complete and delicious afterthought. If you want nothing more than an upgrade from the standard light lager, there's a Chicago beer for that. If you want a more ambitious pairing, there's a locally produced beer for that, too.

Here are the beer styles—and the essential Chicago beers—that pair perfectly with some of the range of pizza styles available in Chicago:

LIGHT LAGER

Light, easy-drinking lager has long been the domain of the big guys—Bud, Miller, and (this being Chicago) Old Style. But after years of sneering at such beers, craft brewers have gradually seen the appeal.

For a crowning example, Lemont's Pollyanna Brewing has the hardware to back up the quiet genius of its Lite Thinking, a light lager that offers a touch more heft than Bud Light or Miller Lite, but remains far easier drinking than, say, Budweiser. Lite Thinking has been twice honored by the Great American Beer Festival, with a gold medal in 2019 and a bronze medal in 2020. It's a *very* light beer—but that's the point. It's a faultless beer beside any pizza, with a bright and refreshing character that resets the palate after each sip.

Other options include Spiteful Lager, a beer that's as light as it is fascinating, with very soft white wine aromatics, and Dovetail Brewing's Helles lager.

ALTBIER

Except in Düsseldorf, Germany, where it is the house beverage, altbier is mostly an afterthought across the globe. But it is perhaps *the* perfect pairing with pizza.

Altbier? Really? Yes, really. Altbier.

Germans are mostly known for their lagers, but altbier is a German-style ale that lands somewhere between bronze and brown—malty, lightly roasty, a tad spicy, and just bitter enough to be brawny while refreshing. Altbier complements every wrinkle of a pizza, all the way down to the tang of the tomato sauce. It's pairing perfection.

There was virtually no chance of finding fresh altbier in this city before the rise of craft beer. Today, a handful of breweries make the style, usually in spring and fall, including Dovetail Brewery, Oak Park's Kinslahger Brewing, and Pollyanna, which plans to release an altbier (which it plans to market as an "amber ale") in the spring of 2021.

PILSNER

One step beyond light lager is pilsner: clean, crisp, and refreshing, but muscular in its hop bitterness. It's that bold hop-forward character that makes pilsner such a faultless pizza pairing, cutting through the grease and cheese, mingling nicely with the bready crust, and shining especially brightly alongside any meat topping. Pilsner's key is that it showcases herbal, bitter European hops, rather than the fruity American hops found in most India pale ales. German- and Czech-style pilsners provide a stiff, pleasing backbone that complements virtually any pizza spectacularly.

Fortunately, Chicago is rife with pilsner production. Among the very finest are Maplewood Brewing's Pulaski Pils, Pipeworks Brewing's Premium Pilsner, and Revolution Brewing's Rev Pils.

FARMHOUSE/SAISON

Farmhouse ales, which include saisons, are among the most food-friendly beers, no matter the dish. When it comes to pizza, that's particularly true at the fancier end of the spectrum: those high-end ingredients—prosciutto, roasted or pickled vegetables, imported *bufala* mozzarella—deserve high-end beer. At their best, farmhouse ales are complex and fascinating beers with a bright mix of lively flavors, ranging from fruity to peppery to tart rustic funk.

Off Color Brewing's Apex Predator and Whiner's Le Tub are two of the most dependable farmhouse ales in town, and both are flagships available throughout the year. Two smaller purveyors worth looking for are Is/Was brewing and Lombard's Afterthought Brewing.

AND DON'T FORGET . . .

- ☞ In 2020, Off Color launched a "Beer For" series that includes beers "for" golfing, burgers, beaches, and, yup, pizza. Beer For Pizza is meant to evoke cola, made with ingredients that include dark candy syrup, kola nut, lime juice, vanilla, and lemon and orange zests. It's meant to evoke the pizza-and-soda parties of your youth. It threads the needle beautifully and is a wickedly fun pairing to boot.
- ☞ Kölsch is a style that has had moments of popularity that never last, and that's too bad; it's a bright, crisp, and lightly fruity ale—fruitiness that comes from the yeast, not from actual fruit—that pairs wonderfully with pizza. Several breweries dabble in the style, though two excellent year-round options are made by Metropolitan Brewing (Krankshaft) and Dovetail (Kolsch).
- ☞ Craft beer's most popular style is far and away IPA. It's not a style that pairs particularly well with pizza, but it certainly *can* work, especially one with a malty backbone (such as Revolution Brewing's Anti-Hero IPA, Hailstorm Brewing's Prairie Madness, or Spiteful Brewing's Spiteful IPA) to stand up to the crust, cheese, tomato, and toppings.
- ☞ Haymarket Brewing, which operates a brewpub in the West Loop and a production brewery in southwest Michigan, released a pitch-perfect pizza-pairing beer in late 2020, all the way down to its no-frills name: Chicago Tavern Beer. The amber brew is a crisp dortmunder lager, which is yet another German style of beer that sits expertly alongside cheese, grease, and meat. It's a bit heartier and maltier than pilsner, but not quite as roasty as altbier. Its crispness, hop bitterness, and malt character complement pizza splendidly.

Josh Noel *has written about beer and the beer industry for the* Chicago Tribune *since 2009 and is the author of the 2018 book* Barrel-Aged Stout and Selling Out: Goose Island, Anheuser-Busch, and How Craft Beer Became Big Business.

Clockwise from upper left: *Bar Cargo, Roebuck, Tripoli Tap, Sapori Napoletani*

PERO

15 SUBURBAN STARS

I REALIZE THIS BOOK, UNLIKE ITS PREDECESSOR, excludes a lot of suburban pizzas. As I mentioned in the introduction, I wanted readers to use this guide as a resource if they were only in Chicago for a couple of days, which prohibited me from repeating places like Joe's in Wheeling or Pizzeria Deville in Libertyville. There's just no way a visitor with limited time is going to get in a car and schlep thirty miles for a pizza. That said, if you are looking for great places to find pizza in Palos Park, Lake Forest, or Homewood, please pick up a copy of *Pizza City, USA*. It's got Top 5 picks, maps, and a ton of thin, tavern-style joints in it.

My goal with this chapter was twofold: first, I wanted desperately to include places I missed last time due to publishing deadlines—places like Lefty's in Wilmette, Grateful Bites in Winnetka, and The Wooden Paddle in Lemont. Second, I felt it necessary and important to include the suburban icons that have sustained our region for decades. Joints like Freddy's in Cicero and Louisa's in Crestwood, or Barnaby's on the North Shore, with their perfectly crimped crusts. Even though there are Lou Malnati's located in practically every suburb and throughout the city, I felt it was important to go back to the mother ship in Lincolnwood and talk to Marc Malnati about how his dad and "papa," Adolpho, helped shape the deep-dish pizza we know today.

Classic deep-dish at Lou Malnati's

Generations of Chicagoans have grown up on pizzas in the suburbs, and so if you're going to talk about pizza here, you can't really ignore the collar counties. I realize I've left out Aurelio's in Homewood; also Phil's in Oak Lawn and Armand's in Elmhurst. Some of them were mentioned in the first book, but after return visits in the past two years, I just haven't felt as strongly about recommending them. Part of the reason lies with them. I think that may be the case at places like Fox's in Beverly and Fasano's in Summit—just careless cooks not keeping an eye on consistency. But the other part of this Third Wave of pizza is that there are now *so many* great pizzas being made, the newer ones are pushing some of the older, more tired versions to the back of the line.

My criteria for inclusion in this chapter was simple: if you're going to be in the suburbs for any reason, these independents are certainly worth a visit, either because of nostalgia, their significance and impact on the local pizza scene, or simply because they make a unique pie that is consistently outstanding.

When I was growing up in the 1970s, my mother and father worked hard to support the family and we never wanted for anything—but things like vacations, beyond a drive to Michigan, or dinners in restaurants were not part of our world. Most Fridays, we'd have pizza for dinner, usually from Jewel—but about once a month, my dad would come home with a large cheese and sausage pizza from the Aurelio's in South Holland, and that was like Christmas any time of the year! (At the time, we kids didn't appreciate just how much of an expense that was to my mom and dad, who had to make every penny count while raising four children.) To this day, I can picture the whole family at the Formica-topped kitchen table, with everyone talking at once and sharing stories of their day while we tore into that pizza like it was our last meal.

I've had the luxury of dining out hundreds of times at fine restaurants in Chicago and many places around the world, but nothing will ever top those Friday night pizza dinners.

—**RICHARD ROEPER**, *Chicago Sun-Times* critic and columnist, author, and the former cohost of *Ebert & Roeper*

The counter at Freddy's in Cicero (top) *and a "Quatro Stagione" (Four Seasons) pie* (below left); *deep-dish at Louisa's* (below right)

BARNABY'S OF NORTHBROOK

960 Skokie Boulevard, Northbrook
847-498-3900
www.barnabysofnorthbrook.com
@barnabyspizza
Style: Tavern-style thin

There are Barnaby's locations in Niles and Arlington Heights, as well as a temporarily (but likely permanently) closed one in Des Plaines. They are all unrelated to the original in Northbrook.

Talk about PIGUE (Pizza I Grew Up Eating) Syndrome. After I posted a picture following my unannounced visit to Barnaby's, my Facebook and Instagram lit up with breathless melancholy. "I went there all throughout high school" and "Been going there for twenty years" came the reactions to my nattily crimped, thin, tavern-style pizza photo post.

No question it's a good pie. Although despite North Shore myth, they do not make a cornmeal crust. They simply use cornmeal—as many other places do—beneath the pizza to keep it from sticking to the oven deck. That cornmeal forms a lovely, even shield across the undercarriage, adding a pleasant, corn-fueled crunch to each bite. And everyone who grew up within five miles of the original Barnaby's, located in Northbrook, claims it to be the center of the pizza universe. So to get the true Barnaby's experience, I headed to the Northbrook mother ship. Filbert's root beer and Green River soda—both a source of nostalgia for Chicagoans of a certain age—wouldn't color my opinion.

First, a few words about the other Barnaby's in the area, which sow a lot of confusion. According to the manager on duty the day I bought my pie, the founders tried setting up a corporation with branches for family members only. But in order to get the exact recipe, they would have to pay a licensing fee. They all declined. The only rule, according to this manager, is that they have to relinquish the Barnaby's name if they ever sell to anyone outside of the family. Now that the Des Plaines location is temporarily closed—and the owner is in his eighties—if he sells to someone outside of the family, the name must change. This is why the mother ship goes by "Barnaby's of Northbrook." The "Barnaby's Family Inn" in Arlington Heights and the "Barnaby's of Niles" *each* have separate websites, and according to the Northbrook original, the other locations are working with a different recipe, despite all of them using the same imagery and backstory. The pizza boxes from Northbrook say they opened in 1968; the other ones say 1969. Yikes!

Getting down to my pizza, the sausage side (covered in cheese) was respectable, and I loved how the surface contained tiny, brown specks from the oven's heat. On the other side, my pepperoni was decent—thin circles, about an inch across, just barely beginning to "cup" from the heat, although not quite as crisp as I would have liked. The crust is what you're coming here for. At first glance, the perimeter looks like it was baked in a mini tart pan, with its rippled crimping all the way around. It's thin 'n'

crispy, and when you take a bite, the sound is actually audible.

That's a pretty good sign. I saw some air pockets in the cutaway section of the pie, indicating there might be some fermentation or at least a decent period of resting for the dough. The sauce is innocuous, like a BTS song—not offensive, not particularly notable, but its presence is pleasing. You must eat this pizza no more than five minutes out of the oven for optimal appreciation. Sure, you could bring it home, but the experience isn't the same. Many years ago, my wife and I attended a wedding reception across the street. We arrived in the early afternoon, following the ceremony, but had several hours to go until the dinner. Guess what we brought back to our room at 3 p.m.?

Is this the best thin crust in the region? Definitely not. Is it worth a detour if you're heading down the Edens Expressway and feel the urge to devour a pizza? Absolutely. There's a reason generations of families (including my wife's) have been coming here since 1968.

B SQUARE PIZZA

601 N. Milwaukee Avenue, Wheeling
(delivery only, five-mile radius)
224-676-0312
www.bsquarepizzadelivery.com
@bsquarepizza
Style: Detroit

DURING THE PANDEMIC, Chicago's Lettuce Entertain You Enterprises launched a pair of ghost kitchen pizza concepts, available only for pickup or delivery. One of them, Bill's Original Tavern Pizza, operates out of the same kitchen as Portofino. The other one—B Square Pizza—is a Detroit-style concept operating out of Saranello's restaurant inside the Westin Hotel in Wheeling; a downtown Chicago location for delivery only exists as well (see chapter 9, "Detroit-Syle").

They deliver within a five-mile radius of the hotel, so if you live near Wheeling, Northbrook, Riverwoods, or Deerfield, you're eligible.

Based on the height of the pizza, it appears more grandma than Detroit, but chef Mychael Bonner says that's the plan. There is a crispy-cheesy edge and a mildly crispy undercarriage that I thought could use some more attention (Bonner admitted after I posted a picture of the blond undercarriage it was an execution error, and it should be more caramelized).

They include small containers of marinara, ranch and extra Parmesan on the side, which I guess will come in handy for some, although providing extras like these in pizzerias always makes me think there's something amiss with the pizza. Do you really need extra tomato sauce, sour cream, or cheese to give the pizza the appropriate flavor combination? Is the slice that bland if you don't? I've been out with my New Yorker friends and have witnessed them reflexively reach for the dried cheese, pepper flakes, and oregano without even tasting the pizza first. I think you need to give it a try before dunking thoughtlessly into ranch (looking at you, Andrew Dordek).

Their cheese blend contains the traditional Wisconsin brick as well as mozzarella and Parmesan, while the tomato sauce is pleasantly mild and vaguely sweet, which was just fine. And even though this synopsis may at first glance seem unenthusiastic, I do think if you live up on the North Shore and there isn't a Jet's nearby, B Square is a great alternative.

CHEF BILL KIM'S PIZZA & PARM SHOP

1225 Twenty-Second Street, Oak Brook (inside Michael Jordan's Restaurant)
630-828-2932
www.cbkpizzaparm.com
@cbkpizzaparm
Style: Detroit

Bill Kim is one of the city's most respected chefs, having served two (!) separate terms in the kitchen at Charlie Trotter's. The Korean American chef grew up in a Chicago neighborhood with a colorful quilt of immigrants, including a lot of Italians. Those memories convinced him, eight months into the pandemic, to dive into the deep end of pizza research. He had already built loyal followings at Urban Belly, Belly Shack, and Belly Q for his riffs on Korean comfort food, but with two of those stores closed, and a single Urban Belly remaining in Wicker Park, a lot of his attention in 2019 and 2020 turned to Oak Brook. It was there that he partnered with Crate & Barrel to create the vegetable-forward menu at Table at Crate, which is conveniently located across the street from Michael Jordan's Restaurant, a property owned by his business partners from Cornerstone Management.

With a staff in place at Table, Kim began experimenting with pan pizzas, specifically, Detroit-style. The kitchen at Jordan's became the test site. He consulted Peter Reinhart's excellent *Perfect Pan Pizza* and began making doughs in the fall of 2020. He lets the doughs rest overnight before panning them out for an hour or so the next day. Topped with brick cheese and some Pecorino, plus his homemade marinara, there are just a few options to choose from: sausage, pepperoni, and cheese. The pepperoni is thin and curls up nicely when baked, revealing slightly charred edges. Since he wasn't baking on a stone deck at the time I visited, there wasn't a ton of oven spring in the dough, although I preferred the corners to the rest of the pie, as they had some height and more open crumb than the middle. My only quibble: since he removes the pizza to finish baking for three minutes directly on a preheated sheet pan, the pizza's undercarriage leans a tad too dry for my taste. I think baking in the sturdy Lloyd steel pans from beginning to end is one of the keys to great Detroit-style pizza. Having the ability to properly oil them in advance, then let them do their magic to the bottom, is one of the payoffs, in addition to the formation of the burnt cheese edge.

By the time you're reading this, they will probably have added a new deck oven, allowing him to do just that. The pizzas are pick-up or delivery only, based out of Michael Jordan's Restaurant at the base of an office building on Twenty-Second Street. Oak Brook has had the wonderful La Barra down the street for years, with its excellent artisan, thin, and deep pies; Labriola's Neapolitans are practically next door. Now with Kim's Pizza & Parm a short drive away, the western suburbs have some great options for both pan and hearth-baked pies (and while you're there, might as well get a delicious chicken Parm sandwich to go).

Note: They also opened another location tucked within the Urban Belly space in Wicker Park.

FREDDY'S PIZZA

1600 S. Sixty-First Avenue, Cicero
(708) 863-9289
www.freddyspizza.com
Styles: Thin and Sicilian

EVEN IN AN AGE where old-school mom-and-pops have embraced social media, it's still charming (and not at all surprising) the Quercias have either shunned Instagram or more likely haven't had the time to set up an account. No matter when you enter this charming brick Italian deli, Joe or his wife, Ann Marie, are always hustling behind the wood-and-glass counter, running between the kitchen and the gelato maker or unloading the ovens and bringing some sort of salad or pizza or baked Italian grandma dish to the front counter while they greet the regulars and restock the imported containers of Partanna olive oil on the shelves. When I went in to shoot photos for this book, Joe insisted on showing me his new meat curing cooler and eventually sent me home with some hot soppressata.

A trip to Freddy's is as close as Chicagoans can get to the feeling of stumbling into a midcentury throwback in Brooklyn or Queens, but this deli happens to be in Cicero, just nine miles west of downtown, not far from where Al Capone used to have a house. It's the kind of place where most of the cooks are older dudes with graying hair and generous bellies; where the owners give the regulars a little something extra to snack on while they wait for their orders on busy Friday afternoons. If you never had an Italian grandma stuffing your face with mostaccioli or eggplant Parm as a kid, spend twenty minutes here talking to Ann Marie, asking questions about what you see before you, and you'll be full before you even get to the gelato.

In 1955, Francesco (Frank) De Luca—who previously worked at Sunny Boy Bakery in Chicago—named his place Freddy's in honor of his father, Ferdinando. The old man owned a fish store in Cicero back then and made Italian ice there. Joe Quercia started working at the original Freddy's location in 1968 at the age of thirteen. As a recent immigrant from Cimitile (Naples), Italy, he could neither speak nor understand English. If there's a more impressive worked-your-way-up-from-the-ground-floor story in Chicagoland, I've yet to hear it.

There are several types of pizzas offered at Freddy's, including their legendary Sicilian-style, but in terms of thin, they offer a few types, like a rectangular sheet-pan-style they call "Margherita" and a more standard round pizza. I tried one of each.

The Margherita is affordable, typically sold by the slice, and you should know that a full sheet will feed a small army of hungry teenagers. It's a different dough from the one they use for their Sicilian, and the key is fermentation—at least a day and a half. Baked in a giant Blodgett deck oven, the pizza emerges charred on the edges and bubbling in the middle, with more *fior di latte* cheese than most delis have in their entire cheese section. Basil is sprinkled on liberally, like the sprinkles at Mandy B's, and the sauce is as ruby red as Dorothy's shoes—full of imported tomatoes bursting with flavor and acidity.

I like this pizza. It's not really a classic VPN or DOP Neapolitan, but the Quercias—who try to visit a part of Italy every summer and have been to Naples—say that locals sometimes don't want one of those soggy and wet Neapolitans, preferring something with more heft. This one certainly delivers.

Same goes for their thin pizzas, as well as their sturdy Sicilians, which will typically get finished directly on the stone hearth (make sure you ask that this has been done, to ensure a fantastic, crispier undercarriage). The slices are puffy and generous, and the toppings are sourced as meticulously as at any hipster kitchen downtown. I particularly enjoyed the "Quatro Stagione" (Four Seasons) Sicilian, with quadrants of broccoli, mushroom, spinach, and paper-thin pepperoni. One reason you find yourself reaching for another piece is the slight tanginess and sourness that comes from a long fermentation as well as a solid OBR. There are also some interesting little air pockets here, which lend the pizza even more character and chew.

Do yourself a favor and save room for the gelato. Trust me.

GRATEFUL BITES PIZZA SHOPPE

899 Green Bay Road, Winnetka
(847) 386-9141
www.gratefulbites.com
@gratefulbites
Style: Wood-fired artisan

GRATEFUL BITES PIZZA SHOPPE is a very personal little place hidden among upscale boutiques, women's clothing stores, and a Walgreen's. The dough is clearly the focus here, and it is fermented for at least seventy-two hours.

"We're about three days. It's a sourdough starter so there's no commercial yeast. Literally the only thing that's in there is flour, water, salt," said owner Matt Halack.

Halack certainly wasn't aiming for a place with a ton of foot traffic. Located on a sleepy stretch of downtown Winnetka on the North Shore, this is a place most customers come to pick up pizzas to go since the dining room has only a handful of seats. That's a shame, since this exceptional wood-fired artisan pie doesn't travel well—like most wood-fired pies.

"I wish it traveled a little better, but they seem to have embraced it pretty well so far," he said.

A standard red with tomatoes, Pecorino Romano cheese, and mozzarella can be topped with pepperoni and fired for about two minutes; it's finished with a hot honey to balance the flavors.

"If you have hot, you can add sweet to balance. Acid, sweet, it's always kind of yin and yang," said Halack.

The same principle applies to his elote pizza, topped with corn and then drizzled with Japanese Kewpie mayo, crumbled cotija cheese, fresh cilantro, and a dusting of chili.

Chicago Italian beef fans will really dig the sausage with Halack's homemade giardiniera. There are always six red pizzas on the menu, and three white pizzas. You could certainly customize yours by adding your own ingredients, but if you like the taste of sausage, the version with the sausage and giardiniera is a true taste of Chicago. Just do yourself a favor and eat the pizza in the dining room or in your car; waiting until you get home—even if you reheat it in a skillet as is typically recommended for this style—will result in a completely different (and less thrilling) experience.

LA BARRA

3011 Butterfield Road, Oak Brook
630-861-6177
@labarraristorante
www.labarraristorante.com
Styles: Artisan and deep-dish

IN 2015, AFTER decades in the artisan bread business, Rich Labriola took over a vacant space in Oak Brook to set up his pizza fantasyland. This was after he had already opened his namesake café in the adjacent strip mall, where he served Neapolitan-style pizzas from a wood-burning oven. He recruited a chef from downtown with a good reputation, and they tried to come up with something truly unique for his sophomore effort—La Barra; it's as big as its ambitions.

The restaurant offers three types of pizza: tavern-style, deep-dish, and their signature coal-fired artisan pie, which emerges from the brick oven with some of the most beautiful crusts in the tri-state area. Labriola excels with anything fermented, deploying *bigas* (pre-ferments) and natural starters like James Bond dialing up the features on his tricked-out car. While I absolutely love their artisan pie (the "Dante Margherita" still haunts me), it's the deep-dish the purists will really love.

I never saw it coming. I'm hit like a quarterback on the blind side by Singletary on the blitz when my twelve-inch deep-dish with sausage is placed in front of me, and I like what I see: generous, chunky icebergs of fresh tomato, lightly seasoned with dried oregano; jagged-edged pieces of sausage, fragrant and juicy, embedded with fennel seed, tucked within melted Grande mozzarella; and then the best surprise of all—as I lift out my first piece, I see that outer edge, just like Pequod's. There's a caramelized, darkened, thin layer of cheese clinging to the perimeter, all the way around like a Detroit-style *frico*. This dough is so firm you don't need a knife and fork. In fact, I dare you to simply use your hands. The other benefit here is the OBR—Labriola spent countless hours trying to get that balance right.

It seems strange to say it, but out in a quiet Oak Brook mall, next to a corporate plaza, overlooking a man-made lake, an Italian guy has cracked the code—after a lot of trial and error, no doubt—and is creating the best deep-dish in Chicagoland, now available in the suburbs as well as just off Michigan Avenue.

HUGE GALDONES

LEFTY'S PIZZA KITCHEN

1156 Central Avenue, Wilmette
847-920-5401

600 Central Avenue, Highland Park
847-926-7194
www.leftyspizzakitchen.com

@leftyspizzakitchen
Style: Deep pan

LOOK AT SLEEPY little Wilmette go! I wrote about the Neapolitan pies coming out of the oven at Napolita (one of just six AVPN certified pizzerias in the region) in *Pizza City, USA*. I returned to the North Shore community to check out their latest addition—an homage to one of Morton Grove's beloved pizzerias. If you love Burt's and Pequod's, you're definitely going to appreciate Lefty's. It's an offshoot of sorts, created in that tradition of Sicilian-style dough, but Chicago deep pan–style, with a caramelized cheese perimeter along the upper half of the pie known as a *frico*.

Not something you're likely to find at most pizza joints in the region, but this recipe—and technique—dates back to the 1970s.

The finished pies, with their light brown undercarriages and fennel-jammed chunks of sausage, certainly look familiar to anyone who grew up in the northern suburbs. That's because this deep pan—currently the featured item at Lefty's Pizza Kitchen in downtown Wilmette—has roots in Morton Grove, since the owner here used to be involved with Burt's 2.0.

"After the rehab and grand reopening [of Burt's], I left, sold my stake back, came here, opened up, and brought some of the recipe with me—I had to change it a little bit," said John Munao, the owner of Lefty's.

They still add oil to the dough and let it proof overnight, then shape it into balls, placed in a well-oiled deep pan to proof again for a few hours at ambient temperature. The Sicilian-like dough is pressed out into the round pan, spread evenly; then thin slices of whole

milk mozzarella are layered on top, some of them touching the interior wall so they'll caramelize during the bake..

Once the mozzarella barrier is installed, a thick, reduced tomato sauce is ladled over the top, spread thin and even. Then toppings of your choice: pepperoni if you're from elsewhere, raw sausage if you're a Chicagoan, with the legendary "pinch-and-press" method in effect here. Finally, a healthy shake of dried oregano, followed by a generous sprinkle of Parmigiano—a bit of saltiness to balance that rich mozzarella. The pan goes into the oven for about thirty minutes.

"It's not your typical deep-dish. Burt did not call it a deep-dish. Burt called it a pan pizza. It's a breadier, Sicilian style," Munao said.

Pizzas are cut with a knife the size of a sword from *Game of Thrones*, and you can see immediately, there's a difference inside the crust, which is indeed breadier, denser, and not nearly as light and airy as a Sicilian. They also make thin-crust pies here, but they're started in the deep pans first, then removed to finish on the stone deck. Munao said thin remains the most popular, until customers realize they're actually known for deep pan.

"Once they figure out the style, then they start to order the pan. But both have been very popular," he said.

Munao opened a second location in Highland Park in early 2021.

LOUISA'S PIZZA AND PASTA

14025 S. Cicero Avenue, Crestwood
708-371-0950
@louisaspizzapasta
Style: Deep-dish

While there are dozens of places you can find deep-dish pizza in Chicagoland, only a handful can truly claim a direct link to the original recipe. Current owners at Pizano's and Lou Malnati's are actually related to one of the early employees from Pizzeria Uno—Adolpho (Rudy) Malnati. Gino's East opened its doors in 1966 with the help of Alice Mae Redmond, who spent years in the kitchen at Uno and Due. The only other restaurant with a direct link to those original recipes would be Louisa's, in south suburban Crestwood.

Louise DeGenero's family came to America from Abruzzo and settled in West Virginia, where her father was a coal miner. At the beginning of World War II, Louise moved to Detroit briefly as part of the "Rosie the Riveter" movement of young women helping out the war effort. By the end of the decade, her father moved the family to Chicago, where he worked as a longshoreman. Louise found work in a local hotel before landing a job at Due's in 1959.

"Lou and Rudy [Malnati] loved my mom," said Linda Fitzgerald, now in her seventies. She remembers her mom starting the job at Due's when she was in the seventh grade. "She would go up to their houses on the North Shore and cook for them: gnocchi, pastas . . . They were all very close."

DeGenero worked as a waitress at Due for twenty-two years, learning every aspect of the famous "deep-dish" pizza: the type and source of the tomatoes, the blend of sausage, and, most important, the amount of oil in the dough. By 1980, she left to open her own place, Louisa's Pizza and Pasta, on a stretch of South Cicero Avenue that has about as much charm as the border town Sarah Conner retreated to in *Terminator 2*. I was reminded of the mind-numbing series of featureless strip malls along the Roosevelt corridor between Lombard and Villa Park for comparison. The space has a cozy bar and a pair of dining rooms that transport you to another era—think Harvey Wallbangers and Long Island Iced Teas. But you come here for the pizza, and Louise's granddaughter—Kara—is now in charge of carrying on the tradition into their fifth decade.

The pizzas exist somewhere in the purgatory between full-on deep-dish and thin (sort of like My Pi in Bucktown). Assembled and baked in two-inch-deep, round, carbon steel pans that have built up years of wear and tear on the outsides, the oily

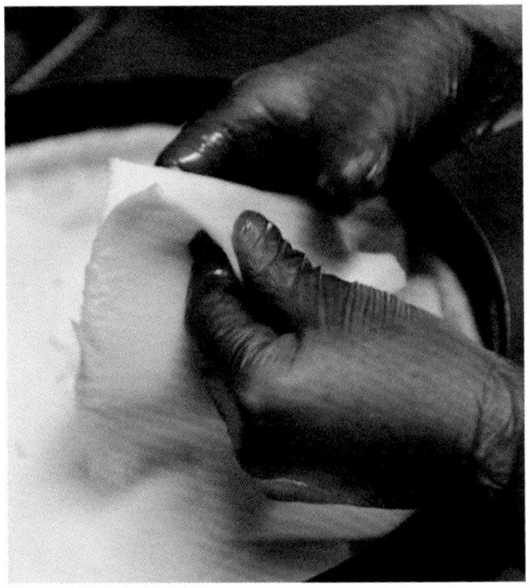

bread dough, made with Ceresota flour, is pressed thin into the pan, and only rises on the sides about an inch. Definitely shorter than a traditional East Coast Sicilian.

"She never made it thick," said Linda. "It was always a thinner pan and the sides were lower than most places today."

If you're familiar with grandma-style pizzas on the East Coast (I talk about them in chapter 8), imagine the same height and construction, only assembled in a round pan rather than a rectangular one. And like an "upside-down" grandma, the cheese always goes first. The thin slices of Wisconsin part-skim serve as a barrier to the sauce, to prevent the bottom dough from getting soggy. Sausage is the most popular topping by a long shot, and Anichini Brothers makes theirs, based on a recipe perfected by Louise that's exclusive to them. California tomatoes with a hint of basil are as chunky as a bowl of Texas chili, strained to reduce the liquid. Just before the pies are placed into the oven, they're given a healthy shower of grated Parmesan.

Figure around forty-five minutes for baking—the steel pans rotate from the bottom oven (a gas-fired, stone-lined Blodgett) after twenty minutes, finishing in the top oven for the remainder—and you typically need to ask if you want the pizza cut into slices.

At the bottom and up along the sides, a sturdy, slightly rich, buttery—and yes, flaky—crust holds in the bottom layer of mozzarella; extra-large hunks of cooked sausage embedded with fennel add substance to the middle layer; and a blanket of slightly thick, deep-red tomatoes lies across the top. Like at Lou's and Pizano's, the sausage is hidden beneath the sauce, rendering its fat into the bottom layer of cheese, ultimately mixing with the oil-enriched dough, enhancing the flavor. The ingredients cover everything except the outermost ring of crust, which is remarkably crispy. The edge, which has risen only slightly during the bake, is browned in spots, yielding to a fork, but somehow riding that beautiful middle ground between crispy exterior and softened, cheese-riddled interior.

"Ours is just like Due's in the 1950s," said Linda Fitzgerald. "We've kept it exactly like it was."

LOU MALNATI'S PIZZERIA

6649 N. Lincoln Avenue, Lincolnwood
847-673-0800
www.loumalnatis.com
@loumalnatis
Style: Deep-dish

Located almost everywhere in Chicagoland, with more than fifty locations in the city and suburbs.

Why did I choose to place Lou's in the "Suburban Stars" chapter? Because even though there are literally dozens of locations now, the mother ship in Lincolnwood is where it all started, and the business celebrates an impressive fifty years in business in 2021. Thousands of people and several generations grew up going to that quaint building on Lincoln Avenue over the years, so it's only appropriate any discussion about this iconic spot begins and ends in Lincolnwood. It's been the site of countless birthdays and post-game Little League celebrations, and for a lot of people on the North Side, it's like going home again—if you grew up nearby. Not unlike a visit to Hackney's or Vito & Nick's or Charlie Beinlich's, there is a large amount of nostalgia served up with the house special: deep-dish pizza.

Lou Malnati worked at Pizzeria Uno and Due for more than twenty years, along with his father, Rudy, who was one of the early employees who joined Ric Novaretti ("Riccardo") and Ike Sewell, shortly after Riccardo created a deeper pizza than locals were accustomed to. (I discuss more of the Uno's backstory in the introduction to chapter 5.) In 1970, Lou asked Sewell about equity and potential ownership (Riccardo had passed away in '54 and Rudy's health was not great—he had been hit by a car). According to Marc Malnati, one of Lou's sons, Sewell told Lou he loved him like a son, but for whatever reason, he wasn't going to sell Uno and Due to him. Instead, he sold to a Popeye's Chicken franchisee from Boston, and the company has been based there ever since. News flash: Pizzeria Uno hasn't been owned by a Chicagoan for more than thirty years.

That was Lou's cue to leave, and so he quit to figure out his next move.

"We got our dad back," said Marc Malnati, after years of missing him while he opened, closed, and

Lou and Rudy at Uno's tenth anniversary

Lou and his dad, Adolpho ("Rudy"), in the 1960s at Su Casa

Lou at his namesake in Lincolnwood

essentially ran both pizzerias downtown plus the Su Casa Mexican restaurant next door to Due's.

Lou spent the next fourteen months plotting his return. A few weeks after an Albanian kid from Wheaton named John Belushi premiered at The Second City, on St. Patrick's Day 1971, in what was then the predominantly Jewish neighborhood of Lincolnwood, the Italian guy opened his namesake . . . a line stretched down the block. "My dad was a brilliant marketer," said Malnati. That fateful first day provided another story the younger Malnati would tell for years to come: a Cadillac crashed through the front wall, knocking out the bricks and breaking the arm of a customer inside. Fortunately, Lou knew some masonry guys who patched up the wall and they reopened on Day 2.

Sadly, Lou passed away just seven years later, and so Marc, by then in his twenties, his brother, Rick, and their mom took over the business. In the decades since, Lou's offspring have stretched the brand into nearly every Chicagoland nook and cranny. They've also set up a nationwide shipping apparatus, so your homesick cousins in California can get their deep-dish fix anytime, thanks to FedEx and Goldbelly.

I met my brother-in-law for lunch on the day set aside for this tasting, since he's a huge fan, and we ordered both the standard deep-dish plus a personal pizza featuring

Malnati's trademarked Buttercrust for an extra seventy-five cents.

Both versions arrive with a crispy-edged crust about two inches high on the outside and a tad shorter on the interior. That crust is sturdy, holding up the layer of Wisconsin mozzarella, lean sausage, and chunky tomato sauce.

In fact, like very few pizzerias in the region, Lou's understands OBR. Each bite is a perfect blend of cheese-to-crust-to-topping-to-sauce. And that sauce, a rough mix of chunky California tomatoes sprinkled with grated Pecorino Romano and seasoned with oregano, offers excellent acidity to balance the rich, melted cheese.

Pro tip: unless you specify "crumbled" on a sausage order, it will arrive as one mass, like a wide sausage frisbee set down onto the bottom layer of cheese. I'm not a fan of the sausage disc, as it covers the entire bottom, making an OBR difficult. (I still prefer the old-school, handmade style of breaking off

sausage pieces and spreading them around the pie, so the edges crisp up rather than just steam beneath cheese or sauce.) The pepperoni definitely has a stronger spice profile than most, offering a good contrast to the oozing mozzarella.

As for that Buttercrust, it's pretty tasty—but it's overkill. The fatty, melted mozzarella provides plenty of richness already, and adding a buttery crust just gilds the lily. There's nothing wrong with the regular crust, but in both cases, we noted how the whole pizza changed character after about ten minutes at the table. I'm guessing most customers aren't going to let their pizzas sit that long, since these slices are somewhat addictive.

NAPOLI PER TUTTI

181 Barrington Road, Schaumburg
224-653-9464
napolipertutti.com
@npt.pizzeria
Style: Neapolitan

You've got to check a lot of boxes in order to call what you're making a true Neapolitan pizza. The crust has to be made with "00," a finely milled flour from Italy; there's got to be San Marzano tomatoes, preferably from near Mt. Vesuvius; there must be *fior di latte*, or fresh mozzarella; and of course, it has to be baked in a wood-burning oven that reaches temps north of 900 degrees.

All of these boxes are checked at Napoli Per Tutti in Schaumburg, where a former cook from Ravenswood's Spacca Napoli makes the pies.

"Flour, tomatoes, cheeses. And also you have to have a really good oven," said co-owner and chef Henry de Leon, most likely the only suburban *pizzaiolo* who is APN certified. "Everything comes together, not just one item. It's everything. We use Caputo flour, "00" blue, and for cheese we use Grande that is from Wisconsin. It's really, really good."

The pizzas take about ninety seconds to bake. Beware, those of you used to crispy, crunchy crusts—this is a wetter pie, softer in the middle and on the edge. There's no getting it "well done."

There are several flavors to choose from, including prosciutto or crumbled sausage with rapini and smoked mozzarella.

Once the pies are drizzled with a bit of olive oil, de Leon stretches them ever so gently around the base of a pizza peel and promptly transfers them to the oven, where that stone deck starts baking them instantly.

De Leon said even though this softer, wetter style of pizza may not be as well known here, once guests get a look—and a whiff—things change.

"As soon as they see the plate with the pizza, they getting in love, and they see the steam and they smell the flavors," he said. "The simplicity in this pizza is the best."

COURTESY NAPOLI PER TUTTI

Here's another sign to show you just how authentic the Neapolitan pizza is here at Napoli Per Tutti: the dough is so delicate that you get the pizza served whole and cut it yourself at the table to preserve the integrity of the crust as long as possible. That's a trick the chef learned when he was working at Spacca Napoli in Ravenswood.

PALERMO'S 95TH ITALIAN CUISINE

4849 Ninety-Fifth Street, Oak Lawn
708-425-6262
www.palermos95th.com
@palermos95th
Style: Tavern-style thin

PALERMO'S HAS BEEN a South Side institution since 1961, serving the same local families, watching their children grow up, go on to college, and start families of their own. Lasagna, pasta, and pizza are its calling cards. Popping in unnoticed on a Wednesday afternoon, I found the brick-arched dining room with grape-vine wallpaper pretty quiet. Tony Bennett crooned on the speakers, serenading the families and nearby hospital workers on their lunch breaks.

Ben Calderone opened the original Palermo, named for the Sicilian city of his family's origins, at 2507 West Seventy-Ninth Street. Calderone made thin pizzas on the city's Southwest Side for about five years, until his brother and sister joined the company, eventually moving it to 3751 West Sixty-Third Street in the late '60s.

Ben's son, Tony, grew up in the business. Sadly, like a lot of other pizza businesses that take in too many relatives, tensions began to rise over everyday decisions. By the late '60s, locals had begun calling the business "Palermo's" and with Tony poised to assume a larger role, he and his family broke away in 1970 and moved one last time, to Oak Lawn, while his uncle remained on Sixty-Third Street. Tony stresses the two pizzerias are not connected. This is a refrain I hear often, as a result of riffs between family members results in two competing brands. Vito &

Nick's vs. Barraco's is one of the more well-known splits. One of Tony's other uncles helped open Phil's, another popular tavern-style joint in Oak Lawn.

So while there is a Palermo's of Sixty-Third Street (with locations in Frankfort and Merrillville, Indiana), they have no connection to Palermo's Ninety-Fifth. One of the key points of difference, Tony says, is the sauce. Palermo's of Sixty-Third promotes the fact they have a sweet sauce, and offers the Chicago triumvirate of deep-dish, thin, and stuffed. The Ninety-Fifth Street location sells the same three styles, but also makes the distinction between a regular pizza and a thin-and-crispy style. Tony says they're known for "thin with a rolled edge." Because his dad never liked when cheese would fall off the edge of a tavern-style pie, he instructed his cooks to leave an uncovered perimeter, pinched and raised slightly. As for that sweet sauce myth, he says that for decades, people thought they were using grape jelly.

"We had a guy come in every morning to do cleanup, and he loved peanut butter and jelly sandwiches. One day, a manager put the large jars of peanut butter and jelly up on a kitchen counter you could see from the dining room," said Calderone. "From then on, people thought we used it in our sauce!" He says only imported San Marzano tomatoes are used to this day.

They still make their bulk sausage in-house (he says about 80 percent of the pizzas sold are sausage), use Grande whole milk mozzarella, and dust each pizza with Romano just before it goes into their rotating Middleby Marshall bread oven. They bake at 525 for about fifteen minutes.

This being the South Side, many folks prefer giardiniera on their pizza. Calderone says a lot of their Calabrian guests would use the hot oil on their pizzas instead of using dried red pepper flakes. When these South Side pizza places originally began serving people back in the fifties and sixties, it was to accommodate larger families. Calderone says cutting pizzas into squares had less to do with fitting slices onto cocktail napkins and providing a snack to people on their way home for dinner, but rather, it was a way to feed an entire family. Cutting a whole pie into eight slices just wouldn't have been enough to go around.

"Ours is more of a meal, not a traditional bar pie," he said.

My server said without a doubt "thin and crispy" was their specialty, so that's what I ordered, with the usual toppings. Fifteen minutes later, he placed a beautifully crisp, square-cut pizza in front of me, set on top of a cooling rack that rested over the pizza pan. Elevating the pizza, just like the Japanese tonkatsu houses do for their breaded-and-fried pork cutlets, keeps that bottom crust crisp.

I don't think I've ever seen tomato sauce so red. It is almost like tomato paste, as thick as something out of a jar. Sausage is cut into large, amorphous hunks, tucked beneath a substantial (but not overwhelming) layer of oregano-flecked cheese. I ate about three pieces, including a good edge slice, so I could really taste the cracker-thin crust.

It's very different from Vito & Nick's, but worth a try. I hesitate to call it tavern-style, since it's served in a proper restaurant with a wine list and uniformed waiters, but there's no denying Palermo's 95th makes a square-cut, thin, light-as-a-cracker crisp crust—a true hallmark of Chicago-style thin pizza.

UNION SQUARED

1307 Chicago Avenue, Evanston
224-714-3100
www.unionpizza.com
@unionpizzasquared
Style: Detroit

There is also a Union Pizzeria in Evanston (same owners) but it offers no Detroit-style pizza, only artisan wood-fired.

FOR A BRIEF TIME, before Derrick Tung started making his Detroit-inspired pizzas at Paulie Gee's Logan Square, Vince DiBattista had cornered the market on Detroit-style pizza in Chicago. DiBattista and his business partner, Heather Behm, had a corner stall inside the Revival Food Hall in the Loop, followed by a first-floor space in a hotel just south of Wrigley Field, both of which ran their course, forcing them to regroup back at the original Evanston location. The whole project started after a visit DiBattista made to see his in-laws in Detroit. He had never had pizzas from the Motor City before, but they literally changed his life. The soft, focaccia-like interiors, the crispy-cheesy edges with the buttery bottoms, and the thick tomato sauce applied in stripes across the top were just too irresistible. He had to offer this kind of pizza back home in Chicago. But first he had to get his hands on a few dozen square steel pans.

Union offers two choices: a whole pie (serves three to four) or a slice (only available for two of their flavors—the four cheese or the pepperoni). They offer plenty of special pies among the whole options, including broccoli and potato, burrata Margherita, and a Corktown-inspired barbecued chicken.

My sausage arrives with large pieces of green pepper embedded in a red lake of zesty tomato sauce resting on a soft pillow of mozzarella. The highlight is the caramelized border, or *frico*—consisting of a Wisconsin brick cheese and mozzarella combo. It all lends nice color and texture to each bite. The fennel-heavy sausage comes from the well-regarded Joseph's Finest Meats on the city's Northwest Side. Since Detroit is more of a pepperoni town than a sausage one, I'd highly recommend the cup-and-char pepperoni (from Ezzo Sausage) with pickled jalapeños and Mike's Hot Honey.

DiBattista models the pies after Buddy's and Cloverleaf in Detroit. I've been to both, and after tasting Union's thick, delicious pieces of cheesy, caramelized pleasure, I can say that you'd have a hard time discerning the difference between the slices from Detroit and Evanston in a blind tasting.

VILLA NOVA PIZZERIA

6821 W. Pershing Road, Stickney
708-788-2944
www.villanovastickney
@villanovastickney
Style: Tavern-style thin

Villa Nova also has locations in Lockport, in New Buffalo, Michigan, and in Chesterton, Indiana, but they are operated by different owners who pay a licensing fee to the original (previous) owners.

CHILDHOOD FRIENDS Ted Lagios and Tom Sekulich grew up in Berwyn. Making regular trips to Villa Nova in nearby Stickney with their families was as much a part of growing up as "dibs" are to saving shoveled-out parking spaces in the winter. As adults, their job the past few years has been running The Corned Beef Factory in the West Loop, a wholesale-retail business that sells terrific sandwiches during lunch.

In 2020, an old friend from high school sent Sekulich a link on Facebook, announcing the legendary pizza joint was for sale. "I was surprised," he said. "I told Ted about it. Business was struggling and we were looking for other ways to drive revenue."

The business was started in 1955 by Al Tornabene. His daughter, Mary, had taken over, and after having sold licensing rights to three other locations, was ready to sell the original on Pershing Avenue.

This is the part of the story where my first book, *Pizza City, USA*, comes into play. "We saw how you rated it so highly, and thought, well that's impressive," said Lagios. "It just felt good to know that our little Stickney place had potential. Customers were coming in from Hinsdale, Naperville, Chicago. That was a turning point. We said, 'We're doing this.'"

The priority was a systems upgrade: phones, POS system, menu design, logo—even social media and website. By the time you read this, all of those external, structural, and back-of-the-house elements should be in place. The other part of the equation—the process for making the pizza—won't change a bit. For starters, they're inheriting a staff

with decades of experience. Lisa, the manager, has been there for thirty years; Vic for twenty; one driver can boast of thirty-five years on the job. Even the young cooks, most of whom are still in their twenties, started a decade ago. "We made it clear to all of the employees we're not firing anyone and we're gonna make sure everything is perfect," said Lagios. "We don't want it to change. That's why we bought it."

So the flour-splattered sheeter stays; the giant Cutler carousel oven too. They join forces every few minutes creating an edge for the ages. Oh, that edge! That glorious, crispy, cracker-like edge—it's a remarkable thing, especially when the rest of the pie is topped with beautifully melted mozzarella (a private label the owners won't disclose) and golf balls of sausage, all formed by hand, dusted with oregano, and placed as meticulously as a jeweler would set a diamond. The sauce—like that at many of the South and Southwest Side joints—leans a bit sweeter and darker, but I don't think that would turn off a purist from elsewhere.

This is what Chicago pizza was a half century ago and remains in many pockets of the city today. If you ever plan on being near Midway Airport, it's a worthwhile stop. But even if you're not taking Southwest Air somewhere, do a fly-by anyway. You won't find a pie like it anywhere else in the region.

WOODEN PADDLE

212 Stephen Street, Lemont
630-326-8150
www.woodenpaddle.com
@woodenpaddle
Style: Wood-fired thin

THE TINY TOWN OF Lemont in the southwestern suburbs is a bit sleepy when it comes to bars and restaurants. The main street looks like a movie set. A new adventure park with rope climbing, mountain bike loops, and a zip line just opened in 2020, and downtown businesses will likely benefit as a result of visitors. One of those restaurants sure to attract curious pizza lovers is the Wooden Paddle. The quaint restaurant is the brainchild of a couple who fell in love with the area, bought the building, and moved to town.

The *pizzaiola* (yes, a woman for a change) works quickly and quietly, stretching dough made with high-gluten flour, topping it with ingredients exclusively made in the US, and baking the pizzas in a jet-black, wood-fired Marra Forni oven that's about 200 degrees cooler than the typical Neapolitan joint.

"I call it American wood-fired pizza. We didn't want to step on the Neapolitan's toes by calling it something it's not," said owner Jonathan Cowan. "A wood-fired pizza that's more local. More local flavorings, like a Chicago sauce and things like that."

In one case, fresh Wisconsin mozzarella and soft ricotta are first baked on a crust; after two minutes, the naked pie is removed. It's whisked over to a counter, where it's topped with paper-thin sheets of prosciutto and dotted with a sweet, rustic fig jam. Another option features crumbled gouda cheese and roasted mushrooms. Again, about two minutes in the oven, before being removed, and then post-bake, garnished with a few spoonfuls of oily black truffle bits along with fresh thyme. Eat them while they're hot; these delicate crusts don't last long. You absolutely do not want to pack these up for a long drive elsewhere as they'll deteriorate just as quickly as a traditional Neapolitan.

There are traditional red-sauce pizza joints pretty much everywhere in the region, but finding an artisan, wood-fired pizza this far southwest? Wooden Paddle is pretty much your only choice.

GLUTEN-FREE PIZZAS IN CHICAGOLAND

We've been offering weekly pizza tours in Chicago since 2018 (www.pizzacityusa.com), and every year, I notice a few more requests for gluten-free options. We typically don't offer them on the public tours, but with enough notice, we can definitely work something out for private tours. We've assembled a few great options here, and if you need more guidance in the city, here's an excellent resource: www.findmeglutenfree.com/us/il/chicago/pizza.

CHICAGO (CITY)

AURELIO'S PIZZA
1212 S. Michigan Avenue; 312-374-4459
aureliospizza.com

CHICAGO'S PIZZA
3114 N. Lincoln Avenue; 773-477-2777
4520 W. Irving Park Road; 773-427-0100
1919 W. Montrose Avenue; 773-348-1700
www.chicagos-pizza.com

D'AGOSTINO'S PIZZA & PUB
752 N. Ogden Avenue; 312-850-3247
1351 W. Addison Street; 773-477-1822
www.dagsdelivers.com

FORNO ROSSO PIZZERIA NAPOLETANA
1048 W. Randolph Street; 312-243-6000
3719 N. Harlem Avenue; 773-295-5697
www.fornorossopizzeria.com

FOXHOLE
3335 N. Southport Avenue; 773-687-8568
(located on the side of Code di Volpe)
Code di Volpe
3335 N. Southport Avenue; 773-687-8568
www.cdvolpe.com

PIZANO'S PIZZA & PASTA
61 E. Madison Street; 312-236-1777
864 N. State Street; 312-751-1766
800 N. Dearborn Street; 312-335-8833
2106 S. Indiana Avenue; 312-842-0777
www.pizanoschicago.com

PIZZA CAPRI
1501 E. Fifty-Third Street; 773-324-7777
1733 N. Halsted Street; 312-280-5700
www.pizzacapri.com

PIZZERIA PORTOFINO
317 N. Clark Street; 312-900-9080
www.pizzeriaportofino.com
*Cauliflower crust

POMPEI
1531 W. Taylor Street; 312-421-5179
www.pompeiusa.com

ROBERT'S PIZZA AND DOUGH CO.
465 N. McClurg Court; 312-265-1328
www.robertspizzacompany.com

ROOTS
1924 W. Chicago Avenue; 773-645-4949
220 W. Lawrence Avenue; 773-433-5959
1610 N. Wells Street; 312-210-7788
744 S. Dearborn Street; 773-645-4909
www.rootspizza.com

SPACCA NAPOLI PIZZERIA
1769 W. Sunnyside Avenue; 773-878-2420
www.spaccanapolipizzeria.com

STELLA BARRA PIZZERIA & WINE BAR
1954 N. Halsted Street; 773-634-4101
www.stellabarra.com

SUBURBS

ARRENELLO'S PIZZA
325 E. Glenwood-Lansing Road, Glenwood; 708-758-6160
9420 W. 179th Street, Tinley Park; 708-532-2424
arrenellos.com/locations/

D'AGOSTINO'S PIZZA & PUB
3131 N. Thatcher Avenue, River Grove; 708-453-3247
7530 W. Oakton Street, Niles; 847-318-8700
2350 Lehigh Avenue, Glenview; 847-729-0909
241 S. Milwaukee Avenue, Wheeling; 847-808-8200
www.dagsdelivers.com

DA LUCIANO
8343 W. Grand Avenue, River Grove; 708-453-1000
www.dalucianos.com

GAETANO'S
7636 Madison Street, Forest Park; 708-366-4010
www.gaetanosforestpark.com

JIMBO'S PIZZA
12257 Walker Road, Lemont; 630-257-1712
www.jimbospizza.com

PALERMO'S 95TH ITALIAN CUISINE
4849 W. Ninety-Fifth Street, Oak Lawn; 708-425-6262
palermos95th.com

PIZANO'S PIZZA & PASTA
1808 N. Waukegan Road, Glenview; 847-486-1777
www.pizanoschicago.com

UNION SQUARED
1307 Chicago Avenue, Evanston; 224-714-3100
www.unionpizza.com/union-squared-evanston

ZAZZO PIZZERIA
7360 IL Route 83, Darien; 630-655-4788
200 W. Ogden Avenue, Westmont; 630-796-2220
www.zazzospizza.com

FRANCHISES

BLAZE
www.blazepizza.com

CALIFORNIA PIZZA KITCHEN
www.cpk.com

GIORDANO'S
giordanos.com

LOU MALNATI'S PIZZERIA
www.loumalnatis.com

PIZZERIA DUE
www.pizzeriaunodue.com

PIZZERIA UNO
www.unos.com

CONCLUSION

ONE OF THE MOST PERPLEXING THINGS TO ME when it comes to the world's understanding of what "Chicago pizza" means—more puzzling than how Gavin Newsom was actually married to Kimberly Guilfoyle for *four years* or what the hell actually happened in the series finale of *The Sopranos*—is where did we lose the narrative? Was it in the 1970s and '80s, when annual conventions for radiologists, auto parts reps, and the National Restaurant Association would come to town? Was it with the legions of comedians who lived here for a year, subsisted on weak pizza, but then used that as an excuse for a lifetime of punchlines? Why is it that a poor excuse for a Netflix series like *Emily in Paris* gets away with ripping on Lou Malnati's and there's no recourse? I love John Stewart, but his infamous deep-dish rant (google it) was likely workshopped by a writer's table of white guys who may or may not have lived in the suburbs or went to Northwestern, but never actually spent time living in the city, eating tavern-style pizza. How is it that stuffed became our official logo?

These are the kinds of questions I find myself asking every time there's a "Top 10 Pizzas in Chicago" listicle in some national magazine or private equity–funded website. I'll take some of the blame for not calling people out more frequently, but it's like trying to take a sip from a waterfall, especially since the city's tourism arm generally supports any and all coverage of Chicago. Being the lone voice in a sea of Yelping influencers hasn't helped amplify the message (or to be more precise, the rebuttals).

Majestic duck prosciutto pie at Robert's Pizza and Dough Co.

Given the issue of economic disparity among Americans, I often ask myself: Where are the well-funded pizzerias owned by Black, Indigenous, and People of Color ("BIPOC") in Chicago? Why haven't publicly traded pizza companies (i.e., Domino's, Papa John's, and YUM Brands) adopted McDonald's model for grooming would-be entrepreneurs and supporting supplier diversity programs to strengthen communities and bolster their brands? While it's heartening to see African American staff employed at Italian Fiesta stores in predominantly African American neighborhoods, and at Lou Malnati's Pizzeria in Lawndale, on the West Side of Chicago, these companies are missing a larger opportunity to expand their appeal and enhance investor returns. They are also missing potentially lucrative opportunities to enlarge their respective pieces of the pie on the North and South Sides of Chicago.

Perhaps the answer to this quandary is Don Thompson, former CEO of McDonald's and the founder and current CEO of Cleveland Avenue, a private equity incubator for restaurant concepts and food technology and beverage companies. The company nurtures the development of businesses that benefit entrepreneurs, investors, and neighborhoods. Perhaps Don can establish the Cleveland Avenue Challenge to fund African American entrepreneurship in the pizzeria industry. Does anyone reading this know Don Thompson? Hey Don, if you are reading this, I'd like to support the development of more African American entrepreneurs and would be honored to support you in this effort!

In a fractured society, pizza is a great uniter. It's apolitical and helps us create indelible memories. Connoisseurs may have their preferences; the only real concern today is the opportunistic gouging by some third-party delivery apps. Pizzerias are community assets that become gathering places. They create virtuous circles of customer loyalty enmeshed with a business's long-term survival. I've seen this happen up close for nearly thirty years. The fortunes of pizzerias have only accelerated during the pandemic.

My only caveat would be to consider the source of your pizza intel. Is the writer of the article local, or did they parachute in for two days to slap together a story? How much on-the-ground eating did they do, or did they rely on a producer or tourism employee as a proxy for them in the data collection (eating) process? Is the writer an "influencer," which may compromise the content created?

If I leave you with anything, I've hopefully convinced you there are so many other options in Chicago besides the stuffed and deep pies you've been hearing about for years. Chefs, artisans, bakers, and scrappy entrepreneurs are all hustling to produce memorable pizzas, rarely in round, deep pans. The Windy City's pizza scene is as varied and exciting as a food hawker stall in Singapore or a Japanese fish market.

Try to think about deep-dish and stuffed like you would if you were visiting New York City for the weekend. Would you spend all of your time in Times Square? Of course not. Once you leave the theater, it's time to go explore one of the dozens of different pockets of the city: Flatbush, Queens, Bushwick, the Lower East Side, Harlem . . . each one offers a different experience, immersing you in a neighborhood with its own personality. The pizza experience in Chicago these days isn't that different.

PIZZA CITY, USA
STEVE

ACKNOWLEDGMENTS

THIS BOOK WOULD NOT HAVE BEEN POSSIBLE without the help of a lot of wonderfully patient people. Primarily, my family. Specifically, my wife, Amy, who calmly reassured me that yes, we could visit another three places on a Wednesday night to try more pizzas. Your support, love, and understanding have made this project all the more satisfying. I promise to always supply you with Barnaby's and Vito & Nick's whenever you feel like it.

My kids—Madeline and Max—played a larger role in my first book, *Pizza City, USA*, since they were around the house more, scooping up extra pizzas for themselves and their friends. Now that Madeline is abroad, our pizza check-ins have been by WhatsApp—and I'm looking forward to pairing some of the local beers Josh Noel suggested with pizza on your next visit with Dammas. Max, fortunately, still has a bottomless stomach, and so I thank you and your roommates for your help in dismantling a number of pizzas I had no intention of finishing in the winter of 2020.

Thanks also to my new neighbors at 1156. Your willingness to stop by and pick up the remains of a stuffed, artisan, Neapolitan, or Sicilian pie were helpful, in that nothing went to waste (hat tip to Charles upstairs). I hope you enjoy this finished result of our pandemic project of 2020.

Big thanks to Celine Macura, intern extraordinaire, for making phone calls, taking notes, fact-checking, laying out photo assignment itineraries, and just generally chasing down quotes while in the midst of moving home from Northwestern back East during a pandemic. Your steady presence and quick responses were immeasurably helpful. Good luck on graduation!

TODD ROSENBERG

Speaking of the little college in Evanston on the Lake, thanks also to the team at Northwestern University Press: Parneshia Jones for giving me the green light to do this, Dino Robinson and Anne Gendler for their help with organizing my thoughts and figuring out how to make this project come together so quickly, Morgan Krehbiel for her terrific design and layout, and Mary Klein for her meticulous proofreading.

Thanks to Peter Regas for sharing his historical insights. I know only you, I, Scott Wiener, and a handful of pizza nerds really care about the minutiae, but as someone who got a double major in history and journalism (Go Badgers), I find an odd pleasure in uncovering long-forgotten facts and being able to debunk popular urban myths—especially ones about pizza.

Tip of the hat to Michael Lucas for his input on my conclusion, to Dan Bransfield and Rich Lo for their illuminating illustrations, and to Josh Noel for sharing his passion for local beer. I've always been a big supporter of our local brands, and I know what I like to drink, but I'm terrible at articulating it. After reading his summary, I now have plenty of options the next time I visit a pizzeria with a good beer list.

Finally, I want to thank all of the pizza owners who gave me their precious time to talk about what they do every day and share their stories. They are each time capsules of a place and time in Chicago. Whether they represent a corner of a neighborhood or an entire suburb, what they do has a direct impact on the lives and memories of millions of people who call Chicago home. I could not have finished this project without you. Just a sampling reveals volumes about our past. As much as outsiders know Capone, Jordan, and Winfrey, locals should also regard these names with reverence: Labriola, Davino, Barraco, D'Amato, Pianetto, Salerno, Malnati, Grittani . . . just a few of the names who built Chicago's pizza scene and will hopefully continue to nurture it for generations to come.

If you haven't bought a pizza this week, go do it now. Better yet, try a pie from somewhere you haven't been before, and expand your horizons. Remember, there's a lot more to Chicago than just deep-dish.

INDEX

Page numbers in *italic* refer to photographs that are separate from their restaurant listing.